The Complete Guide to

Greece

The Complete Guide to
Greece

John & Maureen Freely

GEORGE PHILIP LONDON

George Philip & Son Limited
12–14 Long Acre, London, WC2E 9LP

First published 1974
© 1974 John and Maureen Freely

Filmset and printed in Great Britain by
BAS Printers Limited, Wallop, Hampshire

ISBN 0 540 07088 2

To the Rest of the Family:
Toots, Eileen, and Mister B.

Colour photographs by: Ralph Bates, Tom Davis, Susan Hunter, and
Cindy Peslikis
Black and white photographs by: James Lynch
The authors wish to express their appreciation to the National Tourist
Organization of Greece in Athens and New York for their help in providing
information and photographs

Cover photograph courtesy of Michael L. Beazley

Contents

An Introduction to Greece

There is something quite extraordinary about Greece, and most visitors sense this immediately upon arrival. Is it the clear and pellucid air, which lends clarity to sight and thought, the intensification of light and colour, the unforgettable sight of a white village perched on the hillside of a tawny island floating between the blues of sea and sky? Or is it the knowledge that you are making a spiritual pilgrimage to the place where Western civilization began: science, philosophy, drama, the concept of free men debating in a democratic society and their tragic failure of two thousand years ago repeated once again today? It is surely this and more, the feeling that you have come to an exceptional land and found there a brief home among its high-spirited and hospitable people. *'Kalos orisate!'* (Welcome), says the Greek when you set foot in his house or in his country, and you realize that this will not be a vacation from life but a memorable human experience.

Greece is one of the smaller countries of Europe, with an area (48,000 square miles) somewhat less than that of Great Britain. Nevertheless, its landscapes and topography exhibit a quite astonishing variety. The mainland is, for the most part, extremely mountainous, with such a jagged coastline that no spot in the country is more than eighty miles from the sea. Thus the impression one retains of Greece is that of sea and mountains, the two elements which have shaped the history of its hardy and independent inhabitants. 'Greece is a factory for making Greeks,' wrote Niko Kazantzakis a generation ago, explaining how this rugged land has impressed its qualities upon the men and women who have lived out their lives here, as much in Homer's time as in our own.

The political history of modern Greece has been for the most part a troubled one. Today the country is officially a republic, since in a referendum on 29 July 1973 the Greek people voted to abolish the monarchy and to elect Colonel George Papadopolos as President (he ran unopposed). On 25 November 1973 Papadopoulos was ousted and replaced by General Phaidon Gizikis. A new government, headed by Adamantios Androutsopoulos, was formed. Their often bitter past has made the Greeks cynical about politics, but it has not at all spoiled their good humour or their zest for life.

In attempting to understand the Greeks one must remember that they are a very religious people and that their religion plays a central role in their life. In this they are conservative to the core, which is why their church is called Orthodox. One is often surprised to find how pious are one's otherwise hard-headed and worldly-wise Greek friends, watching them at their devotions or at a religious procession. (Don't be alarmed when your taxi-driver crosses

1

himself when racing past roadside chapels at ninety miles an hour—he is under the protection of the many saints whose icons obscure his windscreen.)

Athens, the capital of modern Greece, dominates the political, economic and intellectual life of the country as much today as it did in classical times. Nearly two million of the country's nine million people live in greater Athens, and most of Greece's power and money is concentrated there. The nation's two leading sources of income are tourism and shipping. Athens is the focal point of the tourist industry, for virtually every visitor who comes to Greece spends some time in the capital, while the Piraeus, the port of Athens since ancient times, is one of the busiest and most important harbours in the Mediterranean. Greece is also rapidly developing its heavy industries, and these too are largely located in and around the Piraeus, giving it that rough and ready working-class atmosphere which was so well pictured in the film *Never on Sunday*.

The country's third most important resource is agriculture, and one need not travel very far out of Athens to enter a pastoral Greece that Hesiod would recognize across the gulf of centuries, with ox-drawn wagons lumbering along dusty country roads, between furrowed fields which have been cultivated in much the same way since remote antiquity. 'Begin your harvest when the Pleiades are rising, and plow again when they are setting', wrote Hesiod more than eight hundred years before the birth of Christ, and under these celestial signs Greek farmers still till their lands today.

Although it may not be a significant source of foreign exchange, fishing is still basic to the country's life, for the Greeks have always been a race of fishermen and farmers. Watch the caïques sailing out at twilight from an island port, and see their lanterns twinkling like floating constellations far out in the dark Aegean, the night sky a lighter blue above. Walk out on the quay at sunrise when they return, salt-encrusted argonauts wolfing down a breakfast of bread, white cheese and olives, and then later spreading out their nets to dry on the shore, singing to the music of a home-made bagpipe while they work, occasionally swigging draughts of cold white wine from an earthenware jug. They might be Odysseus and his shipmates, but the year is 1973 and the captain's name is Petros.

Foreigners flock to Greece for a variety of reasons. Some come to view the country's wealth of antiquities: the incomparable Parthenon in Athens, the superbly situated shrine at Delphi, the evocative ruins at Olympia, the historic palaces of Knossos and Phaistos in Crete. Others are drawn by these and by the unique cultural activities offered at many of the classical sites: performances of Greek drama in the theatre of Herod Atticus in the shadow of the Parthenon, or in the theatre at Epidauros, where the works of the great Greek dramatists were originally performed in the age of Pericles. Perhaps the largest number travel primarily for a holiday in the sun, for the unspoiled Greek seaside has some of the finest beaches in the Mediterranean, and certainly the cleanest. And where else in this crowded and polluted modern world could one walk for miles along a deserted beach of pink sand, and then picnic under an olive tree among the picturesque ruins of an ancient temple?

But whatever reasons one had for coming to Greece in the first place, one returns with something more, the enduring memory of having lived for a while a free and joyous life in beautiful and harmonious surroundings. Sudden moods of total happiness are apt to come upon one quite unexpectedly. (The Greeks call it *kefi*, the Turks *keyif*; the feeling crosses national boundaries in this part of the world.) Where in Greece did we first experience this sense of transcendent happiness? Was it in the village square in Naxos one night twelve years ago, drinking retsina with Yorgo and Sotiris, listening to Michali Karavoula playing haunting melodies on his fiddle while a silver moon soared across the luminescent sky? Or was it when Yorgo Mavromataki sang for us in his garden in Ano Potamia, strumming softly on his lute while we listened to the sound of the wind sighing among the spectral cypresses, and watched the Gothic Naxian mountains grow purple in the fading twilight? These are the happy moments you are apt to remember with a pang on a gloomy winter day in London or New York, when you begin counting the days till you can return once again to Greece.

HISTORY

The beginnings of Greek civilization go back to the Neolithic Age, to about the sixth or seventh millennium B.C., when settlers in considerable number first moved from Anatolia into the southern regions of the Balkan peninsula. In the early Bronze Age (*c.* 3000–2000 B.C.) a new wave of immigrants arrived from Anatolia and spread out to the Aegean isles and Crete. There they laid the foundations of the highly advanced and sophisticated Minoan culture, which was to flourish for nearly two thousand years until its sudden destruction in about 1450 B.C. For the next three centuries the dominant civilization in mainland Greece was the Mycenaean; this was the heroic age of which Homer wrote, the time of Achilles and Odysseus.

In the twelfth century B.C. the Mycenaean world was destroyed by an invasion of barbarous northerners, the people whom the Greeks called Dorians. For the following two centuries the arts of civilization declined in Greece, a Dark Age which lasted until the renaissance of the ninth century. The revival of culture then was part of a great expansion of the Greek world, for by the eighth century the city-states of mainland Greece were establishing colonies all over the Mediterranean. This was the beginning of the Archaic Age, which produced the first philosophers of nature in Asia Minor, and gave birth to the poets Homer and Hesiod. It was also a time when the Greeks manifested a sense of national unity in such activities as the Olympic Games, which were first held in 776 B.C. The Archaic Age culminated in the great victories of the Greeks over the Persians in 480–79 B.C. at the battles of Marathon, Salamis and Plataea.

The century-and-a-half following the Greek triumph over the Persians, the so-called Classical Age, was the most brilliant period in the early history of mankind. This was the time of Pericles and the rise of Athens to dominance in the Greek world. It was an age which produced the philosophers Socrates, Plato and Aristotle; the dramatists Aeschylus, Sophocles, Euripides and Aristophanes; the historians Herodotus and Thucydides; the sculptors

Pheidas and Praxiteles; and the architect Iktinos, the builder of the Parthenon —the symbol of the Golden Age.

But even the Golden Age was marred by the internecine struggles which seem endemic to the Greek world. The most tragic of these in its consequences was the Peloponnesian War (431–404 B.C.) in which Athens and Sparta fought for dominance and in the process eventually destroyed Greece as a nation. The final defeat and surrender of Athens in 404 B.C. was followed by another half-century of battling between the various city-states, and by the middle of the fourth century Greece was so irreparably weakened as to be unable to resist the rising power of Macedonia.

The military might of Macedonia was first manifested in the battle of Chaeronia in 338 B.C., when King Philip and his young son Alexander crushed the armies of the Greek allies, bringing Greek democracy to a sudden and final end. Alexander succeeded his father to the throne in 336 B.C. as ruler of all of Greece, and two years later began his great campaign into Asia. Over the next decade Alexander and his armies swept all before them, and by the time of his death in 323 B.C. his empire extended from the Adriatic Sea to the borders of India.

The two centuries following the death of Alexander are generally called the Hellenistic Period. Politically, it was marked by an almost continuous struggle between the successors of Alexander the Great and eventually resulted in the dismemberment of his Empire. Though democracy and the concept of the independent city-state were dead, Greek culture continued to flourish throughout the Hellenistic Period and even beyond, though failing to achieve the brilliant creative genius of the Classical Age.

Beginning in the second century B.C., the Greek world was caught up in the eastward expansion of Rome, and in 146 B.C. all of Greece and Macedonia became a Roman province. For the next five centuries Greek history is just a footnote to that of Rome, though Athens continued to be one of the intellectual centres of the Empire. The latter part of this period was marked by the rise of Christianity in the Greek world, and by the spread of Greek language and culture all over the eastern Mediterranean and Asia Minor, factors which were to be of profound importance in later centuries.

The next chapter of Greek history begins in the year A.D. 330, when Constantine the Great transferred the capital of the Empire from Rome to Constantinople. During the next two centuries barbarian invasions over-ran most of Western Europe and the Balkans, and the Roman Empire was reduced to little more than Greece and Asia Minor. During the sixth century the fortunes of the Empire revived under Justinian the Great, whose dominions extended from Italy through the Balkans and the Middle East. But the Empire over which he ruled was no longer really Roman, for it was centred in lands populated principally by Greek-speaking Christians—a nation which eventually came to be called the Byzantine Empire.

The Byzantine Empire lasted for over a thousand years, continually fighting off invaders who attacked it from all sides, preserving some precious fragments of ancient Greek traditions and culture. Then, in the early thirteenth century, Greece was overrun by the Latin armies of the Fourth Crusade, who took and sacked Constantinople in 1204. Although the Byzantines eventually regained their capital in 1261, the Empire never fully recovered from this disaster. For the last two centuries of its existence Byzantium fought a losing battle against the advancing forces of the Ottoman Turks, and by the middle of the fifteenth century the Empire comprised little more than Constantinople itself, with some fragmentary possessions in Greece and Asia Minor. Nevertheless, Byzantine culture reached unprecedented heights in those last years and did much to stimulate the Italian Renaissance. But the Byzantine Greeks themselves were to be denied the benefits of this cultural rebirth which they had done so much to bring about, for their world came to an end when Constantinople fell to the Turks on 29 May 1453.

Greece literally disappears from history during the first three-and-a-half centuries following the Turkish conquest. The once proud city of Athens declined to the point where it was little more than a village clustered around the Acropolis, upon which stood the scattered ruins of the Parthenon. The sad memories of this long period of Turkish occupation survive in romantic ballads and in the heroic sagas of the *klephtes*, the brigands who fought and died for some small measure of independence in remote and mountainous regions like Epirus and the Mani.

The struggle for independence began in earnest in the early nineteenth century, when the Ottoman Empire fell into a state of weakness and decadence. The Greek Revolution itself began on 25 March 1821, when the uprising was proclaimed by Germanos, the Archbishop of Patras. The Greeks were aided in their fight for independence by Britain, France and Russia, and by philhellenic volunteers such as Lord Byron, who gave his life to the cause at Mesolongi in 1826. After a long and heroic struggle the existence of the independent state of Greece was finally formalized in the Protocol of London on 11 May 1832.

The original Greek kingdom, whose first ruler was King Otho from Bavaria, consisted of little more than Attica, the Peloponnese and the Cyclades. During the next century successive accretions of territory were obtained, mostly from the declining Ottoman Empire, to form the boundary of present-day Greece. During the present century Greece has suffered terribly in a succession of cruel wars, and only in the past twenty-five years has it enjoyed a relatively prolonged period of peace and freedom from want. And now each year Greece is becoming more and more a modern European country, while still retaining strong links to its ancient traditions.

ARCHITECTURE

The long and varied history of Greece is evidenced by its rich heritage of antiquities. This is not to say that the country should be thought of merely as an outdoor museum, for its ancient monuments are an integral part of the classical landscape, the romantic backdrop to any Grecian journey.

The architecture of the Aegean Bronze Age survives mainly in royal palaces and tombs. The earliest monumental remains from this period are the palaces at Knossos and Phaistos in Crete, the original structures of which date back to about 2000 B.C. Their vast size and complexity, and the sophistication of their decoration, reveal the highly advanced level of the Minoan culture. The palaces of the Mycenaeans, successors to the Minoans, are rather different in character. Whereas the Minoan palace was a combination of pleasure-dome and administrative-centre, that of the Mycenaean was more fortress-like, perched on a rocky hill-top and surrounded by massive walls of cyclopean masonry, reflecting the warlike character of the age. Such are the royal palaces and tombs of Mycenae, Tiryns and Pylos—haunted still by the ghosts of their former rulers, who live now only in the pages of Homer.

The flowering of Greek architecture came with the temples and shrines of the classical period. These were designed in three distinct orders or architectural styles: the Doric, the Ionic, and the Corinthian. The oldest example of Doric architecture is the Heraion at Olympia, and its finest and most famous structure is the Parthenon. The Ionic order developed in Asia Minor and culminated in two other temples on the Athenian Acropolis: the Erechtheion and the Temple of Athena Nike. The Corinthian order came into use somewhat later and is responsible for some of the monumental temples of the late Hellenistic age, the most famous of which is the Temple of Olympian Zeus in Athens.

The architectural genius of the classical world is also shown by the many ancient theatres one finds throughout the country, all of them in superb natural settings. The most famous and most perfect of these is the Theatre of Epidauros, now the scene of the annual Epidauros Festival.

Greek architecture continued to flourish throughout the Hellenistic age, but soon lost its creative vigour under Roman domination. The principal monuments of that period which survive are entirely Roman in character, such as the Arch of Galerius in Salonica.

A new period of Greek architecture begins with the Byzantine era, the principal monuments of which are its splendid churches and monasteries. (The incomparable masterpiece of this period, Haghia Sophia in Istanbul, is no longer in the Greek world.) While travelling through Greece one can follow the whole progress of Byzantine church architecture, from the fifth century basilica of St. Demetrios in Salonica, through the cruciform churches in the great monasteries of Daphni and Osios Loukas, two masterworks of the eleventh century, to the lovely churches of the last Byzantine renaissance, particularly those in the ghost city of Mistra in the Peloponnese.

The visitor to Greece will also be struck by the massive fortification walls which ring the heights of many Greek cities. Most of these were originally Byzantine in construction, and were later rebuilt by the Crusaders and later still by the Turks. Most romantic of all in their appearance and associations are the Crusader castles, whose dark ruins brood on remote crags all over Greece. Then there is the magnificent fortified town of Rhodes, constructed by the Knights of St. John, one of the masterpieces of medieval military architecture.

The Turkish period in Greek history is represented principally by their fortifications and defence-towers, the grandest of which is the famous White Tower in Salonica. There are also several historic mosques in the northern part of the country, including some by the great Ottoman architect Sinan. The silhouettes of domes and minarets give an oriental atmosphere to some of the northern towns, such as lovely Ioannina in Epirus.

And after one has seen all of the great monuments of Greek architecture, one is still struck by the harmonious beauty of humble private homes, particularly in Aegean island towns such as Mykonos and Skyros. Little whitewashed cubes with vine-shaded courtyards and with flower-filled balconies overlooking the surrounding sea and mountains; they have not changed in their design since ancient times. If one could live out one's life in peace and happiness it would be there, in a little white house beside the sea.

A GREEK PRIMER

Although a great many people in Athens now speak English, particularly in hotels, restaurants, travel agencies, and in Customs, it is helpful to know some frequently-used words and expressions. Moreover, the Greeks will be quite appreciative if you speak a few words of their language. They are a very talkative and expressive people, and your few words will let loose a flood of conversation on their part, and in this way you will come to know them better, even if you understand only a fraction of what they say. Reading Greek may seem a somewhat more difficult matter at first, since they use a different alphabet. But with a little study one can master this quite easily, and then one takes an almost child-like pleasure in deciphering signs and notices. (MH BΛAΣΘHMEITE TA ΘEIA, (Do Not Blaspheme the Gods) says the sign on the coffee-house wall, where your limited knowledge of Greek prevents you from understanding the eloquent blasphemy of your companions.)

These are the letters of the Greek alphabet (given in upper and lower case, with their transliteration into English and their approximate sounds):

A, α—a as in car. B, β—v as in very. Γ, γ—y as in yes (when followed by an E or I), gh as in go (when followed by consonants or the vowels A, O, or OU). Δ, δ—th (but transliterated as d) as in the. E, ε—e as in red. Z, ζ—z as in zoo. H, η—i as in machine. Θ, θ—th as in these. I, ι—i as in machine. K, κ—k as in king. Λ, λ—l as in lamp. M, μ—m as in mother. N, ν—n as in new. Ξ, ξ—ks as in extra. O, o—o as in toe. Π, π—p as in piece. P, ρ—r as in rose. Σ, σ—s as in sit. T, τ—t as in tough. Y, υ—i as in machine. Φ, φ—f as in fee. X, χ—kh as in khan or in the Scottish loch. Ψ, ψ—ps as in lapse. Ω, ω—o as in toe.

Each word bears an accent above a vowel in the stressed syllable, and Greeks will have difficulty in understanding you if the accent is not correctly placed. There are three genders and the definite and indefinite articles are different in each case. Masculine: *o ánthropos*—the man, *énas ánthropos*—a man. Feminine: *i yinéka*—the woman, *mía yinéka*—a woman. Neuter: *to pedhí*—the child, *éna pedhí*—a child. There is some correlation between gender and sex, but there are many exceptions, e.g.: *mía bíra*—a beer, *éna oúzo*—an ouzo.

Numbers

(The numbers 1, 3, and 4 depend on the gender of the noun they qualify; masculine: 1—*énas*, 3—*tris*, 4—*téseris*; feminine: 1—*mia*, 3—*tris*, 4—*tésseris*; neuter: 1—*éna*, 3—*tría*, 4—*téssera*. This is also true for the numerals 1, 3 and 4 in each decade starting with 20; the following numbers are given for the neuter gender.)

1—*éna*, 2—*dío*, 3—*tría*, 4—*téssera*, 5—*pénde*, 6—*éxi*, 7—*eptá*, 8—*októ*, 9—*ennéa*, 10—*déka*, 11—*éndeka*, 12—*dódeka*, 13—*dekatría*, 14—*dekatéssera*, 15—*dekapénde*, 16—*dekaéxi*, 17—*dekaeptá*, 18—*dekaoktó*, 19—*dekaennéa*, 20—*íkosi*, 21—*íkosi éna*, 22—*íkosi dío*, 30—*triánda*, 40—*saránda*, 50—*peninda*, 60—*exínda*, 70—*evdomínda*, 80—*ogdónda*, 90—*enenínda*, 100—*ekató*, 101—*ekatón éna*, 200—*diakósia*, 300—*triakósia*, 400—*tetrakósia*, 500—*pendakósia*, 600—*exakósia*, 700—*eptakósia*, 800—*oktakósia*, 900—*enneakósia*, 1000—*hília*, 2000—*dío hiliádes*, 1,000,000—*ekatomírio*.

Days of the week, months and seasons, telling time

Sunday—*Kiriakí*, Monday—*Deftéra*, Tuesday—*Tríti*, Wednesday—*Tetárti*, Thursday—*Pémpti*, Friday—*Paraskeví*, Saturday—*Sávato*. Week—*evdomáda*, day—*méra* (pl. *méres*), today—*símera*, every day—*kathe méra*, yesterday—*hthés*, day before yesterday—*prohthés*, three days ago—*tris méres prin*, tomorrow—*ávrio*, day after tomorrow—*methávrio*, three days hence—*tris méres metá*, morning—*proí*, midday—*messiméri*, evening—*vrádi*, tonight—*apópse*.

January—*Ianouários*, February—*Fevrouários*, March—*Mártios*, April—*Aprílios*, May—*Máios*, June—*Ioúnios*, July—*Ioúlios*, August—*Ávgoustos*, September—*Septémvrios*, October—*Octóvrios*, November—*Noémvrios*, December—*Dekémvrios*. Spring—*Anixis*, Summer—*Kalokéri*, Autumn—*Fthinóporo*, Winter—*Himónas*, season—*epochí*. Year—*chrónos*, this year—*fétos*, last year—*périssi*, next year—*too chrónoo*.

Hours—*óra*, minute—*leptó*. What time is it?—*Ti óra ine?* 1.00—*mía*, or *i óra mía*, 3.00—*tris*, 2.30—*dío ke* (and) *misí* (one-half), 7.15—*eptá ke dekapénde* or *eptá ke tétarto* (one-quarter), 3.50—*tris ke peninda* or *tésseris pára* (minus) *déka*, at 6.20—*stis* (at) *éxi ke íkosi*. Now—*tóra*, later—*ístera*. Wait a minute!—*Ena leptó!*

Everyday words and phrases

Hello—*Hérete*. Good morning—*Kaliméra*. Good evening—*Kalispéra*. Good night—*Kaliníhta*. Goodbye—*Adío*. How are you?—*Ti kánis* or *pos iste?* Good—*Kalá*. Very good—*Poli kalá*. Not so good—*Étsi kétsi*. Bad—*Kakós*. Please—*Parakaló*. Thank you—*Efharistó*. You're welcome—*Parakaló*. Excuse me—*Signómi*. Sir—*Kírie*. Madam—*Kiría*. Miss—*Despinís*. I—*egó*, we—*emís*, you—*esí*, he—*aftós*, she—*aftí*, it—*aftó*, I am—*íme*, you are—*íse*, it is—*íne*, mine—*dikó moo*, yours—*dikó soo*. Yes—*Ne*. No—*Óhi*. I want—*Thélo*. I don't want—*Then thélo*. I have—*Ého*. I don't have—*Then ého*. Do you have—*Éhete*. There isn't any—*Then éhi*. I understand—*Katalavéno*. I don't understand—*Then katalavéno*. I go—*Piyéno*. I will go—*Tha páo*. I went—*Éfiga*. I'm coming—*Érhome*. I will come—*Tha értho*. I came—*Írtha*. Who—*piós*, when—*póte*, where—*poo*, where is—*poo íne*, why—*yiatí*, how—*pos*, how much—*póso kostízi* or *póso káni*, what—*ti*, much or many—*polí*, little—*lígo*. All right or OK!—*Endáxi!* It doesn't matter!—*Then birázi!* (two of the most useful phrases in the Greek language).

On arriving

Customs office—*Telonío*. Passport—*Diavatírio*. Luggage—*Ta prámata*. I am English—*Íme Ánglos* (m) or *Anglída* (f). I am American—*Ime Amerikanós* (m) or *Amerikanída* (f). I have nothing to declare—*Then ého típota na dilóso*. Only personal effects—*Prosopiká móno*. Papers for the car—*Hartiá too aftokinítoo*.

At the hotel

Hotel—*Xenodohío*, house—*spíti*, room—*domátio*. Do you have a single/double room with a bath/shower?—*Éhete monóklino/díklino domátio me lootró/dooz?* With/without meals?—

Me/horís ghévmata? Breakfast—*Proinó.* Chambermaid—*Kamariéra.* Please give me the key/ towel/soap/toilet paper—*S'parakaló, dóste moo to klidí/sapoóni/petséta/hartí tis tualéttas.* Can you wash and press my clothes?—*Boríte na plíhete ke na siderósete ta roúha moo?* Please prepare the bill—*S'parakaló, etimáste to logariasmó.*

Money matters

Bank—*Trápeza,* money—*hrímata,* traveller's cheques—*tooristikí epitaghí.* I want to change money—*Thélo na káno sinálagi.*

Travelling

Street—*ódos,* road—*drómos,* avenue—*leofóros,* main road—*ethnikí ódos,* square—*platía.* Right— *dexiá,* left—*aristerá,* straight ahead—*ísya* or *efthía,* slow—*argá,* fast—*grígora.* Station—*stathmós,* bus—*leoforío,* railway—*sidiródromos,* aeroplane—*aeropláno,* airport—*aerodrómio,* ship—*plío* or *karávi,* harbour—*limáni.* Tourist Organization—*Grafíoh Tourismoo.* Police—*Astinomía.* When does the boat leave/arrive?—*Ti óra févgi/ftáni to karávi?* I want to go to Athens—*Thélo na páo stin Athina.* Where/which is the road to Athens?—*Pou/pios íne o drómos ya tin Athina.* One- way ticket—*issitírio aplo,* return ticket—*issitírio me epistrofí,* first/second/third class—*próti/ défteri/tríti thési.* Have a good journey!—*Kaló taxídi!*

At the service station

Car—*aftokínito* or *amáxi,* motor-repair shop—*sinerghío aftokiníton,* petrol station—*pratírio venzinis,* tyre repairs—*voulkanizatér,* petrol—*venzíni,* litres—*lítra.* Fill it up—*Yémisto.* Check the oil/radiator water/battery water/tyre pressure—*Kitáxte to ládi/neró sti mihaní/igro batarías/ aéra sta lástiha.* Wipe the windows—*Skoópise ta paráthira.* I have a flat tyre—*Ého éno tripi- méno lástiko.* My car has broken down, can you repair it?—*To aftokínito moo then hálase, boríte na to ftiáxete?* Garage—*Garáz.*

Miscellaneous

Post Office—*Tahidromío,* telephone—*tiléfono,* telegraph—*tilegráfio,* postcard—*kart postál,* letter—*grámma,* stamp—*grammatóssimo,* envelope—*fákellos,* newspaper—*efimerída,* map— *hartís,* cigarettes—*sigára,* cigars—*poúra,* pipe-tobacco—*kapnós pipas,* matches—*spírta,* pen— *stiló,* film—*film fotographikó.*

Emergencies

Policeman—*astifilax,* police station—*astinomikó tmíma.* I am ill—*Íme árostos.* I want a doctor/ dentist/oculist—*Thélo énas iatrós/odontíatros/ofthalmíatros.* I am hurt—*Íme travmatisménos.* Bring help quickly!—*Voíthia grígora!* Telephone for an ambulance!—*Tiléfonise sto asthenofóro!* First-aid kit—*Tsánta me tis protés voíthies.* Artificial respiration—*Tehnití anapnoí.* Accident— *Distíhima.* Hospital—*Nossokomío.*

A GUIDE TO GREEK FOOD

'Hurry up and eat, the food's getting hot!' This surely apocryphal remark, attributed by a wag to an Athenian housewife, sums up the typical foreigner's reaction to Greek food, perhaps as he sees his rubbery omelet floating in a sea of rancid oil. But the more adventurous gourmet will be pleasantly surprised by the discovery that Greek food can be quite delicious, particularly in the better Athenian restaurants, or in private homes.

Few foreigners really get to know Greek hors d'oeuvres, or *mezedes,* because normal restaurants offer only a small selection of these dishes. A meal in a good taverna, however, can consist almost entirely of *mezedes*. One usually orders between five and fifteen different items for a good sized group and then eats small portions of each as slowly as possible. Such meals can last for hours, and must be accompanied by litres of wine. Cold hors d'oeuvres include *tsatsiki*, thick yogurt mixed with shredded cucumber and garlic; *melitsanosalata*, crushed aubergine salad; *ktapodi*, octopus, boiled or in a light sauce; *garides*, boiled shrimp; *dolmadakia*, stuffed grape leaves; *taramosalata*, fish roe salad; *fasolia salata*, white bean salad; and *feta*, salty, white goat cheese. In addition to these, a good restaurant will have a few of its own mysterious specialities, such as cheese and pepper purée, or an uncommon kind of shrimp salad, and these are always worth trying. Hot hors d'oeuvres include many versions of *tiropitakia*, or tiny cheese pies made with paper thin pastry; *patata keftedes*, fried potato balls; *keftedakia*, small meatballs; *tirakia*, fried cheese balls; *kolokithakia tiganita*, fried baby squash; *piperies tiganites*, fried peppers; *melitsanes tiganites*, fried aubergine; and *loukanika*, small spicy sausages. The custom of eating a slow meal of *mezedes* is carried out with most grace by the Istanbul Greeks, who have recently flocked to Athens and set up new restaurants there, but the city's very old and established tavernas also do a good job.

Octopuses may look grotesque in the afternoon sun, but they are delicious when grilled and served with ouzo

As far as main dishes are concerned, the foreigner who has heard horror story after horror story about 'heavy, oily, workman's food' will be surprised to hear that grilled foods are very popular. In fact, there are certain restaurants which offer only *brizoles*, or steak; *souvlaki*, beef or lamb on a skewer; *hirines brizoles*, large pork chops; *biftekia*, or meatballs; *sikoti*, liver, and so on. Restaurants with the right equipment will also offer *kotopoulo souvlas*, chicken cooked on a spit; *arni souvlas*, similarly prepared lamb; and *kokoretsi*, or sheep intestines, which everyone finds delicious until discovering what they are. Food cooked on a spit can make a very good evening meal—unless it was cooked for lunch and has been turning ever since. These dishes are usually served with fried potatoes and large plates of *horiatiki salata*, the famous Greek salad of tomatoes, peppers, onions, white goat cheese, olives, and olive oil.

And despite the much-repeated horror stories, most tourists grow to love the very substantial 'minced meat dishes'. Not only are they incredibly filling but they are infinitely cheaper than anything else on the menu. *Pastitsio* is a 'brick' of macaroni with a layer of minced meat in the middle, and a rich bechamel and cheese mixture on top. *Moussaka* is most commonly a series of layers of fried aubergine with minced meat topped once again with bechamel and cheese, but the aubergine is sometimes replaced with potatoes or squash. *Domates yemistes* and *piperies yemistes* are tomatoes and peppers stuffed with a rice and minced meat mixture. Less frequently seen but still delicious are *kolokithakia papoutsakia*, which are halved squashes filled with rice and meat and covered with a very rich cheese, bread crumb, and egg sauce. Finally, there are *dolmadakia avgolemoni*, larger stuffed grape leaves covered with a light egg and lemon sauce. These dishes are cooked in an oven, usually in the morning, and never reheated, so those who demand a hot and filling meal had better eat at midday.

Moshari psito, roast veal; *moshari kokkinisto*, veal cooked in tomato sauce; *moshari youvetsi*, veal and macaroni casserole; *kotopoulo kokkinisto*, chicken in tomato sauce; *arni psito*, roast lamb; *keftedes*, spiced meatballs, are to be found in every single restaurant in the country and therefore many unhappy tourists come to think that they make up the entirety of Greek cuisine. Fortunately, this is not so, because although the dishes are often very well made, they can seem awfully dull after a while. Some special dishes to look for are *moshari stifado*, veal cooked with whole onions in a slightly sweet tomato sauce; *arni yemisto*, lamb stuffed with rice and chopped meat; *splini yemisti*, similarly stuffed spleen; *sofrito*, steak cooked in a rich garlic sauce; *pastitsada*, veal cooked in a tomato sauce with macaroni and cheese; and *hirino krasato*, pork chops cooked in wine.

And if one is in Greece during the winter, one should not miss the delicious game dishes. A few of these are *perdikes krasates*, partridges cooked in wine; *pitsounia krasata*, pigeons cooked in wine; *kounelli stifado*, rabbit cooked with whole onions and a wine and tomato sauce (this is also sometimes available in the summer); *ortikia pilafi*, quail with rice; and *becatses krasates*, woodcocks in wine sauce. There are special tavernas in Athens which specialize in game.

Although it is now becoming increasingly difficult to find a wide variety of fish and other seafoods in many parts of the country, Greece as a whole still has a lot to offer. The most popular kinds of fish are *barbounia*, or red mullet, *glossa*, sole; *xifias*, sword fish; *bakaliaro*, cod; *sinagrida*, sea bream; and *marides*, or whitebait. These fish are most often grilled (*skara*) or fried (*tiganita*) and, are delicious when fresh. Fish baked in casseroles with wine, spices, and tomatoes—*psari sto fourno, psari plaki,* and *psari a la spetsiota*—is also worth trying, as is the Corfiot speciality, *bourdeto,* several varieties of white fish cooked in a hot pepper sauce. *Kalamarakia tiganita,* fried squid, can be found almost anywhere, but *kalamarakia krasata,* squid in wine sauce, and *kalamarakia yemista,* squid stuffed with rice, currants, and pine nuts and cooked in tomato and wine sauce, are very special dishes. Two other specialities are *ktopodi me salza,* octopus in tomato and wine sauce, and *garides me feta,* shrimp cooked in a tomato sauce with crumbled feta cheese. And, of course, there is the outrageously expensive *astakos ladolimoni,* lobster served with an oil and lemon sauce.

Even the most modest island restaurant offers a variety of omelets, usually cooked in olive oil. Two interesting variations are the potato omelets (*omelleta me patates*) and the feta cheese omelets (*omelleta me feta*). The most common vegetables are *patates; fasolakia,* beans; *bamies,* okra; *melitsanes,* aubergine; and *kolokithakia,* squash. Less common are *anginares a la polita,* artichokes cooked in oil with small potatoes, carrots, and onions, and *briami,* baked summer vegetables.

One rarely finds sweets or coffee served in restaurants; instead one goes to the *Zakoroplasteion,* or sweet-shop for these. Each sweet-shop offers its own 'original' ice-cream concoctions, as well as the most traditional sweets, such as *baklava,* the honey-soaked nuts and pastry layers; *kadaifi,* honey-soaked shredded wheat; *galakto bouriko,* milk pie; and *rizogalo,* rice pudding. The occasional shop will make *loukoumades,* hot honey puffs, which are worshipped by sweet-toothed Athenians.

One can get Nescafe throughout the country—*nescafe sketo* is black coffee, *nescafe me gala* is coffee with milk. However, once one is accustomed to it, Greek coffee is preferable as an after dinner drink. There are four preparations of Turkish or Greek coffee, which vary in strength and sweetness. *Sketos* is without sugar, *metrios* is medium strong with a little sugar, *varisglikis* is strong and sweet, and *glikis vrastos* is sweet and boiled. Most Greeks drink *cafe metrio.*

There are also a large number of traditional snacks sold both at open stalls and in sweet shops for minimal sums. *Tiropittes,* cheese pies; the less common *kreatopittes,* meat pies; and *spanakopittes,* spinach pies; all of these are ideal for a quick stand-up lunch. *Souvlaki* cooked on wooden skewers and served with tomato, onions, yogurt and herbs on unleavened bread; and *yiro,* slices of pressed meat sliced off from a large hunk of meat on a vertical spit and served the same way, are both delicious and very filling.

Finally, Greeks eat a good deal of fruit and cheese. During the summer, the most popular fruits are watermelon (*karpuzi*), canteloupe (*peponi*), grapes (*stafilia*), figs (*sika*), and peaches (*rodakina*). The visitor will inevitably taste the ubiquitous *feta,* the white, salty, goat cheese, and *kasseri,* the sharp yellow semi-hard cheese, but one should also try to find *mizithra,* a very soft, unsalted white cheese; *manouri,* also unsalted and soft; *kefalotiri,* a hard salty cheese like Parmesan and used similarly; and *graviera,* which is like Gruyère.

Although one could question the extent to which Greek cuisine is original, the fact that the Greek diet is varied and healthy is indisputable. There is a national conspiracy, particularly among island cooks, to convince all visitors that Greeks live and die on oily roast chicken and an occasional plate of potatoes, but one only has to look at the elephantine proportions of anyone over thirty years of age to realize that they must be eating a lot more than that.

GREEK WINE

Since remote antiquity the Greeks have been noted for their love of wine, 'the gift of bountiful Dionysus'. Although the best Greek wines cannot even begin to compare with the better vintages of France, they are nonetheless quite pleasant. (Or is it the felicitous surroundings that enhance their flavour, sipping *retsina* in a taverna garden while listening to a lutist singing under a silver moon.)

Retsina, the resin-flavoured white wine of Greece, is very definitely an acquired taste. But for the fastidious foreigner, for whom *retsina* will always taste like turpentine, Greece now produces a wide variety of non-resinated (*aretsina*) table wines. These come mainly from the three principal wine-producing areas in Greece: the Mesogia district in Attica, just north-east of Athens; the region around Naoussa in Macedonia; and the vineyards south of Patras in the western Peloponnese. The best wines from the Mesogia are Hymettos, Courtaki and Pallini, all of them dry white wines. Naoussa is noted for its heavy dry red wines, Boutari and Tsantalis; while the Peloponnese is famous for its Demestica, the most popular unresinated white wine in Greece. The island of Samos bottles several varieties of medium-dry aromatic wines ('Fill high the bowl with Samian wine'), the volcanic isle of Santorini produces white wines with a heady taste of brimstone, Rhodes exports two brands of quite passable champagne—C.A.I.R. and Achaia Klauss, and Epirus is justly proud of its sparkling Zitsa. Other popular wines are:

Red. Castello Danielli, Santa Laura, Caviros, Cellar, and Chevalier de Rhodes.
White. Santa Laura, Cava Cambas, Santa Helena, Elissar, and King.
Rosé. King, Kokkineli, and Roditis.
Retsina. Plaka and Malamatina are the best of a mediocre lot.

But the best wines in Greece are never bottled; you will find them in huge barrels set into the walls of little tavernas, where they are served in half-litre (*miso-kilo*) aluminium flagons. As our dear friend Manoli Lavaris taught us to say: '*S'parakaló, dóse moo kaló krasí ápo to varéli!*'—'Please give me some good wine from the barrel!' One can usually predict the quality of the wine served at such tavernas by the state of preservation of the ancients tippling there—the older and healthier the drinkers, the better the wine—to coin an alcoholic proverb.

Modern Greeks have recently taken to drinking beer (thus leaving more wine for the ancients). Greek beers are not yet up to European standards,

Yorgos, happy with his wine, laughs at the refrain of a popular song—'Wherever there is Yorgos, there is gold'

but they are fast improving. The best are Henninger, Amstel, and Fix Hellas (the latter a quaint corruption of Fuchs, the German brewer who accompanied King Otho to Athens).

By far the most popular appetizer is the famous Greek *ouzo*, best taken with a few slices of grilled octopus. The best-known brands of *ouzo* are Metaxa, Boutari and Sans Rival. Greeks of Anatolian extraction prefer *raki*, similar to ouzo, but less sweet and with more kick. And if you find yourself on the isle of Chios, try some *mastika*, a resin-flavoured aperitif with reputed curative powers. In case you wonder why there are so many well-preserved gaffers leaping around on the Greek islands, it is because of their daily potion of *tsíporu* (also called *strofilía*), that clear and deadly last pressing of the fig. (Although Barba Stelio, a *tsíporu*-sipping octogenarian friend of ours on the isle of Naxos, has another explanation for the longevity of the island Greeks. As he says, 'Eh! A man can't die until he's finished with his sinning!')

A drinker's vocabulary

Wine was anciently called *oínos* (a name which still appears stamped on the ubiquitous aluminium wine-cans), but in modern demotic Greek it is known as *krasí*. White wine is *aspró krasí*, red is *kókino*, or if it is very dark *mavró*, or black, and rosé is *kokinélli*. (Local wines are often given appropriate nicknames, such as a delicious rosé retsina which floored us one evening in a little Naxian village—its name meant literally 'a soft blow to the forehead'.) A bottle of wine is *éna bookáli krasí*, a glass is *éna potíri* (or the diminutive *ena potiráki*), another glass is *éna akóma potíri* (*éna akóma potiráki* is the title

14

of a very popular old drinking song), a half-litre flagon of wine is *míso-kílo krasí*, a last quarter-litre for the road is *éna kartótsi*, and the proper phrase for moaning on the morning after is '*Egó ta koópso to krasí!*' ('I'm going to cut out wine!'—the title of still another old drinking song, where the celebrant is promising to abstain in order to demonstrate the magnitude of the love he bears his mistress, and not because of the transient misery of a hangover).

HOW TO ORDER IN GREEK

Soup—*soúpa*, salad—*saláta*, beef—*vodinó*, pork—*hirinó*, veal—*moshári*, lamb—*arnáki*, chicken—*kotópoulo*, liver—*sikóti*, steak—*brizóla*, fish—*psári*, tomatoes—*domátes*, potatoes—*patátes*, onions—*kremídia*, aubergines—*melitsánes*, okra—*bámies*, courgettes—*kolokithákia*, rice—*rízi*, cheese—*tirí*, yogurt—*yaoúrti*, eggs—*avgá*, omelet—*omeléta*, milk—*gála*, beer—*bíra*, wine—*krasí*, unresinated—*aretsínato*, bread—*psomí*, water—*neró*, fruit—*froúta*, oil—*láthi*, vinegar—*xídi*, butter—*voútiro*, salt—*aláti*, pepper—*pipéri*, lemon—*lemóni*, boiled—*vrastó*, fried—*tiganitó*, roasted—*psitó*, broiled—*tis scháras*, oven baked—*tou foúrnou*, stuffed—*yemistó*, hot—*zestó*, cold—*krío*, with—*me*, without—*horís*, fork—*piroúni*, knife—*mahiéri*, spoon—*koutáli*, napkin—*petséta*, glass—*potíri*, plate—*piáto*, table—*trapézi*, chair—*karékla*, one portion—*mía merída*, two portions—*dio merídes*.

Waiter!—*garsón!* Boy!—*mikré!* The menu, please.—*To katálogo, parakaló.* What food do you have today?—*Ti fayitá éhete símera?* I want . . .—*thélo* . . ., we want . . .—*thélome* . . ., bring me . . .—*fére moo.* I am sorry, but this is not on the menu today.—*Lipoome, allá aftó then ine ston katálogo simera.* I did not order this.—*Then paringíla afto.* We ordered only one portion.—*Paragílame móno mía merída.* The food is cold.—*To fayitó ine krío.* The beer is not cold.—*I bíra then ine kría.* The bread is stale.—*To psomi ine bagiátiko.* You did not bring enough forks and knives.—*Then férate arketá piroonia kai mahiéria.* These potatoes must have been made yesterday.—*Aftés i patátes prépi na ine apó hthes.* The bill, please.—*To logariasmó, parakaló.* Immediately—*Amésos.* We did not eat any bread—*Then fágame psomí.* We had . . .—*Íhame . . ..* You made a mistake in the bill—*Kánate láthos sto logariasmó.* Excuse me. You are right.—*Signómi. Éhiete díkio.* Do you have change?—*Éhete psilá?* Unfortunately, no—*Distihós, óhi.* Certainly—*Vevéios.* May I pay tomorrow?—*Boró na plíróso ávrio?*

GREEK MUSIC AND DANCING

One of the pleasant discoveries the visitor soon makes is that the Greeks are a very musical people, as much so in their own way as are the Italians and the Welsh. It is a rare Greek who cannot sing or play a musical instrument, and it is a sad evening when one does not hear the sound of music and song enlivening the streets and squares of a Greek town.

One wonders from whence comes the Greek love for music, which goes back as far as the myths of Orpheus. Is it because of the way in which music and song allow them to express the deepest feelings of their hearts and souls, or is it because they are born performers and show-offs? And so you come to realize that a Greek musician is playing and singing not only for you, but for himself. As Niko Katzanzakis wrote in *Zorba the Greek*, describing Zorba's love for his *santuri*, an old Turkish instrument from Asia Minor:

> I looked at his hands, which could handle the pick and the *santuri*. They were horny, cracked, deformed and sinewy. With great care and tenderness, as if undressing a woman, they opened a sack and drew out an old *santuri*, polished by the years. It had many strings, it was adorned with brass and ivory and a red silk tassel. Those big fingers caressed it, slowly, passionately, all over, as if caressing a woman . . . .

'When I'm feeling down (says Zorba to the narrator), or when I'm broke, I
play the *santuri* and it cheers me up. When I'm playing you can talk to me and I
hear nothing, and even if I hear I can't speak. It's no good my trying. I can't!'
'But why, Zorba?'
'O don't you see? A passion, that's what it is!'

When one hears the lyrics of their songs, one learns that the Greeks are
(or pretend to be) hopeless romantics, for many of their melodies are of
unrequited love. One soon notices the constant recurrence of such words as
kardía (heart), *fegári* (moon), *agápi* (love), and *agonía* (which needs no
translation). The *agonía* songs and poems form a class of their own, with
origins going back to medieval Greece. (A poet-musician friend once presented us with a slim volume of his own *agonía* compositions, heart-breaking
love-songs by a man who has been happily married to a fat wife for thirty
years.)

The folk-songs which one usually hears in Greece are of two general types:
cantádes, and songs accompanied by the *bouzoúkia*. *Cantádes* are the Italianate
choral songs which developed in the Ionian isles during the centuries of
Venetian rule. These songs can be quite lovely and melodious, and one is
often astonished at the exceptionally fine voices of one's otherwise ordinary
friends, the tenor-carpenter, the baritone-baker, and the basso-fisherman.
Singing together around a table in a humble taverna, a few citizens can often
produce music of great lyric beauty, the more so if they have downed a dozen
tankards of *retsina* during the recital. In times past, particularly on Corfu
and the other Ionian isles, *cantádes* were a very important part of the ritual
of Greek courtship, when a love-stricken swain, accompanied by a carefully
chosen chorus of good friends, would stand below his beloved's balcony and
serenade her through the evening hours. (Hence the frequent occurrence in
cantádes of the word *balcóni*.) Our own favourites are *Ta Mátia* (The Eyes),
Prássina Mátia (Green Eyes), *Kalaidíste* (The Song of Birds), and *Yírisse*
(Return), perhaps the loveliest of all *cantádes*. Request these when the strolling
musicians stop at your table, and they will probably be so moved and carried
away by the sound of their own voices that they will sing a dozen more
cantádes.

Bouzoúkia music is quite another matter altogether. Like *retsina*, *bouzoúkia*
music is an acquired taste, with its seemingly discordant melodies and its
whining, nasal songs, but, like *retsina*, it is quintessentially Greek. This despite
the fact that the *bouzoúkia* is not really a Greek instrument at all, for it and
its music were first brought to Greece by refugees from Asia Minor after the
war of 1919–23. The Anatolian origins of *bouzoúkia* music are betrayed by
its marked similarities to Turkish music; and why not, for these two peoples,
who have fought against each other for so many centuries, have shared the
same tribulations and ways of life, and so their music is much the same too.
(Ask for an old Turkish ballad in a taverna some night, and observe the
emotional response of some of the older people, hearing a song from their
childhood in Asia Minor.) The *bouzoúkia* first achieved popularity in Greece
in the 1930s, largely through the songs of Tsitsanis, and soon it became the
music of the working classes, particularly in the Piraeus.

Though many *bouzoúkia* songs are lugubrious, others proclaim that mad and irrepressible joy which is one of the most marvellous traits in the Greek character. Get together a *bouzóukia*-player, a fiddler, a mandolin-player and a guitarist, have them working really great with one another late one evening, passing improvised melodies back and forth like four drunken jugglers with a silver ball, their hands moving across their instruments as rapidly as the wings of humming-birds, creating a twanging, tinkling, jingling folk-symphony which fills the room with its exciting sounds and exhilarating rhythms, themselves so carried away at the finale that they leave the bandstand and move out among the tables to finish with one last orgasm of song, and you will soon see the air filled with flying plates and saucers which come crashing down onto the dance-floor, where the bowing players are now ankle-deep in shards of crockery. (This wild display of enthusiasm is in clear violation of the law sternly advertised above the bandstand; ΑΠΑΓΟΡΕΥΕΤΑΙ ΤΟ ΣΠΑΣΙΜΟ, it says simply, DO NOT SMASH—implying the crockery, of course, for what else would one do in a taverna after hearing such music?)

And so a night in a taverna will tell you more about the Greek spirit than a shelf of books, and is immeasurably more fun. (But you will pay for the plates you break, for they will be added to your bill—a neat example of how the Greeks (or at least some of them) remain practical even when they are otherwise out of their minds with excitement.)

Dancing is as essential a part of Greek life as is music, and is connected with all the joyous experiences of Greek life: weddings, baptisms, religious festivals, or just a few friends drinking together in a taverna. Each region in Greece has its own characteristic dances; the *Pentozali* and the *Sousta* of Crete; the *Malamatianos* from Kalamata in the Peloponnese; the *Hessapico*, or Butcher's Dance, from Macedonia; the *Zeybekiko* from Asia Minor; the *Balo*, a lovely courting-dance of the Cyclades; the *Syrtaki*, a circle dance which takes on a variety of forms all over the country. In all of these dances, especially in the *Zeybekiko* and the *Syrtaki*, the Greek male is at the very peak of his manly form (the woman is usually just a modest accompanist), handkerchief sticking out of his back pocket, cigarette dangling from his lips, head thrown back proudly and arms outstretched like an eagle in flight, soaring through the air in acrobatic leaps and slapping his hand sharply on his shoe, flinging a week's salary at the musicians with a disdainful expression on his face. 'Yasu, Manoli *leventi!*' (the hero), his admiring friends shout encouragingly to Manoli, who tomorrow morning will be hauling crates of fish on his motor-cycle in the Piraeus, but who tonight feels as lordly as Achilles.

But there will be other evenings when Manoli cannot be persuaded to dance, even though his friends beg him to, and he sits in the taverna with a distant expression on his face, staring off into a far corner of the smoke-filled room. He may dance later, when the time is right and if his spirit moves him, but not now.

Traditional Greek music and dancing are best seen at *paniyíri*, the religious festivals which are celebrated throughout the country on the feast days of the innumerable saints of the Orthodox Church. These *paniyíri* are the thinly-disguised survivals of the ancient Dionysiac revels, and some of them go on day and night for the better part of a week. These festivals are especially lively and colourful in remote mountain villages on the Aegean isles, and are

A young man struts like an eagle round the dance floor at a village festival—no longer just a farmer

accompanied by spirited music and dancing in the church courtyard or in the village square. The island music is different again than that heard in mainland Greece, and its origins go back much farther in time, to an age now dimly recalled only in archaic lyrics.

One of our old favourites is *Samiotissa* (The Girl from Samos), which begins and ends with this simple but touching chorus: 'Samiotissa, Samiotissa, when will you come back to Samos? We will wait by the sea till you return one day, and then we will build for you a golden bower on the shore.' And through the night the music and dancing continue under the stars, as arthritic ancients prance gaily around the square, reducing three generations of their women to joyous exhaustion, with proud young blades showing off their gymnastic prowess in courting dances with their demure fiancées, and with lines of shy young girls circling gracefully in ancient choral processions, their hands raised and joined daintily by kerchiefs, looking like classic figures in an Attic frieze.

And so one should not leave Greece without going to at least one *paniyíri*, for there one can best hope to catch the spirit of this magnificent country and its wonderful people. As Michali Karavoula sang to us one night in a mountain village on the isle of Naxos: 'Yani (John) and his family have danced at our *paniyíri* for twelve summers; may they be spared to dance together with us for a hundred summers more!'

SPORTS IN GREECE

SWIMMING. The coasts of mainland Greece and its islands in the Aegean and the Adriatic are blessed with some of the finest beaches in Europe. Many of these beaches are equipped with organized facilities, but visitors may prefer to swim in the isolated sandy coves which are to be found all along the coasts. There are more than a dozen beaches in the immediate vicinity of Athens, the most popular of which are Agios Kosmas (11km from Athens), Glyfada (17km), Voula (20km), and Vouliagmeni (25km). There is a large public swimming-pool in Athens, the Olympic, at 4 Vass. Olgas Ave. (Athens Map E4), next to the Temple of Zeus. The Athens Hilton also has a large swimming-pool, which one can use by becoming a member.

WATER-SKIING. Fast motor-boats for water-skiing can be hired near organized beaches and at villages all along the coasts. There are a number of water-skiing schools along the Saronic Gulf, the most popular of which is at Vouliagmeni. Water-skiing contests are held off the island of Salamis during the summer months.

ROWING. Regattas are held in the summer months in the Saronic Gulf and also on Lake Ioannina. Amateur rowing enthusiasts can enjoy their sport by joining any of the rowing clubs which are to be found all along the Saronic Gulf; boats may be hired for about 30drs an hour. For detailed information contact the Greek Rowing Club, 61 Akadimias St., Athens. Tel: 612-109.

SAILING. The National Tourist Organization of Greece maintains nearly a hundred yacht-supply stations throughout the country. Detailed information on yachting can be obtained from the NTOG, 2 Amerikis St., Athens, Tel: 3223-111. Yacht races are usually held in Faliron Bay on Wednesday, Saturday, and Sunday afternoons. For information, contact the Royal Yacht Club, 15a Xenofondos St., Athens, Tel: 3236-813.

FISHING. The Saronic Gulf is one of the richest fishing grounds in Greece, and it is possible to rent boats for fishing at any of the small harbours along the coast. There are also opportunities for trout-fishing in the lakes and rivers of central and northern Greece. For information, contact the Amateur Angler's Club, Akti Moutsopoulou, Zea Harbour, Piraeus, Tel: 415-731. Underwater fishing with a spear gun is very popular in Greece, particularly on the Aegean islands. Instructions and information on underwater swimming and fishing are provided by the Greek Federation of Underwater Sports, Agios Kosmas, Tel: 9817-166.

GOLF. There is a good 18-hole golf course just outside Athens, the Glyfada Golf Course, Tel: 8946-875. There is also a 9-hole course, the Varibobi Golf Club, Tel: 8014-276.

TENNIS. The most centrally located is the Athens Tennis Club, 2 Vass. Olgas Ave., Tel: 911-672. There are also tennis courts at all of the beach resorts along the Saronic Gulf.

HORSE-RACING AND RIDING. The largest track in Greece is the Faliron Race Course, at the end of Syngrou Ave., Tel: 966-511. There are two meets a week, on Wednesdays and Saturdays (afternoons in winter, evenings in summer). For information concerning opportunities for riding in Greece, contact the Athens Riding Club, Tel: 6815-630.

WINTER SPORTS AND MOUNTAINEERING. Greece has several majestic mountain ranges with peaks over 1800 metres, and there are opportunities for skiing from late November until early May. There are hostels and ski-lifts at the following locations: Mt. Parnes, just outside of Athens; Mt. Parnassos, 150km west of Athens; Mt. Pelion, above Volos; Vitsi, near Florina; Metsovon, a very attractive mountain village in the Pindus range; and Menalon, near Tripolis in the Peloponnese. Late spring and early autumn are ideal times for hiking and mountaineering in Greece, particularly in the Pindus and Olympus ranges. For detailed information apply to the Hellenic Alpine Club, 7 Karageorgi Servias, Tel: 234-555.

HUNTING. The best region for hunting is in northern Greece, particularly in the River Evros Delta along the Turkish border. The hunting seasons are as follows:
September—October: quail, turtle-dove, partridge.
November: woodcock, partridge, hare.
December—January—February: woodcock, thrush, partridge, hare, wild goose, and duck.
   Wolves and foxes can be found in the Pindus (Ioannina) and Olympus (Kozani) ranges. Deer is rare and its hunting is prohibited. Wild boar can be found in the mountainous border districts in north-western Greece and in the River Evros Delta. A boar-hunting festival is held annually in the Evros Delta during a two-week period in late January and early February. For detailed information contact the Greek Hunting Confederation, 2 Korai St., Athens, Tel: 3231-271.

FOOTBALL. The most popular sport in Greece. International matches are held at Karaiskaki Stadium, which is located in Neon Faliron, near Piraeus. For information on match schedules apply to the Greek Football Confederation, 91 Akadimias St., Athens, Tel: 622-202.

CRICKET. A quaint relic of the British presence on Corfu. (In Greek it is called *To Game*, literally *The* Game.) In Corfu the Viron (Byron) Athletic Club, 11 Vass. Georgiou II St., arranges cricket matches between local teams and visiting clubs from Britain and the USA.

GAMBLING. There are three big-time gambling casinos in Greece. One is located at the luxurious Mount Parnes Hotel, an hour's drive from Athens; the others are in Rhodes and in Corfu. But if you would rather gamble for fun, learn how to play *tavli*, the Greek version of backgammon, which is always played at the local *kafenion*. (It is absolutely essential to *slap* the tavli counters smartly on the board, or you will be considered a rank amateur, even if you win.)

Many people say that football is Greece's only sport

USEFUL INFORMATION

Travelling to Greece

Tourist Information. The National Tourist Organization of Greece (EOT) operates offices in a number of countries to provide information for prospective tourists. The main office is:
Athens, Greece—National Tourist Organization of Greece, 2 Amerikis St. Tel: (021) 3223-111/9. Cables: GRECTOUR.
The National Tourist Organization of Greece also maintains offices in:
London, UK—195–7 Regent St., London W1R 8DL. Tel: 01-734-5997. Cables: GRECTOUR. Telex: 51-21122.
New York, USA—601 Fifth Ave., New York, N.Y. 10017. Tel: HA 1-5777/8. Cables: GREC-TOUR.
Los Angeles, USA—627 West Sixth St., California 90017. Tel: 626-6696. Cables: GRECTOUR.
EOT also has offices in most of the major towns of Greece to provide information of a regional nature.

Air Travel to Greece. Greece's two international airports. Athens and Salonica, are well integrated in the network of world airlines. Also, the airports of Rhodes, Crete and Corfu are connected by direct flights to London, Paris and Rome, as well as by charter flights to many other cities. British European Airways (BEA) operates several flights daily direct from London to Athens, as does Trans World Airways (TWA) from New York to Athens. The Greek national airline, Olympic Airways, also has daily direct flights to Athens from London and New York, and operates regular flights to major cities in Europe, North America, South Africa, Australia, and the Near and Far East.
  The main office of Olympic Airways is:
Athens, Greece—96 Syngrou Ave. Tel: (021) 9292-251. Cables: OLYMPIC. Ticket Office: 6 Othonos St.; Tel: 9292-555. Reservations: 9232-323. Domestic Terminal: 122 Syngrou. Tel: 9292-333.

INTRODUCTION

Among the many Olympic Airways offices around the world there are the following:
London, UK—Olympic Airways Bld., 141 New Bond St., London W1Y 0BB. Ticket Office, Tel: 01-493-7262. Reservations, Tel: 01-499-8712. Cables: AIROLYMPIC.
New York, USA—888 Seventh Ave., New York, N.Y. 10019. Tel: (212) 956-8400. Reservations: 838-3600. Ticket Office: 647 Fifth Ave. Tel: 956-8462/4. Cables: OLYMPAIR.
Montreal, Canada—800 Dorchester Blvd. West. Tel: (514) 878-3891. Ticket Office: Queen Elizabeth Hotel, 940 Dorchester Blvd. West. Tel: 878-9691. Cables: OLYMPAIR.
Johannesburg, South Africa—Geneva House, 18b Loveday St., P.o.b. 7399. Tel: 835-5583/4. Cables: OLYMPAIR.
Sydney, Australia—54–62 Carrington St., NSW 2000. Tel: 2901777.
Note: In Athens, all Olympic Airways flights (international and domestic) operate from the West Air Terminal, while all other airlines use the East Air Terminal at Hellinikon Airport.

Sea Travel to Greece. Piraeus, the largest harbour in Greece, is a port-of-call for many of the world's major shipping lines. The ports of Patras, Igoumenitsa and Corfu are entry-points for the car-ferries from Italy, and Rhodes is one of the most popular stopping-points for cruise ships. Among the steamship lines which have a regular passenger service from western Europe to Greece are: Adriatica, Black Sea Lines, Epirotiki Lines, Hellenic Mediterranean Lines, Italian Lines, Jadriolinija, Turkish Maritime Lines, Zim, and the Greek Lines, which has a regular service between New York and the Piraeus. The Hellenic Mediterranean and Adriatica Lines also jointly operate a regular car-ferry service between Italy and Greece, as do DFDS Seaways, Efthymiadis Lines, Fragline, Greek Sea Paradise, the Hellenic Italian Line, Karageorgis Lines, and the Mediterranean Sun Lines. Cruises to Greece direct from Britain are sponsored by several firms in London, most notably Swans Hellenic Cruises (Hellenic Travellers' Club, 260 Tottenham Court Road, London W1).

By Rail to Greece. There are three direct express trains with sleeping-cars connecting London and northern Europe with Greece. These are the Direct Orient/Tauern/Athens Express via Calais, Paris and Milan; the Hellas Express via the Hook of Holland and Munich; and the Acropolis Express via Ostend and Munich. For information and tickets contact the British Railway Travel Centre, Rex House, Lower Regent St., London SW1.

By Motor Coach. The Hellenic State Railways operates a weekly motor-coach service—the Eurobus. The Eurobus follows the itinerary Athens—Salonica—Skopje—Belgrade—Munich—Ostend —and thence by ferry and train to London. For information contact the Hellenic State Railway Service, 31 Venizelou Ave., Athens.

By Road to Greece. Motorists from Britain and western Europe have basically two routes to choose from. The easiest route is through Italy and then by car-ferry from Ancona or Brindisi to Igoumenitsa or Patras. (The completion of the new superhighway from Athens to Patras makes the latter the better port of entry.) The other route is through the Balkans, a long, hard drive of about 1200 miles which brings one down through Yugoslavia and northern Greece. Maps and other information can be obtained from the Automobile Association, Fanum House, Leicester Square, London WC2, or from the American Automobile Association.

Student Travel. There are several travel agencies in Greece which cater for students. The oldest and best of these is Lotus Travel, 7 Filellinon St., Athens; Tel: (021) 3232-874; Cables: LOTUS. Each summer Lotus organizes hundreds of charter flights between Athens and all major European cities, including forty-two to London alone, as well as flights to a few cities in North America; the rates are a fraction of the normal commercial fares. Lotus also offers cut-rate fares on trains, buses and ships from western Europe, as well as low-cost tours of Greece itself. Other agencies catering for students are Host Travel, 3 Filellinon; Tel: 3237-778; Cables: HOSTRAV; and Viking Travel, 3 Filellinon; Tel: 3223-684; Cables: VICTRAVEL.

Passports and Visas. Valid passports are required. Tourists from Britain, the Commonwealth and the USA do not require visas; those wishing to remain after three months must apply for a permit at the local police station (two months for citizens of the USA).

Health Regulations. Vaccination and inoculation are not required for tourists entering from Europe, Turkey, Canada or the USA. If you come from or pass through a yellow fever, smallpox or cholera area you will be required to produce the relevant vaccination certificate.

Customs Regulations. Visitors may bring into Greece all personal effects in reasonable quantity entirely free of any import duty or undue formality. Particular care has to be exercised regarding antiquities, for the laws protecting them are especially strict. No antiquity may be taken out of the country without prior permission from the Greek Archaeological Society, 14 Aristidou St., Athens. Firearms: Only one or two sporting-guns and twenty rounds of ammunition may be imported into the country; these are registered in the importer's passport. Automobiles: Visiting motorists may enter Greece with their cars freely on a valid *Carnet de Passage*, or, in the absence of such a document, by a Customs entry on their passport. Insurance of foreigner's cars in Greece is not yet compulsory, but possession of the usual Green Card is strongly recommended.

Currency Regulations. The amount of Greek currency which one can bring into or take out of the country is limited to 750 drachmae, and the amount in one's possession should be declared at the time of entry. If on entering Greece a visitor is in possession of more than $500 (c. £200) in any foreign currency it is advantageous to declare the amount, so that on departure one may freely take out any amount up to that declared on entry. There is no restriction on the value of traveller's cheques carried by foreign visitors either on entry or exit.

Currency Conversion. The basic unit of Greek currency is the Drachma (dr), and there are 100 Lepta to each Drachma. The following are the current rates of exchange in Drachmae (drs) for British and American banknotes:
1 Pound Sterling = 65·54drs   1 US Dollar = 29·85drs
The approximate equivalents of Greek banknotes in British and US currency are:

	50drs	100drs	500drs	1000drs
Pounds Sterling:	0·76	1·52	7·60	15·20
US Dollars:	1·67	3·35	16·75	33·50

Travelling in Greece

By Air. Olympic Airways operates frequent flights between Athens and the principal cities and islands in Greece. There are one or more flights daily to: Aktion (for Levkas and Preveza), Alexandroupolis, Cefalonia, Chania (Crete), Chios, Corfu, Cos, Herakleion (Crete), Ioannina, Kalamata, Kozani, Kythera, Lemnos, Milos, Mykonos, Lesbos, Porto Heli, Rhodes, Salonica, Samos, and Skiathos. There are also several flights weekly to: Agrinion, Andravida (for Pyrgos and Olympia), Larissa, and Volos. There are also the following inter-island flights: Herakleion—Mykonos; Herakleion—Rhodes; Mykonos—Rhodes—Karpathos. Domestic Terminal: 122 Syngrou St., Athens. Reservations: 9232-323. Ticket Office: 6 Othonos St.; Tel: 9292-555.

By Rail. The Hellenic State Railways (OSE) connects Athens with the principal cities of mainland Greece through two main lines. One line goes north through central Greece to Salonica and thence to Alexandroupolis, near the Turkish border. The other line goes from Athens to Corinth and then branches west and south around the Peloponnese. The southern branch goes from Corinth down to Argos, then crosses to Tripolis in the central Peloponnese, and continues to Kalamata and Messini on the southern coast. The western line runs along the northern coast of the Peloponnese to Patras, then down to Pyrgos on the west coast and inland to Olympia. The western and southern branches are connected by a branch line between Kalamata and Pyrgos.

There are two railway stations in Athens: Larissis Station (Athens Map B2); for central and northern Greece. Tel: 813-882. Peloponissou Station (Athens Map B2); for the Peloponnese. Tel: 524-541.

By Bus. The Greek State Railways operate frequent services by Pullman buses from Athens to the principal towns in mainland Greece. Information: Aghiou Konstantinou St.; Tel: 522-491. Buses to all parts of Greece are also operated by the Joint Pools of Bus Owners (KTEL). Booking offices are listed in *This Week in Athens*, on sale at all kiosks. These buses leave from either Terminal A, 100 Kifissou St., or from Terminal B, 260 Liossion St., both some distance from the centre of town.

23

INTRODUCTION

By Road. The Greek highway system has been greatly improved in the past decade and one can now drive with ease to almost all parts of mainland Greece; car-ferries extend the national highway system out to once-remote islands. There are two super-highways which are now nearing completion; from Athens to Salonica and on to the Yugoslavian border; and from Athens via Corinth to Patras. Virtually all main roads are now asphalted, even on the islands, and even some of the secondary roads.

Rules of the road. Traffic regulations and road signs in Greece are the same as those in use elsewhere in Europe, and driving is on the right-hand side of the road. The speed limit in large towns is 50 kph unless a lower limit is indicated on a sign. In unlimited areas the speed limit for cars is 110 kph.

Road assistance. Foreign motorists in Greece are given free technical assistance in case of a breakdown. The service is provided by the yellow vans which bear the sign ASSISTANCE ROUTIERE; these vans cover most of the main highway routes in Greece. The service is sponsored by the Automobile and Touring Club of Greece (ELPA); Head Office, 2–4 Messogion St., Athens; Tel: 604-411.

Camping and caravan sites. There are nearly one hundred camping and caravan sites throughout the country. They are organized by the National Tourist Organization of Greece in cooperation with the Automobile and Touring Club, and information can be obtained by contacting either office.

Car rental. There are car-rental agencies in all of the large towns in Greece. The largest of the many agencies in Athens is Hellascars: 7 Stadiou St., Tel: 3222-230; 148 Syngrou Ave., Tel: 3233-487. Rates at Hellascars (which are about the lowest in Athens) range from about 180–360drs a day, depending on the make and size of the car, plus an additional charge per kilometre ranging from 2·5 to 3·6drs, petrol not included. A deposit is required.

Petrol. Petrol stations are spaced at more or less regular intervals along the main highways; however they are liable to be few and far between along secondary roads, particularly on the islands. Ordinary petrol (84–86 octane) is 12·3drs per litre, super (94–96 octane) is 16·5drs. (Obviously, prices may fluctuate further.) Tourists are exempt from the restriction on weekend driving, and may purchase coupons which entitle them to 150 litres of super petrol at 10drs (regular—8drs) per litre for every ten days of their stay.

By Sea. There are several shipping companies which operate regular passenger services and car-ferries to most of the Greek islands. Most of these companies have their main offices along the quays in the Piraeus, although one can purchase tickets from any travel agent. (There is a central information office in Karaiskaki Square in the Piraeus where one can obtain data on schedules and fares.) Most ships now carry ferry cars, tickets for which are sold at dock-side an hour or two before departure, in a scene of almost unimaginable chaos. It is advisable to obtain a priority number for your car a day or two in advance; this can be arranged by the agent who sells you your personal ticket. Those who desire to island-hop will find it an almost insoluble problem, for the various ferries follow a more or less set route through a particular group of islands and then back again, so that it is difficult, for example, to cross from the Cyclades to the Dodecanese or the Sporades (or even from one island in the Cyclades to another, if they are not on the same route). Nearly all of the islands can be reached from the Piraeus, although it is more convenient to embark from Volos for the Northern Sporades, from Kavalla or Keramoti for Thasos, from Alexandroupolis for Samothraki, and from Patras or Igoumenitsa for the Ionian isles.

Also, several lines operate organized cruises to some of the better-known islands and to the Aegean coast of Turkey. Tickets and information can be obtained from any travel agent in Athens.

For those who desire to charter a private yacht, there are about a dozen reputable yacht-brokers in Athens. Daily rental fees, including crew, range from about £32 ($80) for a small caïque, or fishing boat, with 4 passengers, £80 ($200) for a large caïque with 8 passengers, and up to £400 ($1000) or more for a luxurious yacht. Information concerning ship-charters can be obtained from the Yacht Brokers and Marine Consultants Association, 4 Valaoritou St., Athens. Tel: 623-674.

Travel Agencies and Conducted Tours. Several travel agencies in Athens offer conducted tours, with knowledgeable, English-speaking guides; these include various tours of Athens and of the major places of interest in mainland Greece and on the islands. The mainland tours are by Pullman bus and the island tours are by ship or aeroplane. The principal agencies in Athens which offer such tours are:

Map of Greece

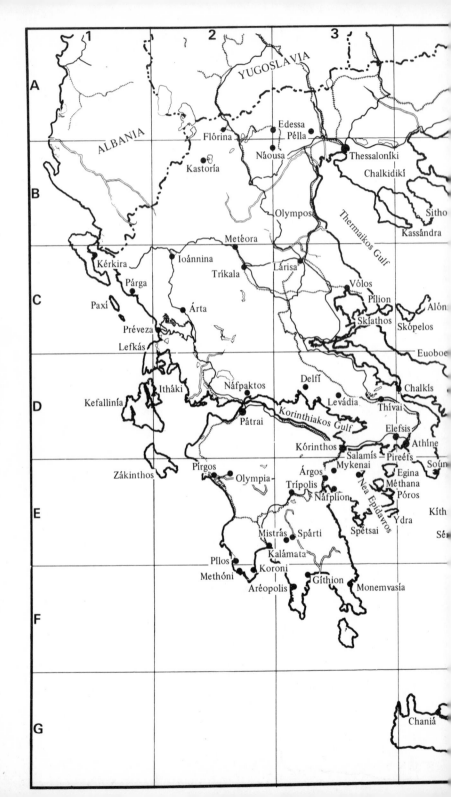

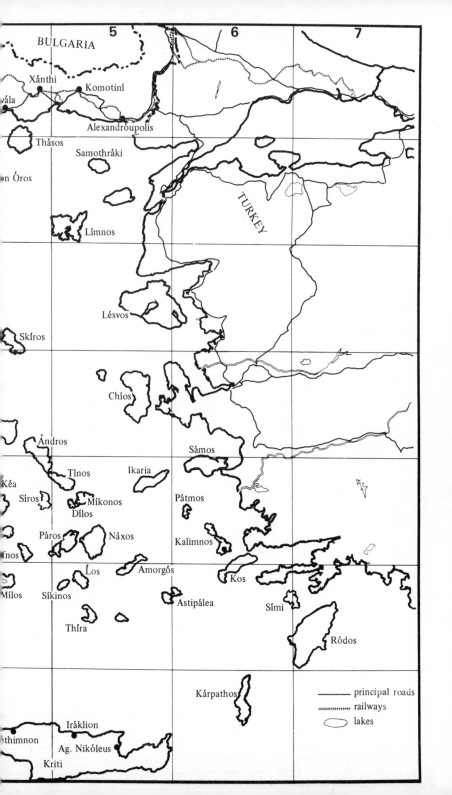

ABC Tours—57 Stadiou St., Tel: 3249-484. Cables: GARIGAN.
American Express—2 Hermou St., Tel: 3230-603. Cables: AMEXCO.
Bamaco Tours—1 Vass. Alexandrou Ave., Tel: 722-800. Cables: BAMACOS.
Bell Tours—3 Stadiou St., Tel: 3224-138.
Chat Tours—4 Stadiou St., Tel: 3223-137. Cables: CHATOURS.
Key Tours—2 Ermou St., Tel: 3232-520.
Lotus Student Tours—7 Filellinon St., Tel: 3225-266. Cables: LOTUS.
Wagon Lits/Cook—2 Karagiorgi Servias, Tel: 3242-281. Cables: SLEEPING.

Youth Hostels. There are a large number of Youth Hostels throughout mainland Greece and the islands. (Individual addresses are given under the listing of hotels for the various localities throughout the country.) For detailed information, contact the Greek Youth Hostels Association, 4 Dragatsaniou St., Klafthmonos Square, Athens. Tel: 3234-107.

Miscellaneous

Opening Hours.
Shops. From May to October: 8 a.m. to 1.45 p.m. and 5 p.m. to 8 p.m. On Wednesdays and Saturdays during July and August shops are open daily from 8 a.m. to 2 p.m. only. (In Salonica, during July and August, shops are open daily from 8 a.m. to 2 p.m. only.) From October to May: 8.30 a.m. to 1 p.m. and 4 p.m. to 7.30 p.m. Shops are closed on Sunday throughout the year.
Offices. Varies, but generally from about 8 a.m. to 1 p.m. and 5 p.m. to 7 p.m. daily; Saturdays 8 a.m. to 1 p.m. Closed Sundays.
Banks. Daily except Sundays from 8 a.m. to 1 p.m. and from 5.30 p.m. to 7.30 p.m. During July and August banks are generally closed on Saturday afternoons and on one or two other afternoons in the week. In order to serve tourists, certain banks provide foreign exchange services from 8 a.m. till 10 p.m. or midnight. Exchange offices at border-points and international airports remain open 24 hours a day.

The opening hours of museums and archaeological sites are different in summer (16 March to 14 October) and winter (15 October to 15 March). The following are the opening hours outside of Athens. (Opening hours in the capital will be given individually in *The Sights of Athens*.)
Museums. In Summer: Daily from 8 a.m. to 1 p.m. and 3 p.m. to 6 p.m.; Sundays and holidays 10 a.m. to 1 p.m. and 3 p.m. to 6 p.m. In winter: Daily from 9 a.m. to 1 p.m. and 2.30 p.m. to 5 p.m.; Sundays and holidays 10 a.m. to 1 p.m. and 2.30 p.m. to 5 p.m.
Archaeological sites. In summer: Daily from 7.30 a.m. until sunset; Sundays and holidays 10 a.m. to 1 p.m. and 3 p.m. to 7 p.m. In winter: Daily from 9 a.m. until sunset; Sundays and holidays 10 a.m. to 1 p.m. and 2.30 p.m. until 5 p.m.

Entry fees to museums and archaeological sites vary from 5–20 drs, depending on their importance.

Public holidays. Museums and archaeological sites are closed on the following holidays: New Year's Day, Independence Day (25 March), Orthodox Good Friday till noon, Orthodox Easter Sunday and Christmas Day.

The official holidays on which shops, banks and offices remain closed are: Christmas Day, St. Stephen's Day (26 December), New Year's Day, the Epiphany (6 January), Independence Day (25 March), Clean Monday (the day following the end of Carnival and preceding Lent), Good Friday, Easter Sunday and Monday, 15 August (Dormition of the Virgin), and National Day (28 October). The various cities and towns of Greece also have official holidays on the feast days of their patron saints; that of Athens is St. Dionysius the Areopagite, whose day falls on October 3.
Carnival. The three-week period preceding Lent is a time for general festivities. Carnival time is particularly gay, even riotous, in Patras and in the Plaka quarter of Athens, where the revels are a reminder of the bacchanalia of ancient times.

Postal Services. Post Offices are identified by the sign TAXYPOMEION. Letter boxes are painted blue and are marked ΓΡΑΜΜΑΤΟΚΙΒΟΤΙΟΝ, those for domestic mail are marked ΕΣΟΤΕΡΙΚΟΥ, and for foreign mail ΕΞΟΤΕΡΙΚΟΥ. Visitors without a definite address in Greece may have their mail sent to POSTE RESTANTE at whatever locality they are residing in, and can then pick it up at the local post office.

Telephones and cables. Both services are handled by a public corporation identified by a sign carrying its initials in Roman letters, OTE. Long-distance telephone calls can be dialled directly to any city in western Europe, the British Isles, and the USA. Information on code-numbers of foreign cities can be obtained from the telephone directory. Cables may be sent at the OTE offices or dictated over the telephone. Local calls cost one drachma; most kiosks have a public telephone.

Tipping. Hotels: Bills include a service charge of 15%, but it is customary to give an additional small tip (perhaps 20–50drs) to any of the personnel who have been especially helpful. Luggage handling is also included in the bill, but porters expect at least 5drs per bag (perhaps 10drs in de luxe hotels). Waiters for room service expect 5–10drs. Restaurants: Bills include a service charge of 15%, so many customers leave only the odd few drachmae to round out the bill. (Perhaps 5drs for each person served to the waiter and 2–3drs per person to the trainee or assistant waiter.) Taxis: Drivers expect a tip of about 10% of the bill, perhaps more at night if they are transporting you home from a revel in the Plaka.

Electricity. Current is 210–220 volts, 50 cycle AC in almost all parts of the country. In some remote localities, particularly on the islands, it is 110 volts DC. And in some happy places there is no electricity at all, so that you can dine by candle-light and hear a guitarist playing without benefit of microphone or electronics.

Water. Drinking water is safe and can even be delicious, particularly in the mountains or on the islands, where it often comes gushing from a village fountain or flowing from an ancient sacred spring beside a church. If you are worried about microbes, take example from the old gaffers sitting with you in the village square, and have your water with an *ouzo*.

Climate. Greece has one of the most agreeable climates in Europe. For those from Britain or the USA who are used to sweltering or rainy summers, there will be few complaints about the occasional heat-wave which strikes Greece in July and August (when the temperature in Athens sometimes reaches 110°F (43°C)), for the air is always dry and the heat tempered by a breeze, particularly in the evening. There is scarcely any rainfall from June through September, except perhaps in the Ionian Isles (a small price to pay for the lush vegetation which there delights the eye). The loveliest months of all are June and September, when the crowds of tourists have thinned out a bit, and when one can enjoy serene weeks of warm and tranquil weather. Even in late autumn and early winter there are still days of brilliant sunshine. If Greece has bad weather it comes in deep winter, when high winds and freezing rain make life difficult in the mountains and on the islands, but your friends there will tell you that they go indoors in those weeks, like any sober man, and drink to stay warm till Carnival. And of course Athens is too preoccupied with its busy life to pay heed to the weather even in the worst of seasons. Spring in Greece comes relatively late, considering how far south the country lies, but when it does come it transforms the land. The rocky hillsides which blinded you with their barrenness last summer are now a soft and virginal green, and withered fields are deep in young grass and brilliant with wild flowers; then the eternal summer returns again.

This is Athens

When walking around Athens, one soon discovers that it is a collection of separate neighbourhoods centring around the city's squares, each with its own distinctive character. Syntagma Square is the centre of official and tourist Athens; on one side stands the imposing edifice of Parliament House, once the focus of Athens' ebullient and frenetic political life, now quiet except for the well-guarded comings and goings of important personages of the realm. Another side of the square is dominated by the massive Grande Bretagne, the oldest and grandest hotel in Athens. (At Christmas 1944, while Winston Churchill was in residence there, the Communist forces briefly considered blowing it up.) The other sides of the square are lined with travel-agencies and air-line offices, and its promenades are given over to pavement cafés where well-heeled tourists sit and stare at one another and at passers-by. Watching the passing parade and catching snatches of conversation is one of the most popular spectator-sports in Athens: camera-slung tourists with their noses stuck in guide-books ('Where's the Parthenon?'), bored American business-men and their blue-haired wives ('You *are* coming to the Sound and Light Spectacle, Harry!'—sounds like Hairy), a freak-show of drifting hippies hitching their way from Nowhere West to Nowhere East ('Hey, Paris was a *drag*, man, no beach!'), and crowds of hurrying, scurrying, gesticulating Greeks. (Although you may not understand their rapid-fire conversations, the subject matter can often be guessed from their dramatic hand-gestures, a silent guide to the national character.)

Greeks generally leave Syntagma to the tourists, unless their business takes them there, and usually prefer to take their evening aperitif and talk in the nearby Kolonaki Square. Their conversation in former times was principally of politics, but since that is no longer of much interest they talk of other things, mostly of money-matters, speaking with all the heat and forceful emphasis of the political past. (The hoary remark that a nation of three Greeks would form four political parties is no longer applicable.) The male Greek voice is stentorian, suited to addressing parliaments or commanding armies, though the speaker be only a humble clerk; and an apparently violent shouting match between two friends, which might elsewhere presage the onset of a fist-fight or a duel, is here just an everyday discussion concerning the merits of two rival football teams. The Greek female speaks in two voices, liquid and dulcet tones if she is talking to her lover or her lady-friends, or a high-pitched staccato shriek if she is arguing with a shop-keeper or calling after her errant son Paniyoti. Kolonaki is much-favoured by well-off Greeks of middle years. Middle age, at least insofar as physical appearance

Syntagma Square is a home away from home for tourists

is concerned, would seem to set in rather earlier in Athens than elsewhere; the lithe and handsome Apollo whom you knew three years ago is now portly and balding and carries a briefcase, and the svelte and beauteous Ariadne has become broad-bottomed and balloon-breasted—the Levantine ideal of feminine pulchritude ('My love is beautiful, she waddles like a duck', wrote a Byzantine poet more than a thousand years ago, describing the girth and gait of many modern Athenian ladies). The so-called Athenian spread is undoubtedly due to the huge meal which Greeks swallow at midday, before taking to their pyjamas for the afternoon siesta. And so if you want to be sure of finding a seat at one of the cafés in Kolonaki, the best time is mid-afternoon, when all of Athens is asleep. But you will be in competition with the local insomniac, who then takes the opportunity of spreading out onto a multiplicity of chairs, one to sit upon, one for his feet, two for his elbows, one for his hat, one for his briefcase, and one for his newspaper, so that two or three Greeks can fully occupy a whole café.

The centre of everyday Athens is the busy Omonia Square. (Omonia means harmony, a word which hardly describes this crowded and clamorous intersection, this whirlpool of traffic, this maelstrom of humanity.) Buses roar from one orifice of the square to another, belching clouds of noxious fumes; taxis and three-wheeled motor-carts race maniacally around the traffic-circle, drivers swearing eloquently at one another; sweating multitudes swarm on and off the underground, which thunders below like an angry plutonic god, and the tourist's only thought will likely be concerned with how to escape as soon as possible. Nonetheless, Omonia Square is a part and aspect of ordinary Athens which one ought to see, though only for the briefest possible span. (How could one possibly avoid Omonia, since all of the main boulevards inexorably lead you there, by the hand as it were, even when you desperately want to avoid it?)

If middle-class Athens has a centre, it is probably Fokionos Negri, a two-block long piazza in Patission, the district north of the Archaeological Museum. The square centres on a fountain surrounded by a pleasant park. Mothers air their babies in ornate carriages, children play tag and ride their bicycles, and old men read their newspapers or doze in the sun. The square is lined with cafés and restaurants which are largely owned and frequented by Greeks who have emigrated from Turkey in the past generation. Many of the restaurants are named after favourite places in and around Istanbul, most notably the Taverna Prinkipo, referring to the idyllic Princes' isles in the Sea of Marmara.

Another Athens altogether is to be found in Monastiraki Square, just to the south of Omonia. Monastiraki is the principal market district of Athens

A busy street scene, with Omonia Square in the background

and is also the site of the endlessly fascinating Flea Market, making it one of the liveliest and most colourful quarters of the city. In the last century Monastiraki was the site of the Turkish Pazar, or public market-place, and it has still a distinct resemblance to a Turkish market town. The kafenions and working-men's tavernas around Monastiraki Square are rough and ready places where the service is informal and the attitude is take it or leave it. But if you sit there and have your food and drink like any other citizen you will perhaps find a warmer and more genuine welcome than at the Grande Bretagne or the Hilton. Who sent that half-litre can of retsina to our table? The waiter who brought it is sworn to secrecy, so we will have to look around the room to find our benefactor. There he is, sitting at a table in the corner with some friends, an old street-vendor with white moustaches and a merry twinkle in his blue eyes. As we catch his eye he and his friends raise their glasses to ours and we toast one another's health. *Stin iyia sas!* His name is Barba Stelio and he is eighty-five years old; he has fought in two wars and suffered and lost sons in two others, but that has not diminished his zest for life nor affected his friendliness and hospitality to strangers. For you are a guest in his country and as such are accorded the same hospitality that Odysseus received when he was welcomed to the palace of King Alcinous. *'Sto kalo!'* May you go with goodness! says Barba Stelio when you bid him and his friends farewell, many convivial hours and wine-cans later. And so one evening in a humble taverna can teach you more about the heart of this city and its citizens than do all the libraries and museums.

Night-town in Athens is the Plaka, the picturesque neighbourhood just under the Acropolis. This is all that is left of Old Athens, the town which Byron knew and loved, and which he immortalized in his poetry. Steep and narrow streets lined with lovely old houses wind their way uphill to the foot of the Acropolis itself, from where one commands sweeping views out over the modern city stretching across the plain below. At night the Plaka is a madhouse, for half of the old houses have been converted into tavernas, and electronic music blasts from every doorway and rooftop. The streets swarm with crowds of foreign revellers looking for a Mediterranean thrill, and the pavements are jammed with restaurant tables, with harried pages and waiters shouting to make themselves heard above the din.

But there are still places in the Plaka where one can catch glimpses of Old Athens as it must have been a hundred years ago. One such spot is Anafiti, virtually a little village nestling right under the rock of the Acropolis itself. This neighbourhood is inhabited by people from the Aegean isle of Anafi, who settled here after their native village was destroyed in the earthquake of 1925. The Anafiotes have created their village here, and one can walk along winding lanes under clambering grapevines, catching glimpses of peasant families sitting serenely in the flower-filled gardens of their whitewashed houses. There are one or two modest little tavernas in Anafiti where one can dine peacefully under the stars, undistracted by the loud and frantic night-life below. Our favourite is the Taverna Panepistimiou, so called because it is housed in the Old University (*Panepistimio*) of Athens, founded by King Otho in 1838. The building is now a crumbling ruin and the taverna occupies an unkempt garden in what was once the courtyard of the University, the

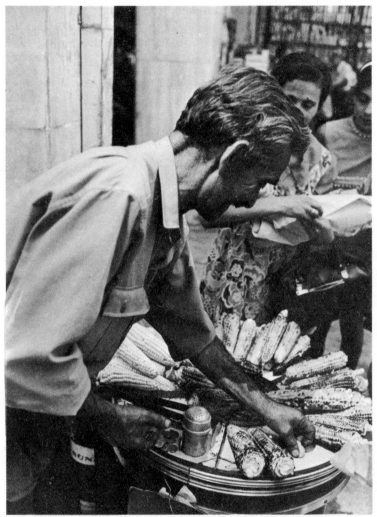

Grilled corn on the cob is sold at every street corner in Athens

scene of the first cultural revival in Greece after the War of Independence. A musician is seated under a wild fig tree in a corner of the garden; he is strumming on his guitar and singing lovely old *cantades* from the Ionian isles, evoking romantic memories of an Athens of times past. Below we see the lights of modern Athens twinkling like a vast constellation across the Attic plain, and above the magnificent ruins of the Parthenon are illuminated with brilliant flood-lamps, making it glow as if with an inner light of its own. . .

31

This is the Athens we have known and loved and to which we keep returning, if sometimes only in our memories.

Note: A map of Athens is available free at the offices of the National Tourist Organization of Greece, 2 Amerikis Street, Athens (just behind the American Express Building on Constitution Square). For convenience, all hotels, museums, monuments etc. mentioned in the sections on Athens are located according to the coordinates on this map.

THE SIGHTS OF ATHENS

Visitors to Athens invariably begin their first tour of the city at Syntagma Square and head straight for the Acropolis. The most direct route begins on Amalias Avenue, which runs past the **Old Palace** (now the House of Parliament), built in 1836–42 for King Otho. Beside the Palace are the very pleasant **National Gardens**, first laid out at the direction of Queen Amalia, Otho's proud and ambitious wife. On the far side of the Gardens is the **New Palace**, still guarded by the picturesquely-dressed Evzones of the King's bodyguard, although the former King is now far away from Greece.

Continuing along Amalias we come next to the **Zappeion Gardens**, an extension of the National Gardens. The Gardens end at Vass. Olgas Avenue, which leads left to the Stadium, built for the first revived Olympic Games of 1896. At the corner of Amalias there is a sentimental nineteenth-century statue of Byron expiring in the arms of Hellas.

Across the vast intersection stands the **Arch of Hadrian**, built by that Emperor in A.D.132 to delineate ancient Athens and the new city of his reign. An inscription on the side nearest the Acropolis tells us that, 'This is Athens, the ancient city of Theseus', while one on the opposite side says, 'This is the city of Hadrian and not of Theseus'.

Behind the archway stand the enormous ruins of the **Olympieion**, or the Temple of Olympian Zeus, the largest in Greece. Taking seven centuries to build, it was finally completed by the Emperor Hadrian in A.D.130. Only 16 of the original 104 columns remain standing; nevertheless it is still one of the most impressive sights in the city, with its immensely tall columns crowned with finely-carved Corinthian capitals. (Open 7.30 a.m. to sunset daily.)

Once past the Olympieion we cross the intersection and take the broad Avenue of Dionysius Areapaghitou, which runs past the **Acropolis**, now looming up before us.

Approaching the entrance to the Acropolis, we pass in succession two ancient theatres built in under the huge rock itself. The first of these is the **Theatre of Dionysos**, where the plays of Aeschylus, Sophocles, Euripides and Aristophanes were performed for the very first time. The present theatre was built by Lycurgus the Law-Giver in 342–26 B.C., but was rebuilt and modified in Hellenistic and Roman times. (Open 7.30 a.m. to sunset daily.)

The second of the two theatres under the Acropolis is the **Odeion of Herod Atticus**. It was completed in about A.D.160 by the eminent rhetorician whose name it bears and is thus one of the last monumental structures built in Athens in ancient times. The theatre is an outstanding example of Roman influence on Greek architecture. It was superbly restored in the last decade and is now the scene of the Athens Festival, in which cycles of ancient Greek drama are given by the National Theatre of Greece, along with performances by some of the world's leading orchestras, theatrical groups and operatic companies. Visually the setting is unbelievably beautiful, mellow amber lights illuminating the Roman arches behind the stage and the floodlit Parthenon glowing on the Acropolis above. Seated there in early evening, waiting for the performance to begin, the lines of Aristophanes inevitably come to mind. 'Come, O muse, tread a measure to the sacred choirs; come to charm our song; come to see the waiting crowds, assembled here in their thousands.'

The **Acropolis** has been the heart of Athens since the beginning of its history. As early as about 1500 B.C. the great rock already bore a stately Mycenaean citadel, whose cyclopean stones are still woven into the fabric of the supporting walls. Athena, the goddess who gave her name to the city, was already being worshipped in Athens at that time, and a succession of temples were built in her honour on the Acropolis across the centuries. After the Greek victory over the Persians at Marathon in 490 B.C., an ambitious project was undertaken to enlarge the area of the Acropolis by building terraces and supporting walls, and work was begun on a new temple to Athena. However, the Persian sack of Athens in 480 B.C. reduced the Acropolis and its temples to fire-blackened ruins. Reconstruction did not begin until a generation later, when Pericles conceived his grand scheme to rebuild the Acropolis and its temples on a truly monumental scale, as befitting the status of Athens as the capital of the Greek world. Work began in 447 B.C. under the direction of the architects Iktinos and Kallikrates, and by 438 the Parthenon was completed and dedicated to Athena, the Virgin Goddess. Work was then begun on the other structures which still survive on the Acropolis; the **Propylaia**, or monumental entryway; the **Temple of Athena Nike**, and the **Erechtheion**. These magnificent structures remained substantially intact for more than two thousand years, till long after the Golden Age of Greece had faded into history. During the Byzantine era both the Parthenon and the Erechtheion were converted into churches and the Propylaia was at one point a Venetian palace, and during the Turkish occupation the Parthenon became a mosque and the Erechtheion a harem. Disaster finally came in the seventeenth century during battles between the Venetians and the Turks, who had fortified the entire Acropolis and converted the Parthenon and the Propylaia into powder magazines. Lightning struck the Propylaia and destroyed it in 1645, in 1686 the Temple of Athena Nike was torn down by the Turks and converted into a gun emplacement, and the following year Venetian artillery fire blew up the Parthenon and demolished it, leaving the scattered ruins we see today. And so the Acropolis and its temples remained in ruination until the past century, when Greece and her friends began the long and arduous work of reconstruction which continues today. But even in ruins these noble edifices are still surpassingly beautiful, and they remain as symbols of the Golden Age of Greece and the dawn of Western Civilization.

We ascend to the Acropolis along any of several paths beyond the Odeion of Herod Atticus, walking through glades of evergreens planted there a century ago by Queen Amalia. We enter through the **Beule Gate**, a reconstructed Roman work of the third century A.D.

(The Acropolis is open from 7.30 a.m. till sunset daily during the summer, and from 9 a.m. till sunset daily during winter. It is also open from 9 p.m. till 11.45 p.m. throughout the year on the four nights around full moon.)

We then ascend a steep ramp which leads to the **Propylaia**, the monumental entry-way which actually cost more to build than the Parthenon itself, and whose construction was eventually halted short of completion in 432 B.C. because of the Peloponnesian War.

Passing through the Propylaia we obtain our first full view of the **Parthenon** itself, across a field strewn with column-drums and fragments of scattered marble. One inevitably pauses here, perhaps sitting upon a fallen column, and reflects upon the glorious past of the temple, certainly the most beautiful and historic structure in the world. One is struck by the perfect harmony of its design and the sheer majesty of its structure, with the brilliant Attic sun blazing upon its honey-coloured columns. The nobility of the Parthenon is not spoiled even by the hordes of tourists who swarm in and around it; although one should see it at its best in early morning or at twilight, when the Acropolis is relatively uncrowded, or better still under a full moon, when the ruins are lovely and serene and you can commune with them almost as if alone.

After an hour or two of wandering through the Parthenon one must tear oneself away to visit the other antiquities on the Acropolis. Just across the way from the Parthenon we see the **Erechtheion**, a temple sacred to both Athena and Poseidon, who in ancient times vied for the worship of the Athenians. This is one of the most perfect specimens of the Ionic order and also perhaps the most original, with its unique and lovely Southern Portico, the Porch of the Carytids, with its roof supported by the statues of six maidens. (The second from the left is a plaster copy replacing one carted away by Lord Elgin.) The North Porch is one of the masterpieces of Greek architecture, with its gracious Ionic colonnade looking out across Athens to the Attic plain and the slopes of Mount Parnes beyond.

Turning back towards the entrance, we see the east front of the Propylaia and to its right the **Pinakotheke**, or Picture-Gallery, where once were displayed the now vanished masterpieces of ancient Greek painting.

To the left of the entrance we find the charming little **Temple of Athena Nike**, Athena the Bringer of Victory, which stands on a giddy platform beside the south wing of the Propylaia. From this vantage point one commands a sweeping view out over Athens and the Piraeus to the Saronic Gulf, where the historic isles of Aegina and Salamis float on a mist-covered sea. From the front porch of the temple we look across to some of the historic hills near the Acropolis. To the left we see the **Mouseion Hill**, topped by the **Monument of Philopappus**, built in A.D.114–16 in honour of a distinguished Athenian. It was from the summit of this hill that a Venetian cannon fired the shot that destroyed the Parthenon. At the foot of the Mouseion there is a rock cave which popular tradition associates with the **Prison of Socrates**, where the philosopher drained the cup of poison hemlock as the sun set behind Salamis. Next to the Mouseion on its right is the **Hill of the Pynx**. On its north-eastern slope we see a huge semicircular terrace supported by a massive retaining-wall, this is the site of the **Pynx**, which in classical times served as the meeting-place of the Athenian Assembly. (The Pynx now serves as a theatre for the nightly presentations of the Sound and Light Spectacle.) To the north of the Pynx rises the so-called **Hill of the Nymphs**, now surmounted by an observatory. Then finally on the far right we see the low **Hill of the Areopagus**, which in ancient times gave its name to the High Court of Justice of the Athenians. Aeschylus, in his *Eumenides*, here placed the trial of Orestes by the Gods for the murder of his mother Klytemnestra. And it was on the Areopagus in the year A.D.51 that St. Paul delivered his Sermon on the Unknown God.

Walking now along the southern wall of the Acropolis, we pass beside the Parthenon and come to the **Acropolis Museum**.

(Open daily, except Tuesdays, from 9 a.m. to 5 p.m. in summer and from 9 a.m. to 4 p.m. in winter. Sundays and holidays 10 a.m. to 2 p.m.)

Here are housed nearly all of the works of art discovered on the Acropolis since archaeological work began in 1835, forming a unique collection of archaic sculpture from the seventh, sixth and early fifth centuries B.C. Among the masterpieces exhibited here are the Moscophorus, or Calf-Bearer (No. 624); the Kritian Boy (No. 698); the Peplos Kore (No. 679), faint traces of colour still tinting her smiling eyes and plaited hair; the Rider (No. 590) and the Running Hound (No. 143)—two works by Phaidimos, the greatest sculptor of the Archaic Age; the gracefully moulded relief of the Winged Victory removing her sandal (Room VIII); and the particularly lovely Korai, or Maidens, dressed in their flowing archaic robes (Room IV). The most highly-treasured sculptures in the Museum are the Fragments from the Parthenon Frieze (Room VIII), all of those which escaped the avid eye of Lord Elgin. They are especially fascinating because they represent scenes from the Panathenaic Procession, which every four years made its way up from the Sacred Gate to the Parthenon for the celebration of the Great Panathenaia, the joyous festival honouring Athena, the tutelary goddess of the city.

Directly across from the Museum there is a belvedere, from where one enjoys yet another panoramic view of the city, this time to the north. Looking down, one sees the red-shingled roof-tops of the picturesque old houses in the Plaka, and off in the middle distance to the north-west the conical **Lykabettos**, the highest (910ft) hill in Athens.

Most of the remaining antiquities in Athens are to be found in the area around the north slope of the Acropolis. Though none of these monuments are comparable in beauty or importance with those on the Acropolis itself, they are nonetheless quite fascinating and well worth seeking out, scattered as they are through the oldest and most picturesque quarter of Athens, extending in time across the whole span of the city's history.

We might begin once again in Syntagma and from there follow Mitropoleos Street, which soon brings us to the nineteenth-century **Greek Orthodox Cathedral** (Athens Map E3). (It was built by four architects using stones

The Byzantine church of Little Metropolis

taken from seventy-two demolished churches!) Just beside it is the old cathedral, known variously as the **Little Metropolis**, St. Elefterios, or the Panayia Gorgoepicoos (the Virgin who grants requests quickly). The Little Metropolis, which dates from the twelfth century, is a very pleasing example of the Byzantine architecture of that period. The walls of the church, both outside and within, are revetted with stonework taken from more ancient structures, making it literally a palimpsest of Athenian history. Most interesting is the fourth century B.C. frieze across the west front, in which the twelve zodiacal signs are represented in terms of their seasonal festivals.

Turning to the right past the Cathedral we come almost immediately to another little church from about the same period as the Little Metropolis. This is the **Kapnikarea** (Athens Map D3), perhaps the best-preserved Byzantine church in Athens. The main structure dates from the eleventh or twelfth century, while the porch, the outer vestibule, and the north chapel are thirteenth century additions.

Continuing past the Kapnikarea on Ermou Street we soon come to **Monastiraki Square** (Athens Map D3), the centre of a busy and colourful market area. The streets leading off from the square are lined with antique shops, clothing markets, shoe shops, coppersmiths' ateliers, blacksmiths' forges, and market barrows; and one has to fight one's way through a mêlée of haggling housewives and itinerant peddlers hawking their shoddy wares to the passing throngs. (A pretty gypsy girl is trying to charm a middle-aged Athenian into buying a garishly-coloured coverlet. 'I'll take it at that price if I can have *you* thrown in!' he jokes. 'It would be a bargain, *kyrios*, but I'm afraid you'd die in bed!' she replies contemptuously and struts away, swearing in Romany.)

Monastiraki takes its name from a Byzantine church which stands at the north side of the square. This is the **Pantanassa**, or Great Monastery, more commonly called Monastiraki, the Little Monastery, because of its modest dimensions. The church dates from the tenth century, but whatever architectural interest it might have had was destroyed by a very poor restoration early in the present century.

At the south-east corner of the square we see the eighteenth-century mosque of Tzistarakis, more usually known as **Pazar Dzami**, or the Market Mosque, one of the very few Turkish antiquities remaining in Athens. The former mosque now houses the **Museum of Greek Popular Art**.
(Open daily, except Tuesdays, from 9 a.m. till 1 p.m.)

On exhibit are a very interesting collection of antique Greek embroideries, vestments, regional costumes, wood carvings, ceramics, and some beautiful medieval jewellery.

At the far end of the square we see the ruins of **Hadrian's Library** (Athens Map E3), dating from the first half of the second century A.D. All that remains of this once-splendid institution are its shattered and fire-blackened walls and a few Corinthian columns. Nevertheless, the ruins have a kind of sombre grandeur, evocative of the vanished splendour of Roman Athens. Unfortunately, they are not presently open to the public.

From Hadrian's Library we follow the street beside the railway line for a short way and then cross it over a foot bridge; this brings us to the entrance of the **Agora** (Athens Map E2,3). Just as the Acropolis and the Parthenon were the focus of the religious life of Athens, so was the Agora the centre of its civic life. The Agora was basically a great market square, where all of the city's merchants met to transact their business and where politicians and intellectuals gathered to discuss public affairs and philosophy. Except for the newly reconstructed **Stoa of Attalos**, all is now in ruins, destroyed when the barbaric Herculi sacked Athens in A.D.267. But it takes only a little exercise of imagination to recreate the scene in one's mind, filling the Agora once again with merchants, politicians, orators and philosophers, living at the dawn of Western civilization.

Perhaps the best way to explore the ruins is to first take the path which leads off half-left from the entrance; this follows the ancient Panathenaic

Way, which led from here up the slopes of the Acropolis to the Parthenon. This soon brings us to the entrance of the **Stoa of Attalos**, the huge building which dominates the east end of the Agora.

The Stoa was originally built in the middle of the second century A.D. by Attalos II, the philhellenic King of Pergamum in Asia Minor. Though Athens was long past its prime by then, it was still an important commercial and intellectual centre, and so the Stoa was designed to fit in with the ancient character of the Agora, a market-place of goods and of ideas. The two floors of the building were lined with retail shops, and from its porticoed arcades Athenians could look out on the busy and exciting scene in the Agora or review passing processions on the Panathenaic Way. The Stoa was destroyed in the Herculian sack, but its stones were built into the defence wall which the Romans later put up to protect the city from further raids. The building was reconstructed on its original foundations in 1953–56 by the American School of Classical Studies, using the stones recovered from the Roman wall and following almost exactly the design of the Old Stoa, altogether a splendid achievement. The Stoa is a colonnaded building in two storeys, with twenty-one replicas of the original shops opening off from the back of the portico on each floor. Ten of the shops on the ground floor have been made into a museum, where the most important of the antiquities discovered in the Agora excavations are exhibited. On the upper gallery of the building there is a model of the Agora as it looked at the time of its greatest extent, in the second century A.D. There are also six plans showing the Agora at various stages in its development from the fifth century B.C. to the fifth century A.D. Using these plans, one can look out from the portico and easily identify the various ruins which litter the site.

The most impressive monument visible from the Stoa is the so-called 'Theseion', the temple that stands at the north-west end of the Agora. This has now been identified as the **Hephaisteion**, the **Temple of Hephaistos and Athena Hephaestia**, patron saints of the blacksmiths and coppersmiths who had their shops in this quarter in classical times and still do today. The Hephaisteion, which dates from the middle of the fifth century B.C., is the best preserved temple in Greece; although failing to achieve the surpassing beauty of the Parthenon, it is nevertheless a fine example of Doric architecture. In the Byzantine era it was converted into a church dedicated to St. George, and from the seventeenth to the nineteenth century it was used as a Protestant cemetery. One of the funerary slabs bears a Latin epitaph written by Byron.

(The Agora and the Hephaisteion are open daily from 7.30 a.m. till sunset. The Agora Museum in the Stoa of Attalos is open daily, except Mondays, from 9 a.m. till 4 p.m. in winter; Sundays and holidays 10 a.m. till 2 p.m.)

Leaving the Agora, we continue as before along Adrianou as far as the Underground station, where we bear right and then continue along Ermou Street. This soon brings us to the entrance of the **Kerameikos** (Athens Map D2), the cemetery of ancient Athens. The Kerameikos was the necropolis of Athens as far back as the twelfth century B.C., and in classical times the central area of the cemetery was reserved for the tombs of great men of the realm and for heroes who died fighting for their city. It was here that Pericles delivered his famous funeral oration for those who fell during the first year of the Peloponnesian War. Many of the finest funerary monuments which have been unearthed over the past century are now either in the National Archaeological Museum or in the **Oberlaender Museum**, which stands just beside the entrance to the Kerameikos. Nonetheless a considerable number of monuments still remain, scattered on either side of the extraordinary Street of Tombs. The most important of these is the **Memorial of Dexilos**, erected in honour of a young knight killed in action at Corinth in 394 B.C. The marble relief on the memorial is a copy of the original, which is on exhibit in the Oberlaender Museum. The Museum also contains a very important collection of Attic vases dating from the eleventh to the seventh century B.C.

At the west end of the Kerameikos we see a short stretch of the ancient city walls of Athens; these include the ruins of the city's two most important gates, the **Dipylon** and the **Sacred Gate**. The Dipylon was the main gate of ancient Athens, where the roads from Piraeus, Eleusis and Boetia converged to enter the city; and the Sacred Gate was the starting-point for the Panathenaic Procession.

(The site of the Kerameikos is open daily from 7.30 a.m. till sunset. The Oberlaender Museum is open daily in summer from 8 a.m. till 1 p.m. and from 3 p.m. till 6 p.m.; Mondays noon till 6 p.m.; Sundays and holidays 10 a.m. till 6 p.m. In winter the Museum is open every day from 8 a.m. till 5 p.m.)

From the Kerameikos we walk back along Ermou to Monastiraki. On our left we pass the quarter known as Psiri, the site of the fabulous Athenian Flea Market, where on Sunday mornings the city's junk collectors spread out their wares on the pavements.

Once back in Monastiraki Square we turn right, passing the entrance to Hadrian's Library, and soon come on our left to the main gate of the **Roman Agora**, which bears an inscription praising the generosity of Julius Caesar. At the west end of the Agora we see the famous **Tower of the Winds**, built in the first century A.D. for the astronomer Andronicus of Kyrrhos. The tower is octagonal in shape, with each wall facing one of the cardinal points of the compass and decorated with a relief depicting the wind blowing from that direction; altogether a unique and striking monument. (In Greek it is known as *Oi Aeridhes*, the Windy Ones.) In Turkish times it was inhabited by a community of Mevlevi dervishes, who probably found this extraordinary building peculiarly appropriate for their mystical songs and dances. Across the square are the ruins of an eighteenth-century Turkish *medresse*, or theological school.

We are now in the oldest and most picturesque quarter of the Plaka, with streets flanked with tottering old houses painted in faded and flaking pastels, and squares out of Italian opera sets. It is impossible to give directions here, for the alleyways of the Plaka are a labyrinthian maze staggering up and down the slope of the Acropolis. This area is particularly rich in Byzantine churches, for it was the centre of Athens during the days of Byzantium. (The tiny size of these churches tells us how humble the status of Athens was in that period.) Just under the Long Rocks of the Acropolis we find the fourteenth-century church of the **Transfiguration**, known locally as **Sotiraki**, or the Little Saviour; directly above it are the caves where in remote antiquity the earliest ancestors of the Athenians worshipped their primitive deities. A short distance below is the church of **SS. Cosmas and Damian**, which unreliable tradition associates with the Empress Eirene, one of the very few women to rule Byzantium in her own right (799–806). Eirene was born in the Plaka and is a revered saint in the Greek Orthodox Church, which seemingly ignores the unpleasant fact that she and her council of eunuchs put out the eyes of her son, the Emperor Constantine VI, and thus brought about his death. And on the same street we find the twelfth-century church of **St. Nicholaos Rhangavas**, another relic of the now almost vanished Byzantine town of Athens.

Continuing past St. Nicholaos on the same street we descend to a pleasant little square where we come upon what is perhaps the most romantic antiquity in Athens. This is the **Monument of Lysikrates** (Athens Map E3), a cylindrical drum surmounted by an entablature and dome, all carved from the same piece of marble, and framed in a circlet of slender Corinthian columns. The monument was erected in 334 B.C. to honour the singer Lysikrates, who in that year directed a boy's choir which won first place in the Athenian musical competition. From 1669 till 1821 it was enclosed within the grounds of a Franciscan monastery—an old print shows it in the monastery garden encircled in flowering vines, with a cowled monk seated beside it gazing at a human skull, obviously reflecting upon the frailty of human existence. Byron lived in the monastery when he first came to Athens in 1810, and it was there that he wrote *Maid of Athens* and began *Childe Harold*. The monastery was burned down during the War of Independence, but fortunately the Monument of Lysikrates escaped virtually undamaged. The site of the monastery is now occupied by a small park, in which a few fragments of ancient columns lie fallen in the grass, and the poet's residence is commemorated with a simple marble tablet bearing his name. The romantic can be forgiven for lingering here for a few moments and reflecting on the vanished scene, evoking the poetic Athens of Byron's time.

Much of Athens' past is preserved in its several museums. By far the most important of these is the **National Archaeological Museum** (Athens Map B3), one of the finest institutions of its kind in the world. It would be folly to attempt even a summary account of the museum's exhibits in a guide of modest scope, and the best one can hope to do is point out a few outstanding art treasures which no visitor should miss.

The main lobby gives entrance to Room 4, the Hall of Mycenaean Antiquities, where articles unearthed from Mycenaean sites over the past century are displayed. The most famous exhibits here are the so-called Death Mask of Agamemmon (No. 624), two gold-inlaid bronze daggers (Nos. 394, 385), a libation cup in the form of a bull's head in silver with golden horns (No. 384), and innumerable pieces of jewellery, all from the royal tombs at Mycenae 'rich in gold'. Also on exhibit here are the famous gold cups (Nos. 1758–9) from the royal tomb at Vapheio near Sparta.

Rooms 5 and 6, to the left and right of the Mycenaean Hall, are devoted to antiquities from the Early Bronze Age. Here we see the enchanting Cycladic 'idols', little marble statuettes found in burial sites from the third millennium B.C. The finest of these is The Harper (No. 3908), who looks as if he was modelled on a musician in a modern village festival in the Aegean isles.

The North Wing, seven rooms to the left of the main lobby, is devoted

The bronze statue of Poseidon of Artemision in the National Archaeological Museum, Athens

to Archaic sculpture from the seventh and sixth centuries B.C. Most striking are the huge statues of young men (*kouroi*), represented nude with the left foot slightly forward and arms rigid at their sides, mocking smiles on their handsome faces. The finest of these is the Anavissos Kouros (No. 3851), the culmination of Archaic sculpture.

Room 15, in the middle of the North Wing, is dominated by the magnificent bronze statue of Poseidon (No. 15161), which was rescued from the sea off Cape Artemision in 1928; this is surely one of the supreme achievements of Greek sculpture. Here also we find the famous votive relief from Eleusis (No. 126), showing Persephone, Kore and Triptolemos in a moving scene of great religious power.

We now turn right, passing through Rooms 17 to 20, which are used largely for the display of votive and sepulchral sculptures of the classical period. Everyone has their own favourites here, but ours is the Stele of Hegeso

(No. 3624), a funerary relief from the Kerameikos, in which the deceased lady is shown gazing sadly at her jewellery—feminine vanity even in the grave.

Room 21, the Central Hall, is dominated by two very famous statues, the Diadumenos (No. 1826), a Roman copy in marble of the lost bronze original by Polycleitos, and the Hermes of Andros (No. 218), another Roman copy of a lost bronze original, this one from the school of Praxiteles.

We now turn left and pass through Room 34 to the New Wing at the rear of the Museum. Two of the many masterpieces which we find here are the magnificent bronze statue of Zeus Soter (the Saviour) (unnumbered, in Room 43), and the strikingly handsome Youth of Marathon (No. 15118)—perhaps the greatest work of art in the Museum. Room 37, at the far left end of the New Wing, is devoted to early bronzes, the best of which are the head of Zeus from Olympia (No. 6440), and Athena Promachos (literally 'fighting in the front rank') (No. 6447).

Returning to the main hall we now enter Room 22, filled with sculptures from Epidauros; then Rooms 23 and 24, both lined with funerary reliefs, some of them possessed of a quite moving loveliness. This brings us to Room 28, in the centre of which we see still another of the Museum's masterpieces, the Ephebos of Antikythera (No. 13396). Here also is the serenely beautiful Hygieia, which may be one of the very few surviving works of the great Skopas.

Room 30 has several excellent sculptures from the Hellenistic Period. The most famous of these is the Jockey of Artemision (No. 15177), rescued from the sea at the same time as the statue of Poseidon; also noteworthy are the head of the pugilist Satyros (No. 6349), and the head of a Philosopher (No. 1340), perhaps so called because of his piercing eyes.

This quick tour of the ground floor of the Museum is culminated by a visit to Room 32. This is given over to the Helene Stathatos Collection of jewellery and gold and silver ornaments, with gorgeous items spanning the entire period from the early Bronze Age to late Byzantium—an absolutely unique and beautiful display.

The upper floor of the Museum, approached from the Central Hall, houses the Museum's tremendous collection of ancient Greek pottery, the most complete in the world. The number and variety of the vases exhibited here are quite literally staggering, with innumerable examples of every type from every period of Greek art. (There were at least two dozen basic types of vase in use in ancient Greece, about half of which were used for wine.) The wondrous names of some of the more famous vases suggest the incredible inventiveness and originality displayed in this distinctively Greek art-form: the Calyx Krater (No. 1666), the Niinion Pinax (unnumbered, Room IX), the Vourva Loutrophorus (No. 991), the superb Nessos Amphora (No. 1002), and the matchless collection of White Lekythoi, or sepulchral vases (Room VIII). The casual visitor can do no more than glance at a few of the more striking vases, for a careful examination of the whole collection would doubtless require several years.

The upper floor also contains a new and fascinating exhibit of the recent Minoan finds from Akrotiri on the volcanic isle of Thira, or Santorini; of particular interest here are the fresh and delightful frescoes.

The visitor is undoubtedly completely foot-worn and mentally exhausted by this time, and so a rest is recommended. There is no more pleasant a place to do so than the Atrium of the Museum, a cool and charming courtyard just below the ground floor.

(In summer the Museum is open daily, except Mondays, from 8 a.m. till 4 p.m. In winter it is open daily, except Mondays, from 9 a.m. till 4 p.m.; Sundays and holidays 10 a.m. till 2 p.m.)

The **Numismatic Collection** of the Museum is housed in the south wing of the building and is entered from Tositsa Street. Nearly half a million ancient Greek coins are stored here, the most interesting of which are the classic 'Owls' of Athens.

(In summer the Collection is open daily from 7.30 a.m. till 1.30 p.m. In winter it is open daily from 8 a.m. till 2.30 p.m. Closed on Sundays.)

The **Epigraphical Collection** of the Museum is also entered from Tositsa Street; here all of the historical inscriptions which still remain in Greece are stored. The most important of these is the Troezen Stele, which records a decree by Themistocles in the year 480 B.C., in which he ordered the Athenians to evacuate their city and prepare to do battle with the invading Persians.

(In summer the Collection is open daily from 8 a.m. till 1.30 p.m. In winter it is open daily from 8 a.m. till 2 p.m. Closed on Sundays.)

For those who are interested, there are two other museums in Athens of some major importance; both are located in the Kolonaki district in the shadow of Lykabettos.

The first of these is the **Benaki Museum** (Athens Map D5), which houses a unique and fascinating collection of oddments from all periods in Greek history. The basement of the museum has on exhibit a very important collection of Greek folk-art and regional costumes, some of which one would dearly love to own and wear.

(In summer the Benaki is open daily from 9.30 a.m. till 1.30 p.m. and from 4.30 p.m. till 7.30 p.m.; Sundays and holidays 9.30 a.m. till 1.30 p.m. In winter it is open daily from 9.30 a.m. till 2 p.m. and from 4.30 p.m. till 7.30 p.m.; Sundays and holidays 9.30 a.m. till 2 p.m. Closed on Tuesdays.)

A short distance away from the Benaki we find the **Byzantine Museum**. (Athens Map D3). The museum contains what is perhaps the world's most extensive collection of Byzantine antiquities in the world; several of its rooms are designed to reproduce the interiors of Byzantine churches of various periods.

(In summer open daily from 8 a.m. till 1 p.m. and from 3 p.m. till 6 p.m.; Sundays and holidays 10 a.m. till 2 p.m. In winter open daily from 9 a.m. till 4 p.m.; Sundays and holidays 10 a.m. till 2 p.m. Closed on Mondays.)

Just up the hill from the Byzantine Museum we find three of the most important cultural institutions in Athens: the **British School of Archaeology**, the **American School of Classical Studies**, and the **Gennadeion Library** (Athens Map D6). Those with a serious interest in Greek culture will find a lifetime of reading in the outstanding libraries of these three institutions.

(The Gennadeion is open daily from 9 a.m. till 2 p.m. and from 5 p.m. till 8 p.m. Saturday 9 a.m. till 4 p.m. Closed Sundays and holidays. The libraries of the other two institutions are not generally open to the public; those wishing to use them should make special arrangements.)

No visit to Athens would be complete without ascending **Lykabettos**. Those who are foot-worn from tramping along hot pavements or hard museum

View of Lykabettos Hill

floors can ride the funicular to the top, but it is a pity to miss the delightful walk, which takes one through scented groves of evergreens, with continually expanding views of Athens through the trees. At the top one can relax at the large outdoor café, enjoying a magnificent panorama of Athens spread out across the plain of Attica, the Parthenon queening it majestically atop the Acropolis. The best time is just before sunset, when the falling sun illuminates the bare slopes of Mount Hymettos, which then briefly casts a violet glow over the whole city. It was this magic moment which Pindar wrote of twenty-four centuries ago, when he sang of 'Athine, violet-crowned'.

WHERE TO STAY

Hotels in Athens are for the most part modern, well-equipped, and reasonably priced. They are clearly divided into six classes: de luxe (L), A, B, C, D, and E. The luxury hotels are comparable to their counterparts in the great European cities; A, B, and C class hotels are clean and efficient almost without exception. D class hotels, which are entirely adequate outside of the big cities, are usually old and oppressive in Athens, and E class hotels are so unpredictable that they are rarely mentioned in official guides. In addition to standard hotels, Athens has several marvellous furnished-flat hotels, which are ideal for groups of people who want privacy and want to cook for themselves occasionally.

All prices are controlled by the Chamber of Hotels. Each hotel class has its own price range, and the hotels in the class determine their prices within those brackets according to their facilities. There is a 6% government tax on room rates. An extra bed in a room is usually 20% of the room cost. Most hotels give winter reductions between 5% and 30%. A continental breakfast (coffee, bread, honey, butter, etc.) is normally 20 or 22drs except in the more expensive hotels, where it can be as much as 50drs.

All rooms in the L and A categories have a private shower or bath; most rooms in B hotels have a private bath. In recommending C class hotels in Athens, we have made an effort to include only those which have at least some rooms with baths. D class hotels seldom have such facilities.

Athens, like most European cities, is completely full in the summer so that it is often very difficult to find a room. If you have trouble, you should go immediately to the Tourist Police, on the sixth floor at 15 Ermou St. The Tourist Police operate a very efficient 24-hour-a-day room-finding service.

The hotel prices for 1974 in drachmae, pounds sterling, and US dollars are given below:

Hotel prices in drachmae

Class	Single room without bath	Single room with bath	Double room without bath	Double room with bath
L	205 min.	350 min.	360 min.	500 min.
A	150–200	265–345	240–355	360–495
B	120–145	180–260	180–235	215–355
C	95–115	120–175	120–175	170–210
D	75–90	105–115	110–115	135–165
E	55–75	75–105	80–110	100–135

Village guest house: 25–40drs per bed.

Hotel prices in pounds sterling

Class	Single room without bath	Single room with bath	Double room without bath	Double room with bath
L	2·85 min.	4·86 min.	5·00 min.	6·95 min.
A	2·08–2·78	3·68–4·80	3·34–4·94	5·00–6·88
B	1·67–2·02	2·50–3·62	2·50–3·27	2·99–4·94
C	1·32–1·60	1·67–2·43	1·67–2·43	2·36–2·92
D	1·04–1·25	1·46–1·60	1·46–1·60	1·88–2·30
E	0·76–1·04	1·11–1·53	1·11–1·53	1·39–1·88

Village guest house: £0·35–0·56 per bed.

Hotel prices in US dollars

Class	Single room without bath	Single room with bath	Double room without bath	Double room with bath
L	6·87 min.	11·71 min.	12·06 min.	16·72 min.
A	5·02–6·70	8·89–11·58	8·05–11·89	12·06–16·58
B	4·02–4·86	6·03–8·72	6·03–7·87	7·20–11·89
C	3·18–3·85	4·02–6·03	4·02–6·03	5·70–7·03
D	2·51–3·02	3·52–3·85	3·52–3·85	4·52–5·53
E	1·84–2·51	2·51–3·68	2·51–3·68	3·35–4·52

Village guest house: $0·84–1·34 per bed.

(L) Acropole Palace, 51 Patission (Athens Map B3). Tel: 533-651. Cables: ACROPALACE. Situated across the street from the National Archaeological Museum, the Acropole Palace is quiet and elegant. Rooms are pleasantly old-fashioned and frequently contain antiques. Dinner and dancing in the roof-garden nightly throughout the summer. Other facilities include a beauty salon, barber shop, tearoom, bar, and air-conditioning.

(L) Amalia, 10 Amalias (Athens Map E4). Tel: 3237-301. Cables: HOTAMAL. Very modern and efficient hotel in a choice location. Rooms are well air-conditioned and many of them have balconies overlooking the Royal Gardens. The Amalia has a bar, tearoom, restaurant, several lounges, a hairdressing salon, and a barber shop.

(L) Athenee Palace, 1 Kolokotroni Sq. (Athens Map D4). Tel: 3230-791. Cables: ATHENEE. Centrally located, this is one of Athen's most delightful hotels. It is elegant without being overbearing, and its graciously decorated rooms have all modern amenities. The gigantic lobby has a marble floor and marble columns; the lounges and other public rooms are reminiscent of a London club. Very helpful management. Air-conditioning, excellent restaurant, cocktail bar, beauty salon, baby-sitting facilities, television, radio in each room.

(L) Athens Hilton, 46 Vasillisis Sophias Ave. (Athens Map D6). Tel: 720-201. Cables: HITELS. Luxurious and ostentatiously comfortable, the Athens Hilton has 480 rooms, a post office, a bank, several women's boutiques, a Rent-a-car office, an art gallery, a TWA office, a heated swimming-pool, a café, a night-club, a pizzeria, and a deluxe restaurant. One could easily forget that one was in Greece, if it were not for the 30,000 square metres of marble distributed lavishly throughout. The Galaxy restaurant/night-club, which is on the roof, has a particularly stunning view; the Byzantine Café, very popular with Greek teenagers, offers all-American snacks, and Ta Nissia, the de luxe restaurant, is reputed to be one of the best in Athens. Completely air-conditioned, of course.

(L) Grande Bretagne, Constitution Square (Athens Map D4). Tel: 3230-257. Cables: HOT-BRITAN. One of the grand old hotels of Athens, the Grande Bretagne has housed every distinguished visitor to Greece for the last century. Largely due to its illustrious reputation, it is now overpriced and overrated. The public rooms are certainly majestic, but the bedrooms are old-fashioned. Service is sometimes gracious. Air-conditioned.

(L) King George, Constitution Square (Athens Map D4). Tel: 3230-651. Cables: GEKING. Right next to the Grande Bretagne, the King George is just as imposing as its neighbour. The décor is discreetly elegant; most bedrooms have satin bed-covers, antique chairs, and marble bathrooms. The restaurant on the top floor, the Tudor Room, is thought to be the best in Athens. Other facilities include a bar, a tearoom, a café garden, and an art gallery. Air-conditioned.

(L) King's Palace, 4 El. Venizelou (Athens Map D4). Tel: 9226-411. Cables: KINGOTEL. Conveniently located on one of Athens' busiest streets, the King's Palace is as luxurious and dignified as its competitors. The management is helpful, the marble staircases impressive, and the bedrooms cosy. The hotel's most charming feature is the two-tiered roof-garden which serves as a restaurant and bar during the summer. The beauty of the view is heightened by the flowers which line the terrace. On the ground floor is a newly opened art gallery. Air-conditioned.

(L) Royal Olympic, 28–32 Diakou (Athens Map F4). Tel: 9226-411. Cables: ROYTEL. Although this hotel is slightly off the beaten track, it is in many ways preferable to the more centrally-located luxury hotels. The view is not only different but spectacular; all front rooms face the Temple of Jupiter and the Lykabettos Hill. Both the bedrooms and the public rooms are bright and modern; the sparkling dining room opens onto a swimming-pool. Air-conditioned.

(A) Ambassadeurs, 67 Sokratous (Athens Map C3). Tel: 534-321. Cables: AMBASHOTEL. Situated a few minutes away from the noisy Omonia Square, this large, sedate hotel does not quite fit in with its surroundings. The spacious lounges are filled with sombre upholstered furniture and the roof-garden, although it has great potential, is forlorn. The bedrooms are quiet and comfortable. Air-conditioned.

(A) Astor, 16 Karageorghi Servias (Athens Map D4). Tel: 3234-971. Cables: HOTELASTOR. A very sensible, modern, conveniently situated hotel, whose main asset, the roof-garden restaurant, offers good international cuisine and a beautiful view of the Acropolis. The Astor also has an art gallery and a well-concealed souvenir shop. Air-conditioned.

(A) Attica Palace, 6 Karageorghi Servias (Athens Map D4). Tel: 3223-006. Cables: HOTELATIC. Situated on one of the streets off Constitution Square, the Attica Palace is a modern hotel with very attractive bedrooms. A colourful semi-partition divides the sleeping area from the sitting area in each room. Other features are a modern bar, a typical hotel restaurant, a large sitting room with television, and a roof-garden. Abstract paintings are distributed judiciously throughout the hotel. Air-conditioned.

(A) Electra, 5 Ermou (Athens Map D4). Tel: 3223-222. Cables: ELECTRA. Directly off Constitution Square, the Electra is simply and elegantly decorated. The cool lobby has potted plants and an aquarium; the bedrooms are attractively wall-papered and have adjustable air-conditioning. The Restaurant Ambrosia, on the ground floor, offers a small but tasteful selection of grilled fish and meats, and the small adjacent café-bar is reminiscent of Italy.

(A) Esperia Palace, 22 Stadiou (Athens Map D4). Tel: 3238-001. Cables: ESPEROTEL. Located half-way between Constitution Square and Omonia, the Esperia Palace is rather joyless despite its marble lobby and studiously elegant bedrooms. Completely air-conditioned, with a restaurant, a bar, and a delightful open-air breakfast room.

(A) King Minos, 1 Pireos (Athens Map C3). Tel: 531-111. Cables: HOMINOS. This modern and spacious hotel is two feet away from the infernally busy Omonia Square. Its large lounges, complete with fountain and birds, its pleasantly modern bedrooms, and its full-length bathtubs fortunately serve as an antidote to the surrounding chaos. The King Minos also has a bar, a barber shop, a beauty salon, and a restaurant with kosher food. Air-conditioned.

(A) Olympic Palace, 6 Filelinon (Athens Map E4). Tel: 3237-511. Cables: OLPALACE. Like so many Greek hotels, the Olympic Palace makes lavish use of marble in the lobby, on the balconies, and in the bathrooms. The bedrooms are tastefully decorated and all front rooms have a good view of the Lykabettos Hill. The hotel also has a restaurant, a barber shop, and a beauty salon. It is five minutes away from Syntagma Square. Air-conditioned.

(B) Achilleon, 32 Ag. Constantinou (Athens Map C3). Tel: 525–618. Located on one of the busy streets leading from Omonia Square, this is a very typical but nonetheless comfortable hotel. There is a bar with a television, and no food served on the premises except breakfast.

(B) Academos, 58 Akademias (Athens Map C4). Tel: 629-220. Cables: ACADEMIAHOTEL. Near the university, the Academos is one of the most agreeable hotels in its category. The rooms are simple but bright, and the management is helpful. Restaurant, lounge, and bar.

(B) Adrian, 74 Adrianou (Athens Map E3). Tel: 3221-553. Cables: ADRIANHOTEL. A small, agreeable hotel at the edge of the Plaka, this well-run establishment has a very attractive roof-garden.

(B) Alfa, 17 Halkokondili (Athens Map C3). Tel: 521-255. Cables: ALFOTEL.

(B) Arcadia, 46 Marnis (Athens Map B3). Tel: 526-571. Cables: ARCADIAHOTEL. Conveniently close to the Archaeological Museum. Simple, clean. Only serves breakfast.

(B) Aretoussa, 6–8 Mitropoleos (Athens Map E4). Tel: 3229-431. Cables: ARETHUSOTEL. Directly off Syntagma Square, this is the most attractive hotel in its category. Very colourful, modern, and compact décor. The roof-garden restaurant has aluminium tables, an orange and green awning, and a view of the Parthenon. Air-conditioned.

(B) Atlantic, 60 Solomou (Athens Map B3). Tel: 535-361. Cables: ATLANTOTEL. A clean, decent hotel with a restaurant.

(B) Cairo City, 42 Marnis (Athens Map B3). Tel: 533-361. Cables: CAIROCITY. A clean but dingy hotel frequented by Arabs of all persuasions.

(B) Candia, 40 Deliyanni (Athens Map B2). Tel: 546-112. Cables: CANDIAHOTEL. A very new hotel near the Larissas train station. Clean, well-run; it has a restaurant and parking facilities. Air-conditioned.

(B) Diomia, 5 Diomias (Athens Map D3). Tel: 3238-034. Cables: DIOMIA. Situated in a noisy but charming part of town, the Diomia is a clean, sensible, and efficient establishment. The public rooms, which include a restaurant and a bar, are decorated with ancient Greece in mind. Air-conditioned.

(B) El Greco, 65 Athinas (Athens Map D3). Tel: 3244-554. Cables: GRECOTEL. Located on another of the busy streets leading from Omonia Square. Pleasant enough. Air-conditioned.

(B) Eretria, 12 Halkokondili (Athens Map C3). Tel: 635-311. Cables: ERETRIAHOTEL. Clean, pleasant, air-conditioned, half price in the winter.

(B) Galaxy, 22 Academias (Athens Map D4). Tel: 632-831. Cables: GALAXOTEL. An air-conditioned hotel with restaurant.

(B) Ilion, 7 Ag. Constantinou (Athens Map C3). Tel: 537-411. Very near Omonia Square, this is a typical but acceptable hotel with television in the lounge and a bar.

(B) Lycavittos, 6 Valaoritou (Athens Map D4). Tel: 633-514. Cables: LYCAVHOTEL. Situated on a charming, quiet street near the Lykabettos Hill. Serene atmosphere, tasteful décor. Very desirable. Air-conditioning. Restaurant attached.

(B) Marmara, 14 Halkokondili (Athens Map C3). Tel: 626-362. Cables: MARMARAOTEL. The generous use of marble makes up for the lack of air-conditioning. Half-way between Omonia Square and Syntagma Square. Hardly luxurious, but inexpensive within its class.

(B) Minerva, 3 Stadiou (Athens Map D4). Tel: 3230-915. Cables: MINERVOTEL. Clean and central. Partially air-conditioned. Only breakfast served.

(B) Minoa, 12 Carolou (Athens Map C2). Tel: 534-622. Small, with a restaurant and a roof-garden. Partially air-conditioned.

(B) Omiros, 15 Apollonos (Athens Map E3). Tel: 3235-486. On the edge of the Plaka, this well-run, air-conditioned hotel has a delightful roof-garden and restaurant.

(B) Palladion, 54 El. Venizelou (Athens Map D4). Tel: 623-291. Very functional and adequate. Located between Omonia and Syntagma, which may or may not be a blessing. Partially air-conditioned.

(B) Pan, 11 Mitropoleos (Athens Map E4). Tel: 3237-816. Cables: PANHOTEL. Well located, but less charming than advertised. Small bedrooms with unforgettably designed bathrooms. Rooms on the front are far preferable.

(B) Plaka, 7 Kapnikareas and Mitropoleos (Athens Map E4). Tel: 3222-096. Cables: PLAKOTEL. Delightful modern hotel which is almost in the Plaka. Bright rooms, and a beautiful roof-garden with swings and fragrant flowers. The restaurant, also on the terrace, is appropriately picturesque.

(B) Sirene, 15 Lagoumtzi. Tel: 922-9311. Whereas other hotels offer roof-garden restaurants from which to gaze at the Acropolis, the newly built Sirene offer a roof-top swimming-pool with the same inevitable view in the far background. To swim here after a hot day of sightseeing can be a real pleasure. The rest of the hotel is cool, modern, and comfortable. The Sirene is a good distance away from the centre, but the weary traveller may tenderly cherish every mile separating him from Syntagma Square. Air-conditioned.

(B) Stadion, 38 Vass. Constantinou (Athens Map D6). Tel: 726-054. Cables: STADIOTEL. Pleasant without being remarkable. Restaurant.

(B) Stanley, 1 Odysseos (Athens Map C2). Tel: 541-611. Cables: STANLEYHOTEL. Large, reasonably-priced hotel with a swimming-pool and a bar on the roof. Magnificent view both for sunbathing and cocktails. Rooms are clean and cheerful. Most rooms air-conditioned; restaurant.

(B) Xenophon, 340 Acharnon (Athens Map B3). Tel: 2020-310. Air-conditioned, restaurant.

(C) Achillefs, 21 Lekka (Athens Map D4). Tel: 3233-197. Cables: ACHILLEFS.

(C) Albion, 6 Carolou (Athens Map C2). Tel: 531-136. Located just off Karaiskaki Square. Cheerful atmosphere.

(C) Alcystes, 18 Platia Teatrou. Tel: 3219-811. Cables: HOTELALKISTIS. Restaurant, roof-garden, partially air-conditioned.

(C) Alma, 5 Dorou (Athens Map C3). Tel: 522-833. Spotless hotel with an espresso-machine in the lobby.

(C) Apollon, 14 Deligeorghi (Athens Map C2). Tel: 545-212.

(C) Ares, 7 Pireos (Athens Map C3). Tel: 534-347. Cables: HOTELARIS.

(C) Aristedes, 50 Sokratous (Athens Map C3). Tel: 532-881.

(C) Artemis, 20 Veranzerou (Athens Map C3). Tel: 529-596.

(C) Aspacia, 26 Satovriandou (Athens Map C3). Tel: 534-211.

(C) Asty, 2 Pireos (Athens Map C3). Tel: 530-424. Cables: ASTYHOTEL. Right on Omonia Square. Conveniently located.

(C) Attalos, 29 Athinas (Athens Map D3). Tel: 3212-801. Cables: ATTALOSOTEL. Modern and well-run, five minutes walk from Omonia. Restaurant and roof-garden.

(C) Banghion, 18b Platia Omonias (Athens Map C3). Tel: 3242-259. Old and central.

(C) Carolina, 45 Kolokotroni (Athens Map D4). Tel: 3220-837. Cables: KAROLINAHOTEL. Charming hotel run by two brothers. Front rooms have wrought-iron balconies with a view on a lively, narrow street. Highly recommended.

(C) Caryatis, 31 Nicodimou (Athens Map E4). Tel: 3224-947. Patrons find this hotel to be homelike.

(C) Ceramikos, 30 Ceramikou and Iassonos (Athens Map C2). Roof-garden.

(C) Continental, 21 Voukourestiou (Athens Map C3). Tel: 612-774. Cables: CONTINENTAL. Close to Syntagma Square on a quiet shopping street; pleasantly old-fashioned. Breakfast is sometimes obligatory.

(C) Diros, 21 Ag. Constantinou (Athens Map C3). Tel: 548-112.

(C) Elite, 23 Pireos (Athens Map C3). Tel: 521523.

(C) Florida, 25 Menandrou (Athens Map C3). Tel: 523-214.

(C) Hermes, 19 Apollonos (Athens Map E3). Tel: 3235-514. Cables: HERMESHOTEL. A reasonably-priced hotel with a bit of style and a nice roof-garden. Near the Plaka.

(C) Iasson (Jason), 3–5 Nikoforou (Athens Map C3). Tel: 548-031. Very pleasant hotel near the inescapable Omonia. All rooms with bath.

(C) **Imperial,** 46 Mitropoleos (Athens Map E4). Tel: 3227-617. Cables: IMPERIALHOTEL. Near Syntagma. Simple and clean.

(C) **Karayiannis,** 94 Leoforos Syngrou (Athens Map G3). Tel: 915-903.

(C) **Kosmos,** 16 Psaron (Athens Map C2). Tel: 539-201. Cables: KOSMHOTEL.

(C) **Kronos,** 18 Ag. Dimitriou (Athens Map D3). Tel: 3211-601. Rather small hotel in a beautiful square.

(C) **Leto,** 15 Missaralitou (Athens Map F3). Tel: 911-526. Roof-garden.

(C) **Marina,** 13 Voulgari (Athens Map C3). Tel: 529-109. Near Omonia, very helpful management. Restaurant.

(C) **Mediterranean,** 28 Veranzerou (Athens Map C3). Tel: 522-631.

(C) **Minion,** 3 Mezonos (Athens Map B2). Tel: 525-959.

(C) **Navsica,** 21 Carolou (Athens Map C2). Tel: 539-381. Quiet, modern, acceptable, near Karaiskaki Square.

(C) **Nestor,** 58 Ag. Constantinou (Athens Map C3). Tel: 535-576. Near Omonia.

(C) **Odeon,** 42 Pireos (Athens Map C3). Tel: 539-206. Cables: ODEONOTEL. Air-conditioned, with parking facilities and a restaurant.

(C) **Olympia,** 25 Pireos (Athens Map C3). Tel: 522-429.

(C) **Omega,** 15 Aristogetonos (Athens Map D3). Tel: 3212-421.

(C) **Omonia,** Platia Omonias (Athens Map C3). Tel: 537-210. Cables: OMONOTEL. Large, very visible hotel on the infamous square. Restaurant, garage, reasonable prices. Very popular.

(C) **Oscar,** 40 Mitropoleos (Athens Map E4). Tel: 3238-198. Centrally located, typical rooms.

(C) **Paris,** 49 Geraniou (Athens Map C3). Tel: 539-955.

(C) **Parnon,** 20 Tritis Septembriou and 21 Halkokondili (Athens Map C3). Tel: 530-013. Cables: PARNOTEL. Clean and functional with a pleasant roof-garden. Near the Archaeological Museum. All rooms with bath.

(C) **Philippos,** 3 Mitseon (Athens Map F3). Tel: 9223-611. Cables: FILIPOTEL. Located in a residential district behind the Acropolis, the Philippos is cramped but friendly.

(C) **Phoebus,** 12 Petta (Athens Map E4). Tel: 3220-142. Located on a quiet street in the Plaka. Clean and well-run. Special group and student prices on request.

(C) **Poseidon,** 16 Victoros Hugo (Athens Map C2). Tel: 541-708.

(C) **Pythagorion,** 28 Ag. Constantinou (Athens Map C3). Tel: 542-811. Just off Omonia Square, this hotel manages to be more cheerful than most neighbouring hotels. Partially air-conditioned with an attractive lobby and bar.

(C) **Rhea,** 31 Neophytou Metaxa (Athens Map B2). Tel: 813-760.

(C) **Royal,** 44 Metropoleos (Athens Map E4). Tel: 3234-220. Near Syntagma and opposite the cathedral, this hotel is spacious and pleasantly furnished. Most rooms are furnished with couches and chairs.

(C) **Solomou,** 72 Solomou (Athens Map B3). Tel: 529-101. Partially air-conditioned.

(C) **Tegea,** 44 Halkokonili (Athens Map C3). Tel: 542-211. Cables: TEGEAHOTEL.

(C) **Theoxenia,** 6 Gladstonos (Athens Map C3). Tel: 600-250. Partially air-conditioned.

(C) **Thession,** 25 Apostolou Pavlou (Athens Map E2). Tel: 367-634.

(C) **Vienna,** 20 Pireos (Athens Map C3). Tel: 525-605. Small, charming, and reasonable. Near Omonia Square.

(C) **Zinon,** 3 Ceramicou (Athens Map C2). Tel: 528-811.

Furnished flats

Classified together with A class hotels, these establishments are ideal for a family. They have all the advantages of a hotel, maid service and 24-hour-a-day desk-service, together with all the privacy of one's own flat. All rooms have kitchens or kitchenettes, and private bathrooms; the larger flats have living-rooms and dining-rooms.

(A) **Ariane,** 22 Timoleontos Vascou (Athens Map F4). Tel: 6466-361. Air-conditioned single and double occupancy suites.

(A) **Ava,** 9–11 Lysicratous (Athens Map E4). Tel: 622-386. On the edge of the Plaka, the Ava has charmingly decorated flats. Rooms have wall-to-wall carpeting, attractive wood furniture, sparkling kitchens, and palatial balconies if they face the front. Air-conditioned.

(A) **Delice,** 3 Vassileos Alexandrou and Vrassida (Athens Map D6). Tel: 738-311. Behind the

Hilton, the Delice has boringly-decorated but spacious flats. A good place for children, because there is less to destroy. Air-conditioned.

(A) Egnatia, 64 Tritis Septembriou (Athens Map B3). Tel: 8811-561. A bit out of the centre, but the suites are very comfortable.

(A) Embassy, 15 Timoleontos Vascou (Athens Map D6). Tel: 6421-152.

(A) Kolonaki Flats, 7b Kapsali (Athens Map D5). Tel: 713-759. Beautiful flats in one of Athens' most fashionable districts. Some of the larger flats have two floors, and most have large balconies.

D class hotels and hostels

There are 66 D class hotels in the city of Athens, and although many of them are spotless, many of them are not. Be especially wary of those establishments which are close to Omonia. The following are a handful of D class hotels which are above average, and a number of very agreeable hostels.

(D) Hermeion, 66 Ermou (Athens Map D3). Tel: 3212-753. Very near the centre, noisy, and clean.

(D) Kimon, 27 Apollonos (Athens Map E4). Tel: 3235-223. Small, well-run, on the edge of the Plaka.

(D) Phaedra, 16 Herofontos (Athens Map E4). Tel: 3227-795. Located on a small square in the Plaka, this hotel is clean and cheerful.

XEN (YWCA), 11 Amerikis St. (Athens Map D4). Tel: 632-734. Cheerful and modern, near the centre. A famous and inexpensive cafeteria below which attracts businessmen at lunch. Building closes at 1 a.m.

XAN (YMCA), 28 Omirou St. (Athens Map D4). Tel: 626-790. Convenient and reasonably priced.

John's Place, 5 Patrou (Athens Map E4). This disorganized but thoroughly charming hotel is between Syntagma and the Plaka. The kind-hearted John charges minimal prices for a dormitory bed and a large breakfast.

Hostel Krist, 11 Apollonos (Athens Map E4). Tel: 323-4581. The Krist is directly above a pastry shop and caters mostly for students.

Residence Pangration, 75 Damareos (Athens Map F6). Tel: 755-763. Advertised as a 'residence for young ladies', this hostel is bright and friendly. A good place to stay if you are travelling alone. Dormitory beds are very cheap, and the residence has washing, cooking, and ironing facilities. Out of the centre of town in the residential district of Pangrati, but easily accessible by the 2 and 12 trolley-buses from Syntagma.

WHERE TO EAT

Restaurants in Athens

Athens has a far greater variety of restaurants than any other spot in the country. There are the highly tourist and noisy tavernas of the Plaka, the fish restaurants of Tourkolimani, the garden restaurants of Halandri and Kifissia. In addition to the establishments in famous 'restaurant areas', there are the excellent Istanbul-Greek restaurants, the steak houses, the French, Italian, Chinese, and Japanese restaurants. If one can afford to avoid the grim, cheap restaurants surrounding Omonia Square, one will quickly forget that Greek food can be monotonous.

Entrées in expensive restaurants are between 90 and 120drs; in reasonable to expensive restaurants they are 40–70; in very reasonable restaurants 25–50; in cheap restaurants 20–30. A service charge of 12% is automatically added to every item on the menu. Of course, one must bear in mind that, due to inflation, the price ranges quoted are hardly constant.

Here is a selection of well-known and/or very good restaurants in Athens proper. The restaurants in Tourkolimani, Halandri, Kifissia, and so on, will be covered in the *Environs of Athens*, while the Plaka tavernas will be treated in the *Athens at Night* section. All luxury and A class hotels have respectable restaurants; only a few exceptional ones are mentioned here.

High class restaurants

L'Abreuvoir, 51 Xenokrantos (Athens Map D5). Thought by many to be the city's top restaurant, L'Abreuvoir has an excellent menu of French food and the most complete list of French wines in the city. Hors d'oeuvres include melon au porto; for the main course there are entrecôtes (marchand de vin, au poivre, bordelaise, etc.), escalopes, frogs' legs, snails, cheese soufflé, ham soufflé, mushrooms with cream, steak tartare, three preparations of mussels, home-made pâtés, and other specialities. For dessert one can choose from the soufflés—Grand Marnier or chocolate— the crêpes, mousse au chocolat, and so on. Situated in a lovely garden towards the top of the Lykabettos Hill, L'Abreuvoir is ideal for celebrations, because it is well-stocked with good champagne. Expensive.

Bagatelle, Hadziyianni Mexi and Ventiri (Athens Map D6). Located behind the Hilton, this small French restaurant is decorated with taste and run with distinction. It is most famous for its 'grillades', which include everything from steaks to red snapper en brochette, but it has also a good selection of well-known entrées, such as frogs' legs Provençal, canard a l'orange, coq au vin, and boeuf stroganoff. Spectacular chocolate and Grand Marnier soufflés for two, and an impressive wine list. Expensive.

Corfu, 6 Kriezotou (Athens Map D4). This efficient indoor restaurant, very popular with ageing and affluent Greeks, has an ambitious collection of international dishes. The Corfiot specialities, *sofrito* and *pastitsada*, are excellent, as is the *sinagrida fournou spetsota*, a special kind of baked fish. The management has a low opinion of foreigners' food tolerance; whereas the Greek menu offers five preparations of brain, the English one only mentions two. Lots and lots of sweets. Reasonable to expensive.

Gerofinikas, 10 Pindarou (Athens Map D5). This delightful air-conditioned restaurant, run by Istanbul-Greeks, has white tablecloths, sparkling wine glasses, huge displays of fresh fruit, flowers, and miniature flags. Emphasis on grilled fish and meat, all of which is displayed in a long showcase-refrigerator. Especially good are the swordfish on a skewer and the 'mixed sea-food', served in a shell and covered with bechamel and cheese. Desserts, *ekmek kadaif* and *creme caramele*, are also worth trying. Reasonable to expensive.

Je Reviens, 49 Xenokratous (Athens Map D5). Je Reviens, which is near the Lykabettos funicular, has a lovely garden with lots of trees and the cushioned wicker chairs which are a prerequisite for Athens' better restaurants. It offers up to ten daily dishes, in addition to an interesting menu of 'embellished' Greek favourites—*moussaka à la je reviens*, octopus with oregon—and European specialities—*baby veal capri à la chef, escalope je reviens*, etc. Expensive.

Lucullus, 6 Valaoritou (Athens Map D4). Connected to the Lycabettus Hotel, this restaurant's respectable European menu—*escalope Marsala, escalope Milanese, tournedo rossini*—does not quite make up for its plain décor, cheerless service, and its flower arrangements. Rather expensive.

Michiko, Kidathineon 27 (Athens Map E4). This very refined restaurant is situated in a beautiful garden with Japanese lanterns and an oriental bridge with a contrived stream running below. The menu, which is in English and Japanese, is long and mysterious. Specialities are *momoyaki* (chicken drumsticks) and *tatsuka* (fried chicken and vegetable in a special sauce) but the connoisseur will find many more entrées of note. Michiko encourages *saki*, but it also has an 80-item wine list. Expensive but unique.

Mr Yung's, 3 Lamarchou (Athens Map E4). Mr Yung's has a shamelessly Chinese décor; this, along with the friendliness and efficiency of the management, makes it one of the most enjoyable places to eat in Athens. The menu is primarily Cantonese, the specialities being sweet-and-sour pork, king prawns in black bean sauce, and fried rice, but concessions are made for people who prefer spicier food. Peking spiced chicken is the best of these token dishes. Most people who want to make the wisest choice, however, merely ask what Mr Yung is eating that day. Reasonable to expensive. (The management also plans to open an Italian restaurant, La Toscana, at 5 Lamarchou, in a few months. The décor is to be fourteenth century Florentine, complete with courtyard and fountain. Both of the cooks have been imported from Tuscany, so it should be worth looking into.)

Pagoda, 2 Bousgou St. (behind 7 Alexandras) (Athens Map D6). This Chinese restaurant is more elegant, more sophisticated, and slightly more expensive.

Stage Coach Saloon, 4 Loukianou (Athens Map D5). Run by two Greeks who met in America, it more than lives up to its Wild West name. The saloon is filled with huge mirrors, buffalo skulls, wheels, statues of Indians, and appropriate signs. The bar is twenty metres long and is reputed to be one of the few places in town where single girls can go and not be bothered. All varieties of sandwiches for lunch, even more varieties of steak, fried chicken, and so on. Piano music in the evenings. Expensive, but you get what you pay for.

Steak Room, 6 Aiginitou (Athens Map D6). Located half way between the Hilton and the American Embassy, Athens' first steak-house has a cool, subdued atmosphere. The hors d'oeuvres include snails; for the main course one can choose from six different cuts of meat. The 'special' is steak with mushrooms and madeira sauce. A well-equipped bar; excellent Irish Coffee. Expensive.

Ta Nissia, Hilton Hotel (Athens Map D6). This is a very elegant restaurant, expensively decorated with 'traditional motifs'—brass ornaments, a small fountain, woven menus, etc. The menu is meant to be typically Greek, but it is so only in a very Hiltonesque way. They have *bouillabaisse*, *tourkolimano cassoulette*, *poulet sauté Venus flambé*, and other specially prepared dishes, all explained at great length on the menu. Reputed to be one of the best restaurants in Athens; certainly one of the most expensive.

Tudor Room, King George Hotel (Athens Map D4). Situated on the top floor of the King George Hotel, this restaurant has one of the more striking views of the Acropolis. The décor is supposed to suggest an English manor, and the excellent menu consists of well-known European dishes. The waiters try very hard to look like butlers, and they raise their eyebrows at improper dress.

Vladimiros, 12 Aristodemou (Athens Map C5). This beautiful restaurant has a gravel garden in the olive groves towards the top of Lykabettos Hill, and it is run by people who take great pride in their rather innovative international cuisine. A few of their specialities are *salade beaucaire*; *paupiettes Vladimir*; *spetsofai*, a sausage and pepper casserole; pork chops with olives, and *makaronia gargadoua*, a ham bacon, and soft cheese casserole. Vladimiros has its own wine, which is unresinated, and delicious desserts—bananas flambé, crêpe chocolat, and crêpe suzettes. Expensive, but definitely worth it.

Less expensive restaurants and tavernas

Bistrot Aristo, Ploutarchou and Haritos St. (Athens Map D5). Very recently opened, this is a pretty little restaurant in the Lykabettos Hill area. There is a very complete menu of pasta, omelets, soups, grills, and so on as well as daily specials. Specialities are *moussaka*; *filet tartare*; *bekri meze Aristo*, a meat stew; *sinagrida ala spetsiota*, fish baked with tomatoes, etc. Long wine list. Attractive and well-stocked bar. Very well-run. All foods are excellent and the atmosphere late at night is delightful. Reasonable.

Delphi, 13 Nikis St. (Athens Map E4). Air-conditioned, noisy, and brightly decorated, the Delphi is a restaurant whose charm has suffered from too many glowing reports in too many popular guides. The menu is primarily European, e.g. grills, *risotto*, *escalope creme Champignon*, *snitzel*, and lots of omelets, and prepared well if without flourish. Open 11.30 a.m. until 1 a.m. Reasonable.

Doris, 36 Loukianou (Athens Map D5). Doris is an extremely simple and charming 'people's' restaurant on Lykabettos Hill. Now it has the appearance of a small island cookhouse, but it is scheduled to be remodelled. Five or six dishes offered daily. A variety of vegetables, delicious *keftedes*, and nothing to drink except for barrel *retsina*. Very cheap.

Fatsio, 5 Efroniou (Athens Map E6). Formerly one of Istanbul's most distinguished restaurants— Facyo—Fatsio offers the same excellent cuisine in more modest surroundings. It has many European entrées, such as *coquille St. Jacques*, but its specialities are Turkish. Try the hors d'oeuvres—brain salad, aubergine salad, fried aubergine, potato croquettes—the *pilaf*, the delicious *yaourtlou kebab*, which is spiced meat, unleavened bread, and yogurt, and *ekmek kadaif*, sponge cake soaked in honey. Very reasonable.

Kentrikon, 3 Kolokotroni (Athens Map D4). Located on a little passageway near Syntagma, the Kentrikon is quiet and cheerful. Its extensive menu includes Greek specialities, e.g. *stifado*, grilled red snapper, aubergine salad, and the inevitable European filet mignons and *snitzels*. Reasonable.

Kostayiannis, Zaimi (Athens Map B4). This taverna is one of the few places in central Athens where one can eat very well for reasonable prices. One enters its bustling indoor garden through the kitchen, where all of the food is displayed. Kostayiannis has exceptional mezedes; try the paprika salad, the *dolmades*, *tiropitakia*, *tsatsiki*, *melitsanosalata*, the fried aubergines, peppers, and squash. It is very well-known for its grilled meats, but its special version of *moussaka gratinée* and its stuffed baby squid are worth trying.

Pringipos, Fokionos Negri. Pringipos is in one of Athens' main café areas, but as it is a good distance from the tourist centre, it is almost completely free of foreigners. Those who go to Fokionos Negri to enjoy an authentic *ouzo* should follow it up here with a delicious meal of Istanbul-Greek mezedes. Try the *taramosalata*, the bean *plaki*, the *tsatsiki*, the *ktapodi*, the fried aubergine, and the fried liver. There is also a good selection of fish and meat for those who enjoy plainer dinners. Reasonable prices.

Rougas, Kapsali 7 (Athens Map D5). This is a small, simple, and charming taverna near Kolonaki Square, decorated exclusively with straw mats. Rougas is run by one family; the father does all the cooking, and very well indeed. For mezedes, try the *ktapodi*; the *loukanika*, sausages; the *kolokithakia*, baby courgettes; and the *bakalario*, cod fish. For main courses there are a few grilled foods, and then some delicious casseroles cooked in individual clay pots—*moshari stifado*, *moshari youvetsi*, etc. Things get lively very late. Inexpensive.

Sintrivianni, Syntagma and 5 Filelinon (Athens Map D4). This is a wonderful garden-restaurant with simple Greek food, only two seconds away from Syntagma. To reach the garden one walks through a long dusty corridor, so many Syntagma habitués content with their steak sandwiches will never even find it. The fish soup is good, as is the *stifado*, the *dolmades*, the *melitsanes imam*, the *moussaka*, and the grills. Good atmosphere and inexpensive.

Steki Tou Yanni, 1 Trias St. (Athens Map A4). Only open in the winter, this is a typical and popular taverna near the Archaeological Museum. The interior is filled with old wine barrels, and very prominent displays of lobster, fresh fish, and suckling pigs. Excellent mezedes. Meals here should be eaten very slowly with lots of wine. Reasonably priced.

To 18, 18 Tsakalof (Athens Map D5). 18 looks like a private home on Lykabettos Hill, and both the bar and the restaurant have retained a certain intimacy and cosiness. It is run by a French woman, so the menu, which changes daily, is a combination of Greek and French foods. A sampling would be shrimp tourkolimano, breaded chicken, *coq au vin*, *veal à la 18*, steak, etc. People come here late to eat, and there is much traffic between the bar and the dining room. Delightful atmosphere, good food, and very reasonable.

Vasilis, 14a Voukourestiou (Athens Map D4). Some people say that Vasilis lost its charm ten years ago; others say that it never had any. Nevertheless, it is very popular with tourists because it serves bland food at 7 p.m. for reasonable prices. Its menu is a mixture of Greek foods, such as 'chicken with baked potatoes', and well-travelled international ones, such as cannelloni, curry, and hamburger steak. Four languages are spoken at Vasilis, and it honours 12 credit cards.

Cafés in Athens

As is the custom in most Mediterranean countries, Greeks spend a good amount of their free time in cafés. The tourist who has recently arrived and strolls past scores of huge, deserted cafés at midday, will marvel at their deluded owner's expectations. The same tourist, however, will not be able to find a seat at eight in the evening.

There are three main 'café districts' in Athens: Syntagma Square, Kolonaki Square, and Fokionos Negri. The first of these caters mainly for the tourists, with its overall seating capacity of 3,000. The **Pappaspyrou** is the most popular café only because it is so close to the American Express; better service can be had at the adjacent **Dionysus**, which offers almost the same selection of coffees, cocktails, ice creams, and sandwiches. Near Syntagma, on Panepistimiou, are Athens' best-known cafés, the elegant **Zonar's** and **Floca**. Both of these serve cocktails, aperitifs, and elaborate ice creams, as well as more sensible things, for high prices.

Those who do not want extravagant desserts or cocktails, however, and are looking for a simple glass of beer and a cheese sandwich, should go to **Orfanidis**, which is right across the street from Zonar's. This is a cheaper and more authentic café, frequented by older Greeks. A Campari is half the price and a cheese sandwich is a third of the price charged across the street. Another authentic and rather unique bar is **Apotsos**, at 10 Panepistimiou. Unfortunately, it has been forced to move from its very cosy former quarters, but it is still a fun place to drink at. The posters which cover the walls are very old and very amusing; one could use the same adjectives to describe the clientele.

The best coffee shop in the area is **Cafe do Brasil**, in the Stoa Kalliga, between Karageorghis Servias and Stadiou. Here all varieties of coffee are served—espresso, capuccino, Viennese, frappé

Sitting in cafés is habit forming!

—for reasonable prices. The toasted sandwiches are also delicious here. If you sit in the upstairs section, you will have a full view of the passing crowds in the Stoa.

There are scores of snack-bars around Syntagma, e.g. Ellysée, Elite, the American, City, but they offer overpriced food and poor service for the most part. One of the best places to get a good quick meal is, surprisingly enough, **Texas Fried Chicken**. Not only does it serve the typical pancakes, coleslaw, 'chicken in the basket', spaghetti, chilli, and hamburger, but also excellent espresso, capuccino, breakfast rolls, and so on for reasonable prices.

The second area, Kolonaki Square, is right at the centre of one of Athens' best neighbourhoods, and the habitués are as distinguished as would be expected. The most noticeable of these cafés is the **Noufara**, which also serves light meals such as pizza, pasta dishes, and *saganaki*, fried cheese with sausages or eggs. Next to this is the **Byzantion**, whose popularity among ageing politicians has become mythical. At the opposite end of the square are the **Piccolo**, the **Nea Lykovrissi**, and the **Snack Bar**, all of which serve hot meals as well as wines and spirits. But since one will probably go to Kolonaki for an aperitif and some atmosphere, it makes little difference where one sits; finding a seat may be an accomplishment in itself.

The Fokionos Negri café area is the residential area of Kipseli, which is beyond the National Archaeological Museum. It can be reached by a 3 or a 12 trolley. Running down the middle of the street is a long plaza-like island, filled with trees, cushioned café seats, grotesque plastic fountains, and, in the evening, hundreds of people taking their evening stroll. The atmosphere is quite charming, because few foreigners take the trouble to leave the centre just to drink the same old *ouzo*. Those who finally go, however, will not regret it, and they will also be able to eat very well in any of the restaurants along the street.

The **Dionysus** on Philopappos Hill, a restaurant as well as a snack-bar, is near the Herod Atticus Theatre, and it has yet another magnificent view of the Acropolis. More spectacular is the café of the same name on the top of Lykabettos Hill.

The above-mentioned cafés are the city's most distinguished, and most expensive, ones, and you need not limit yourself to them. There are thousands of more modest cafés along every street and in the many tiny squares of the residential areas. One of the most picturesque of these tiny squares is the **Platia Pallias Agoras** in the once residential Plaka area. The small cafés here used to cater mostly for neighbourhood families, but the truly excellent *souvlaki* and *giro* stand on the corner has also made them attractive to starvation-budget travellers who can only just afford a lemonade.

Most cafés are open from the early morning until at least midnight, but in Syntagma and

54

Kolonaki there are a handful of all-night places. You can spend days trying to find the right ticket for the right island boat, or hours trying to find an open pharmacy, but no matter where you are and what the time is, you can always find a place to have an ice cream.

ATHENS AT NIGHT

It has often been said that there is no real night life in Athens; in fact everybody in the city leaves his house between 8 and 10.30 p.m. to stroll along the streets and to have an aperitif or an ice cream. Even the staider families will have dinner between ten and eleven, for they have been abed all afternoon dreaming of their evening feast. From ten till twelve the streets are full of portly post-prandial promenaders, and long past midnight one still hears the serenades of tipsy revellers returning from tavernas.

Furthermore, Athens has several night-life institutions to be found nowhere else; the most famous of these 'institutions' is the Plaka, the old city at the foot of the Acropolis. Twenty years ago, the Plaka was merely picturesque and residential; the tavernas on the narrow winding streets were good but inconspicuous. Now the tavernas, with their electric *bouzoukia* and pulsating neon signs, have completely taken over the area, so that the Plaka is reminiscent of an amusement park or a Hollywood set. Nevertheless, even the orthodox will admit that the new Plaka has its own perverse charm. The meals last for hours on end, and those who are in Greece for only a short stay will get perhaps their only chance to hear live Greek *bouzoukia* and *cantades* music. Every visitor to Athens has to see the Plaka at least once.

One should select a taverna with some care, as the food can be bad at the less reputable places. Here is a list of the better tavernas. Unless otherwise stated, a main course at these tavernas will range from 70–90drs. (The tavernas are all located in Athens Map E3, 4.)

Bacchu, 15 Bacchu. Slightly barn-like with a grander music show than most. Excellent food; good selection of mezedes. Specialities are *moshari stamnaki*, a veal, feta cheese, and pepper casserole, and *moshari youvetsi*.

Attalos, 16 Erechtheos. Pleasant terrace, music, delicious baby lamb on a spit, and good grilled fish.

Erotokritos, 1 Erotokritou St. The terrace is four flights up with plants, music, and a good view. Specialities are *moshari youvetsi*; *hirino krasato*, pork chops in wine; *kounelli*, rabbit; and fish on a skewer. Omar Sharif and Belmondo have eaten here. Music.

Kritikou, 24 Mnisikleous. Its menu, littered with drawings of cows, chickens, and pigs, is instructive but disturbing. Specialities are *arni stamnas*, lamb stew; *moshari stifado*; and *bekri meze*, a meat stew aptly translated here as 'drunkard's titbit'. Noisily situated but cheaper than most.

O Geros Tou Moria, 29 Mnisikleous. Situated on some picturesque steps and adjoining terraces. Music is very loud and gay; dancing is wildly encouraged. Standard menu; try *Special Periklis*.

Mostrou, 22 Mnisikleous. Caters for people who prefer variations on Frank Sinatra to bouzoukia music; night-club members and night-club prices. European menu with a few Greek standards. Expensive.

Xinos, Ag. Geronta St. Popular with Athenians; beautiful garden, soft music. *Hirino krasato* is delicious.

Fantis, Lissiou and Mnisikleous. Picturesque to the point of being grotesque; standard menu, music, and better service than normal.

O Thespidos, Thespidos 18. Run by charming people, very reasonable prices. Terrace, music. Specialities are fish on a skewer, and fish *spetsota*.

Lito, Flessa and Tripodon. A more elaborate terrace than most, with candles and orange chairs.

An outdoor restaurant in the Plaka

Music. Emphasis on mezedes; try the *loukanika*, spiced sausages; *pastourma*, spiced pressed beef; and the *tsatsiki*. Good grilled fish and meat.

Ambrosia, Stratonos 1. A large terrace and a clean kitchen. Specialities are *Bekri meze, moshari youvetsi,* and *kounelli stifado,* rabbit stewed with onions in wine. Music.

Taverna Tou Psariou, Erechtheos St. Situated on some picturesque steps, it serves only grills, but a great variety. Very good *biftekia,* grilled meatballs; *souvlaki,* and *swordfish souvlaki.* Much cheaper than its neighbours.

Palaia Plakiotiki, Tripodon 2. In a tiny gravel garden. Meagre menu, but the food is good and relatively cheap. Pork on a skewer is excellent.

Zafiris, 4 Thespidos. Open only during the winter, this is an excellent taverna, specializing in game, with a marvellous atmosphere.

Every year more discothèques open in the Plaka. Most of them are rather unpleasant, with no décor to mention and limited tapes. Exceptions to this rule are **Kariatis** and **Mecca**, located next door to each other on Mnisikleous St.

Discothèques

The city has a surprising number of good discos, but most of them either close up or move to the suburbs for the summer. If you are in town off season, you should try **Annabella**, at 6 Kolonaki Square, one of the very in places (during the summer Annabella moves to the beach at Ag. Cosmas), or the **50-50 Restaurant Club**, on 4 Haritos St., whose upper storey is an elaborately decorated restaurant serving Greek and European food, and whose basement is an ultra-modern discothèque. **Nine Muses**, 43 Akadimos St., **Dolly's**, Kolonaki Sq., **Piper**, 1 Nikodimou St., and **Samantha's**, 6 Alex. Soutsou St., are other good winter discothèques. **Aquarius**, in the inland suburb of Drossia, is one of the best places to go in the summer if you want to avoid the beaches.

The highly original **Architektoniki**, at 10 Venizelou St., is open all the year round. It used to be a display room for architectural innovations, but as it was running at a loss, it was converted partly into a discothèque with loud rock music and psychedelic lighting (with the displays of tiles, toilet seats, light fixtures, and wall-paper designs still on the walls) and partly into a restaurant-bar. There is also a room for card playing, and a permanent display of architectural magazines for the professionally inclined. It is a fascinating place at any time of day but especially very late at night, and it should not be missed.

The Athens Festival

The Athens Festival takes place every summer in the Herod Atticus Theatre from the beginning of July to the middle of September. The scheduled events range from ballet performances and Beethoven's *Missa Solemnis* to ancient Greek and Shakespearian drama. Tickets can be as little as 10drs and as expensive as 250drs, depending on the event. Students can always obtain greatly reduced tickets.

The most attractive events are quickly sold out, but one can buy tickets for the less popular ones only a few hours before the performance at the theatre. The main Festival Office is on 4 Stadiou St., in the Stoa Spyrou Miliou. Those intending to see an ancient Greek play should buy the 30drs English synopsis at the door.

Athens Sound and Light

Starting from the first of April, 1,500 batteries of lights flash at dramatic intervals on the Parthenon in an attempt to evoke the stormy past of Greece for the tourists sitting on Pynx Hill. Although many feel inspired by the melodramatic fusion of light, shadow, and a commentator's deep voice, others find the performance to be overdone and overwritten. Nevertheless, the Acropolis continues to be spectacular in spite of the purple prose which blasts out over the loudspeakers.

There are performances in English every evening at 9 p.m. except on full-moon nights. Tickets are 30drs (15drs for students) and can be bought at the Festival Box Office on 4 Stadiou St. or in front of the theatre on Pynx Hill.

The Dora Stratou Dance Theatre

Founded around twenty years ago, the Dora Stratou Company performs authentic and colourful Greek dances throughout the summer in the Theatre of Philopappos. The performance begins with some music by a small orchestra called the Zygia, which is made up of a violin, a lute, a santouri, a clarinet, and drums. Then out come the dancers in traditional dress. The setting is of course ideal, and ancient Greece is more successfully evoked through these songs and dances than through the monologues and electric beams of the nearby Sound and Light show.

Performances start at 10.15 p.m. on weekdays, with extra shows at 8 p.m. on Wednesdays and Sundays. Tickets range from 35 to 70drs.

Outdoor theatre

Even those who do not speak Greek will enjoy the open-air revues which take place all over Athens in the summer. Although the biting satire of these shows is largely verbal, the whole mentality of the show can be appreciated from the songs, the imitations, the costumes, the casting, and the outrageous scenery. The three major revue theatres are the **Metropolitan** (Alexandras Ave.); the **Bournelli** (Alexandras Ave.); and the **Park** (36 Alexandras Ave.). Information about the current revues can be obtained from *This Week in Athens* or *Athens Life*.

Another popular and, for European audiences, highly original form of outdoor theatre is the Karaghiozis shadow theatre. Every evening at 8.15 p.m., Yorgos Haridimos puts on a performance with his waxed puppets in Lisikratous Square in the Plaka. The comedy has sophisticated overtones at times, but again, even those who do not understand Greek will grasp the slapstick routines which the flat, colourful puppets act out from behind the screen. Tickets are 15drs.

Bouzoukia

Bouzoukia music, like retsina, is an acquired taste

There are great clubs along the coastal highway and in the suburbs of Athens which specialize in *bouzoukia* music. They are growing increasingly popular despite the extremely high prices. Of course, the singers in the Athens' clubs are the best in the country, so one gets one's money worth.

The major clubs are: **Queen Anne**, **To Kanoni**, **Ximeronata**, and **To Oniro** along the Athens-Lamia Highway; **Adynamis**, on 365 Syngrou Ave.; **BB**, on the National Road; **Panorama**, on 37 Possidonos, Moschaton; the **Stork** on the Ag. Cosmas seaside, and **Idolo**, on the Voula Seaside. One chooses the club not for itself but for the singers, so one should look for such names as Tsitsanis, Sakellariou, Zambettas, and so on. *Athens Life* and *This Week in Athens* publish current information about these bouzoukia places. Performances start very late in the evening.

Casinos

The restless can also go to the Casino at Mount Parnes and play blackjack or roulette. One can take a taxi all the way out of Athens and up the treacherous mountain road, but those who prefer to take fewer risks can take the five minute teleferique ride up the mountain. Mount Parnes is one of the largest and most attractive casinos in Europe, attracting a daily crowd of 1,500. It is open every day except Tuesday from 7 p.m. until 4 a.m. The first drink costs 180drs and subsequent ones 90drs; spectacular buffet dinners are served for a blanket price.

SHOPPING IN ATHENS

Things Unique to Greece

One of the advantages of Greece's acute awareness of the past is that it has encouraged the continuation of traditional art forms, such as metal work, weaving, embroidery, carpet making, and pottery making. The National Organization of Hellenic Handicrafts has opened schools, given grants, and provided outlets both within Greece and abroad, in the hope that the talented will not only reproduce the beautiful motifs of the past but also develop and revitalize the art. The intense pride which is necessary for such a 'renaissance' is certainly not lacking; one only needs to study briefly the work of Greece's foremost architects, dress designers, and jewellers to see how emphatically they have incorporated traditional themes into everything they do.

The shopper has myriads of handicraft and jewellery shops to choose from in central Athens, but one will probably enjoy oneself more and make better choices if one has a vague idea of regional specialities. One should know, for example, that the best jewellery comes from Ioannina, the most interesting ceramics from Sifnos and Skopelos, the most original embroidery from Skyros, Lefkas, and Rhodes, and that Crete is famous for alabaster, Kastoria and Siatista for furs, Mykonos for dress fabrics, and Macedonia for the fluffy *flokati* rugs. With a minimum of critical discretion, one can bypass the ubiquitous trinkets and find objects of true worth.

Men haggle over the price of a bargain

Handicrafts

Before going anywhere else, one should perhaps see the permanent exhibit of the **National Organization of Hellenic Handicrafts** at 9 Mitropoleos St., to obtain a visual idea of quality objects from different regions of the country. Other non-profit institutions, with good displays and reasonable prices, are the **National Welfare Organization**, with shops at 10 Stadiou, 8 K. Servias, and the Hilton, the **Greek Women's Institute** at 13 Voukourestiou, and the **Lyceum of Greek Women** at 17 Dimokritou St. The most excellent boutiques for handicrafts are **Tanagrea**, at 15 Mitropoleos, which sells classic and contemporary designs from the Keramikos Factory; **Pandora**, at 12 Voukourestiou, famous for its authentic copper plaques, rings, etc.; **Myconos**, at 10 Mitropoleos, whose four floors are filled with products from its own factory; **Hadjopoulous Jeweller**, at 3 Mitropoleos, which has everything from costumed dolls to hand-painted icons; **Mati**, at 20 Voukourestiou, with a collection which is more interesting and eccentric than most; and **Kouros**, at 2 Syntagma, whose highly original dress fabrics and styles (made to order in no time) and exquisite jewellery are definitely worth buying.

Jewellery

The most distinguished jewellers are **Lalaounis**, at 6 Venizelou and **Zolotas**, at 10 Venizelou (also known as Panepistimiou). Both of these work primarily with gold and are strongly influenced by ancient Greek jewellery, although they do not limit themselves to the old forms. Other truly excellent boutiques are **Pentheroudakis** at 13 Voukourestiou, **Petra** at 20 Voukourestiou, **Piocos** at 4 Ermou, **Adler** at 13 Voukourestiou, and **VIP** at 10 Nikis. Those interested in old coins should not miss seeing the display in **Gold Coin Jewellery** at 17 Stadiou.

Carpets

The **Greek Carpet Organization** at 6 Filellinon, has a large showroom given over completely to handmade carpets, arranged in such a way that the different types and designs of traditional carpets are clarified. At **Karamichos Flokati**, 3 Mitropoleos, there is also a fascinating showroom where one can acquire a brief knowledge of the history of carpet weaving.

Antiques

Two shops worth browsing through are **Antiqua** at 4 Amalias, and **Gallerie Antiqua** at Vas. Sophias and Messioghou, which is also an art gallery.

Furs

George M. Trahou and Sons, at 7 Filelinon, is the best known furrier with the greatest variety. Two other fur shops are **Sistovaris** at Nikis and Ermou, and **Efthatiades** at 27 Mitropoleos.

Other shopping information

Not only is Athens completely in tune with European fashion, but it has three internationally-known designers, all of whom, predictably enough, draw heavily from their cultural heritage. **Yannis Travassaros**, whose boutique is in the Hilton, uses beautiful handwoven fabrics, and specializes in elegant winter wear. The other two big designers, both former painters, **Nikos and Takis**, work together at 10 Lissiou. Due to their striking prints and styles, they are well-loved by various celebrities and therefore by everyone else.

The best women's boutiques are to be found on the small streets between Venizelou and Kolonaki Square. Most of these sell excellent collections of the latest French, English, and Italian styles. A few names are **Annabelle**, 41 Ermou; **Bettina**, 4 Voukourestiou; **Help**, 23 Voukourestiou; **Contessina**, Voukourestiou; and **Ritsi**, Tsakalof, but these are by no means the only ones with quality merchandise.

For chic men's wear, one should go to the same area on the Lykabettos Hill and to the streets leading to the Plaka. A few shops are **Who's Who**, on Amerikis St.; **Jet Set**, at 16 Valaoritou; **Gounaro Menswear**, at 9 Valaoritou; **Ascot**, at 29 Nikis. For extremely expensive men's wear, there is **Pierre Cardin** at 10 Amerikis; and **Cerruti**, at 24 Akadimos.

For books in English one should go to **Eleftherodakis** at 4 Nikis St., **The American Bookstore** at 23 Amerikis St., **Pantelidis** at 11 Amerikis St., and the Athens Hilton. Periodicals and newspapers are to be found at any of the very central kiosks.

For classical, pop, and traditional Greek music, go to **Music Box** at 2 Nikis St.

The most reliable photographic shop is **Suslian**, on Voukourestiou St.

Two good supermarkets are the **AB Delicatessen**, 19 Stadiou, and **Pris-Unic-Marinopoulos**, at 9 Kanaris.

Two prominent department stores, specializing in clothes and sea equipment, are **Athenee** and **Katanzaspor**, both situated between Omonia and Syntagma on Stadiou St. The best store for children's clothes is **Lanti**, at 23 Eolou St. in Monastiraki.

Kiosks (*periptero*), open usually eighteen hours of the day, sell newspapers, aspirin, soap, shampoo, chocolate, envelopes, books, film, pens, and other very necessary odds and ends.

ATHENS—GENERAL INFORMATION

Useful addresses and telephone numbers

Emergency Squad—Tel: 100 or 109.

First Aid Hospital—16 Tritis Septemvriou St. (Athens Map C3; open twenty-four hours daily.) Tel: 525-555.

Tourist Police, Athens—15 Ermou St. (Athens Map D4; open twenty-four hours daily.) Tel: 3227-665.

Tourist Police, Piraeus—43 Akti Miaouli. (Open twenty-four hours daily.) Tel: 4523-670.

Fire Brigade—Tel: 199.

Hospitals on Duty—Tel: 106.

All-Night Chemists—Tel: 173.

Lost Property—16 Messogion St. Tel: 6431-460.

Telegrams Service—Tel: 105.

Touring Club of Greece—Tel: 588-601.

Time—Tel: 141.

Theatres—Tel: 172.

Railways Schedules (Domestic)—Tel: 175.

Railways Schedules (Foreign)—Tel: 176.

Shipping Schedules—Tel: 195.

Flight Schedules—Tel: 196.

News Bulletins—Tel: 185.

Complaints—Tel: 190.

Embassies (e) and Consulates (c)

Australia (e & c)—8 Makedonon St. (Athens Map D4.) Tel: 6425-310.

Canada (e & c)—4 Ioannou Gennadiou St. (Athens Map D5.) Tel: 739-511.

Cyprus (e & c)—16 Irodotou St. (Athens Map D4.) Tel: 737-883.

Great Britain (e & c)—Ploutarchou and Ypsilandou Sts. (Athens Map D5.) Tel: 736-211.

Israel (c)—4 Koumbaris St. (Athens Map D5.) Tel: 6715-012.

New Zealand (c)—63 Vass. Sophias Ave. (Athens Map C7.) Tel: 727-514.

South Africa (e & c)—69 Vass. Sophias Ave. (Athens Map C7.) Tel: 729-050.

United Nations Office—36 Amalias Ave. (Athens Map E4.) Tel: 3228-122.

USA (e & c)—91 Vass. Sophias Ave. (Athens Map C7.) Tel: 712-951.

Religious services

Cristus Kirche (German Evangelical)—66 Sina St. (Athens Map C5.) Tel: 612-713.

First Church of Christ Scientist—7 Vissarianos St. (Athens Map D4.)

Greek Orthodox Cathedral—Mitropolis St. (Athens Map E3.) Tel: 322-1308.

Holy Trinity (Russian Orthodox)—21 Filellinon St. (Athens Map E4.) Tel: 3231-090.

Saint Andrew's (American Protestant)—66 Sina St. (Athens Map C5.) Tel: 714-906.

Saint Denis (Roman Catholic)—24 Panepistimiou St. (Athens Map D4.) Tel: 623-603.

Saint Paul's (Anglican)—27 Filellinon St. (Athens Map E4.)

The Jewish Synagogue—6 Melidoni St. (Athens Map D3.)

Banks. American Express, Syntagma Square. Bank of America, 10 Stadiou St. Bank of Novia Scotia, Syntagma Square. Bank of Greece, Stadiou and Voukourestiou Sts. Chase Manhattan Bank, 2 Vass. Sophias Ave. First National City Bank, 8 Othonos St. Bank of the Piraeus, 3 Paparrigopoulou St.

Libraries. American Library, 18 Akadimias St. British Council Library, 17 Kolonaki Square. USIS Library, 18 Akadimias St.

Postal services. The Athens General Post Office is in Kotzia Square. There are central GPO branches in all parts of Athens and post-boxes are placed at intervals along the streets. The Parcel Post Office is at 41 Sophocleous St. Postal rates: Surface mail (to all destinations): letters 4drs, postcards 2·5drs; airmail to Europe: letters and postcards 4·5drs; airmail to the USA: letters and postcards 6drs.

Telephones. The charge for calls within Athens and the Piraeus is one drachma; there are public telephones at all kiosks. Long-distance calls can be made within Greece and to foreign countries by using the Automatic Telephone Exchange; consult the phone directory for code-numbers.

Telegrams. The main office at 85 Patission St. is open twenty-four hours daily; another at 15 Stadiou St. is open from 8 a.m. till midnight.

Miscellaneous

Barber shops (KOYPEION). A haircut costs about 20–35drs, a shave 10–15 drs, with an additional tip of at least 5 drs.

Ladies' hairdressers (KOMOTHIPION). Most of the high-class hotels have a hairdresser's salon on the premises. The most popular beauty salons in central Athens are: **Angelos**, 2 Amalias Ave., and 17 Omirou St. **Georges**, 2 Kanari St., and at the Hotel Grande Bretagne. **Kammer**, 1 Kolokotroni St. **Mary**, King Minos Hotel. The charges at such de luxe establishments are: shampoo 20–30drs, manicure 20–30, pedicure 30–70, haircut 50–60, tinting 150–500.

Shoeshines. High-class hotels have a free shoeshine service. Itinerant shoeshiners may be found along the main avenues in central Athens, particularly near the University on Panepestimiou Ave. Charge 5drs.

Launderette. Bendix Self-Service Launderette, 9 Erenthiou St. Open 8 a.m. to 2 p.m. and 5 p.m. to 8 p.m. Closed Wednesday and Saturday afternoons and all day Sunday.

Left luggage. Luggage may be stored at many of the larger travel agencies and at the office of the Tourist Police.

English-speaking doctor. Dr. Dimitriades, 75 Skoufo St. Tel: 636-466 or 728-523.

English-speaking dentist. Dr. Destounnis, 12 Lykavitton St. Tel: 675-517 or 635-625.

Taxis are 5 drs for the first 100 metres, 3·8drs for each subsequent kilometre, luggage 2–5drs per bag; supplements: night (midnight–6 a.m.) 5drs; taxi from port, airport, rail or bus terminals 8·5drs. There are taxi stands around Syntagma and the other main squares in central Athens. Taxis are hard to obtain during the midday and early evening rush-hours; to alleviate the situation official taxi-stands are being set up at central locations.

Garages and parking. There are numerous garages for parking in central Athens. The charge is about 20–30drs for each morning or afternoon and 40–60drs for each day. There is also metred parking space in centrally-located streets; the charge is either 5 or 10drs, depending on location, from 7 a.m. to 10 p.m., while parking is free at other hours. In addition, there are free-parking areas for tourists in the centre of Athens.

Baby-sitting. Many of the better hotels have a baby-sitting service. The charge is usually 30drs an hour, with a minimum of 5 hours.

Athens bus services

There are about forty bus lines which operate in Athens and its environs. Fares are usually 2·5drs for rides in central Athens, up to 5drs out to the inland suburbs, and 4–7drs for the seaside suburbs. The principal services are:
Trolley-bus routes
1: Attikis Square—Larissis Station—Omonia Square—Syntagma Square—Kalithea
2: Kipselis—Omonia—Syntagma—Pagrati
3: Patissia—Kaningos Square—Ambelokipi
5: Attikis—Larissis Station—Omonia—Syntagma—Koukaki
16: Koliatsu—Omonia—Syntagma—Pagrati

Bus routes
A: Omonia—Syntagma—Koukaki
B: Omonia—Syntagma—Filopapou
2: Omonia—Kipseli
3/7: Patissia—Kaningos Square—Ambelokipi—Erithros Stavros
6: Omonia—Akharnon
10: Ipokratos—Syntagma—Votanikos
10/170: Averof—Ipokratous—Omonia—Votanikos
12/3: Koliatous—Omonia—Syntagma—Pagrati
16/176: Ambelokipi—Ipokratos—Syntagma—Acropolis—Thission—Egaleo
34/63: Kinossargous—Syntagma—Bus Station B—Tris Gefires
39/52: Polignon—Kaningos Square—Syntagma (Royal Gardens)—Kessariani
50: Kaningos—Akadimia—Kolonaki—Maraslion—Likavitos
62: Omonia—Akadimia Platanos—Bus Station A
72: Dimarhion (Town Hall)—Kato Petralona
113: Viktoros Ougo St.—Bus Station A—Agii Anargiri
114: Viktoros Ougo St.—Bus Station A—Nea Liossia
163: Korai St.—Syntagma—Neon Faliron
181: Larissis Station—Alexandras Ave.—Erithros Stavros
30, 84, 89, 90: Stop at Vass. Olgas Ave., near the Zappeion, and go to the beach resorts at Glyfada, Voula, Vouliagmeni, and Varkiza
1: Leaves from Amalias Ave. for the West Air Terminal
Direct bus to East Air Terminal leaves from 4 Amalias Ave.

Athens underground

The Athens Underground has only a single line

operating between the Piraeus through the centre of Athens and out to the inland suburb of Kifissia. There is frequent service between 5.30 a.m. and midnight; fares range from 2–7 drs. The stations are: Piraeus—Neon Faliron—Moschatton—Kallithea—Petralona—Thission (central Athens)—Monastiraki (central Athens)—Omonia (centre of Athens)—Victoria (central Athens)—Attiki—Agios Nikolaos—Kato Patissia—Agios Elefterios—Patissia—Perissos—Pefkakia—Nea Ionia—Neon Irakilion—Amaroussion—Kifissia.

Funiculars
There are two funicular railways now operating in Athens and environs. One goes up to the summit of Lykabettos, and the other ascends Mount Parnes as far as Metoki, where the Mount Parnes Hotel and Casino are located.

Sightseeing tours in and around Athens

There are several travel agencies which offer conducted tours of Athens and its environs (see listing on page 25). The following are the day or half-day trips offered by Chat Tours, which are typical of those operated by the other agencies: Athens Sightseeing, full or half-day; Athens by Night; Sounion; Ancient Corinth; the Argolis (Corinth, Mycenae, Argos, Nauplia, Epidauros); Delphi; Attica and Marathon; Aegina, Poros, and Hydra.

These men seem involved in intent discussion. Politics? No, meat prices!

The Environs of Athens

The environs of Athens vary in their character and scenery, and the visitor has a wide range of sights and activities from which to choose. There are the many beach resorts which line the coast of the Saronic Gulf, where all of Athens takes to the sea during the summer months. Then there are the exceptionally pretty islands in the Gulf itself, such as Hydra, Spetsai and Poros, so close to Athens but so far away, for out there one first senses that wonderful remoteness and independence of Aegean island life. There are also the sybaritic inland suburbs, where well-off Greeks and foreign exiles escape the heat and frenzy of downtown Athens. And beyond them is all of lovely Attica itself, that classical landscape which has been praised by poets as far apart in time as Pindar and Byron. Modern industry has ruined parts of the land, mainly along the Gulf west of the Piraeus, but there are large areas of unspoiled countryside still to be seen. This is particularly true of the pastoral Mesogeia district of western Attica, behind Mount Hymettos; here one finds farms, olive groves, vineyards, and picturesque villages, reminiscent of the scene described by nineteenth-century travellers. And then there are the lordly hills of Attica: Parnes, Pentelikon and Hymettos, once the dwelling-places of the gods, still remote and austere though they are only an hour's drive from Syntagma Square.

If one can afford the luxury of a car, perhaps the best way to have a first look at the Attic countryside is to drive along the shore to Cape Sounion, and then circle back through the Mesogeia. If not, then one must start from one of the various Attiki Bus Terminals in Athens. (A list of the terminals and the localities they serve is given at the end of this section.) Most of the Saronic isles are served by ferry-boats from the Piraeus; Akti Poseidonos is the starting-point for Aegina, Methana, Poros, Hydra and Spetsai. To reach the island of Salamis, one must first take a bus from the electric train station; this brings one to the suburb of Peramá, from where the Salamis ferry leaves.

THE PIRAEUS

10km from central Athens
Greece Map D3

Most visitors fail to appreciate that the Piraeus is a city in its own right; in fact it is second only to Athens in population and economic importance. Its half-million residents are principally working-class, rough and ready characters with quick wits and acid tongues, but hospitable to the richer foreigner who makes an effort to meet them on their own ground.

No poet has ever praised the beauty of the Piraeus and the chances are that none ever will, but it is not without its own perverse plebeian charm. One notices this first of all along the lively quays, where crowds of shouting, screaming Aegean islanders fight their way on and off the island ferries, accompanied by a cacophonous orchestra of ship whistles, taxi horns, and screeching motor-carts—the ever present sounds of the Piraeus. One senses the spirit of the Piraeus even more acutely in the boisterous food and produce market, where one could soon acquire an extensive vocabulary of blasphemous and obscene demotic Greek of most outrageous eloquence. And finally there are the informal tavernas one finds in the back streets of the Piraeus, where a few flagons of wine shared with a couple of workers will teach one more about what is going on in Greece than will any newspaper.

A short stroll from the waterfront brings one to the centre of downtown Piraeus, now undergoing a cultural renaissance under its dynamic mayor, Aristides Skylitsis. Walking south along the quays from the electric train station, one first passes the bustling Karaiskaki Square, the embarkation centre for the busy inter-island boats. Continuing along, one passes on the left the new Market, less colourful in appearance than the old one it replaced, but every bit as boisterous. A short stroll then brings one to the Tinan Gardens, where the huge cathedral of the Piraeus, **Ayia Trianda**, or Holy Trinity, stands, which was built to replace the older cathedral, destroyed in an air-raid in 1944. From here one takes the Avenue of George I, which soon brings one to the Municipal Theatre, a handsome building in the neoclassical style. One then turns right on Vass. Konstantinou, a broad, tree-lined avenue which runs up the spine of the Akti peninsula, the heart of the Piraeus.

Although the Piraeus has had a long and interesting history, it has little to offer in the way of antiquities. All that remains now are some fragments of its ancient defence-walls, which can be seen along the shore road around the Akti peninsula, and the ruins of the **Theatre of Zea**, built in the second century B.C.

The Theatre of Zea stands next to the **Archaeological Museum** of the Piraeus, at 8 Filellinon St., which houses antiquities discovered mostly in accidental excavations over the past decade. The Museum's proudest possession is a large bronze statue of Athena, an original bronze work done in 375 B.C. by Cephissodotus, father of Praxitiles.

(Opening hours. Summer period: daily 8 a.m. to 1 p.m. and 3 p.m. to 6 p.m.; Sundays and holidays 10 a.m. to 1 p.m. and 3 p.m. to 6 p.m. Winter period: daily 9 a.m. to 1 p.m. and 2.30 p.m. to 5 p.m.; Sundays and holidays 10 a.m. to 1 p.m. and 2.30 p.m. and 5 p.m.)

The **Naval Museum** is situated a short distance away, just off the Akti Moutsopoulou. The Museum houses relics of Greece's long and glorious naval history, with particular emphasis on the War of Independence.

(Opening hours. Summer period: daily 9 a.m. to 1 p.m.; Wednesdays and Saturdays 9 a.m. to 1 p.m. and 6 p.m. to 8 p.m.; Sundays and holidays 10 a.m. to 1 p.m. and 6 p.m. to 9 p.m. Winter period: daily 9 a.m. to 1 p.m.; Wednesdays and Saturdays 9 a.m. to 1 p.m. and 5 p.m. to 7 p.m.; Sundays and holidays 10 a.m. to 1 p.m. and 5 p.m. to 8 p.m. Closed on Mondays.)

Akti Moutsopoulou borders one of the two smaller harbours of the Piraeus. This is the **Zea Marina**, better known by its older name of **Pashalimani**, the

Pasha's Port. Just behind the port is Kanaris Square, lined with restaurants and cafés, a favourite haven for Athenians fleeing their city on a hot summer night.

The second of the two small harbours is a short stroll to the north; this is **Tourkolimani**, the Turk's Port. (This has recently been renamed Microlimani, the Small Port, part of a plan to obliterate all Turkish place-names in Greece, but everyone still calls it by its old name.) The crescent-shaped harbour of Tourkolimani is filled with handsome yachts and lined with outdoor fish-restaurants, which makes it a favourite subject for picture postcards. Although the atmosphere along the port is not as relaxed as it was in past times (waiters sometimes try to drag you in as you pass by), the increased popularity of Tourkolimani has done nothing to lower the quality of the seafood served there, the best in Greece. (The best eating-places in Tourkolimani are listed together with the other restaurants of the Piraeus.)

The heights above Tourkolimani form the district called **Castella**. This is the site of the open air **Skylitsean Theatre**, where performances by Greek and foreign dance groups are held nightly at 9 p.m. during the summer months. From Castella there is a splendid view out over the whole Saronic Gulf.

Just north of Tourkolimani we come to **Neon Faliron**, whose once-pleasant beach is now polluted and unfit for swimming. Here we find the lively Faliron Fairground; the Faliron Race Course, the largest in Greece; and Karaiskaki Stadium, the scene of international track and field meets and soccer matches. Beyond Neon Faliron the coast road is lined with the famous *bouzoukia* clubs which are such a basic part of the Piraeus scene. (A listing of the most popular clubs and current stars is given in *Athens at Night*.)

The most important public holiday in the Piraeus is Naval Week, which begins on the first Sunday in July. This festival, commemorating Greece's naval victories in the War of Independence, is centred in the three ports of the Piraeus. It is a spectacular sight at night, particularly if viewed from the Castella, with warships, yachts and fishing boats bedecked with flags and their rigging strung with lights, and with brilliant displays of fireworks exploding in the air.

Hotels

(B) Homirdon, 32 Harilaou Tricoupi and Alkiviadou. Tel: 4519-932. Air-conditioned. Restaurant and roof-garden.

(B) Noufara, 45 Vass. Konstantinou. Tel: 4519-558. Partially air-conditioned. Restaurant and roof-garden.

(B) Triton, 8 Tsamadou. Tel: 473-457. Cables: TRITONHOTEL.

(C) Argo, 23 Notara. Tel: 471-795.

(C) Arion, 109 Vass. Pavlou, Castella. Tel: 421-425. Partially air-conditioned.

(C) Capitol, Harilaou Tricoupi and Philonos. Tel: 4524-911.

(C) Castella, 75 Vass. Pavlou, Castella. Tel: 473-623. A charming old hotel on the hill above Tourkolimani, with a splendid view out over the Saronic Gulf.

(C) Cavo, 79 Philonos. Tel: 4522-430.

(C) Delfini, 7 Leocharous. Tel: 423-512.

(C) Diogenis, 27 Vass. Georgiou. Tel: 425-471. Air-conditioned. Restaurant, night-club and roof-garden.

(C) Glaros, 4 Harilaou Tricoupi. Tel: 4515-421.

(C) Leroti, 294 Themistokleous. Tel: 4516-640.

(C) Serifos, 5 Harilaou Tricoupi. Tel: 4525-001.

(D) Galaxy, 18 Sachtouri. Tel: 4512-973.

Restaurants

Vassilenas, corner of Vitolion and Aetolikon, Piraeus. No journey to the Piraeus is complete without a visit to this incomparable taverna. There is no menu, and do not try to order for you will be ignored, but simply sit down and the food and wine will come (and keep coming), and if you manage to eat through the cycle of half-a-hundred specialities, you can start a second cycle and continue until you collapse under your own weight. Wine is free and plentiful and the price is moderate considering the quality and abundance.

Of the many restaurants in Tourkolimani, we recommend these favourites, although most of the others along the port have their devoted backers too:

Kanaris. On the far left side of the port as one faces the sea, this is one of the area's best-known restaurants. Most of the fish is priced according to the kilo and not by the particular portion. Try the *kalamarakia,* the *barbunia,* and the *garides.* The special *garides* casserole is excellent. Reasonable unless one chooses lobster.

Kaplanis. Formerly a very popular restaurant in Istanbul, this is the port's newest and most popular restaurant. The *mezedes,* which are beautifully displayed in glass cases, are much better and more varied than anywhere else in Athens. Try the *pigiazi yemista* (bean salad), the *tsatsiki,* the *ktopodi,* the *midia yemista* (stuffed mussel shells), the *tsiroz* (tiny salted fish), the fried aubergines and squash, and the potato croquettes. There is an enormous selection of main fish dishes, but the best is *garides youvetsaki,* a shrimp casserole. If the weather is not good enough for an outdoor meal, go upstairs to the elegant dining-room, whose picture windows afford the same spectacular view.

Semiramis. Despite the indecipherable menu, this restaurant is worth trying. The grilled fish, again sold by the kilo, is beyond reproach, and the service is good.

Kokino Varka (The Red Boat). The K V is one of the oldest restaurants in Tourkolimani; among other things, it offers twelve different kinds of fish, and all for reasonable prices. Although one will probably want to eat outside, the inner hall is highly enjoyable, with its huge wine barrels set into the wall, its cartoons, its score of bird-cages, and its old-fashioned overhead fans.

TO SOUNION AND BACK
10–70km from Athens
Greece Map D, E4

One of the most popular excursions from Athens is to drive out along the coastal highway to Cape Sounion, at the south-eastern tip of Attica. But its very popularity has diminished somewhat the charm of this scenic coast, for during the summer months the coastal highway is congested and the beaches are packed with humanity. Nevertheless, if one doesn't mind crowds this can be a pleasant ride. The beach resorts themselves are very lively, for the Greeks are not content to just sit and brown themselves like northern Europeans. When at the beach they are in a state of constant and ebullient activity, with young men and women vigorously batting balls about, boys kicking soccer balls at imaginary goals, athletes showing off their gymnastic prowess, women stuffing gruel into the mouths of their over-fed babies, children and old folks splashing happily together in the shallows, everyone shouting and laughing except the silent and supine Germans and Scandanavians, who have crossed Europe to bake every square centimetre of their pale skins.

Alimos (10km from Athens). There are only two reasons why a visitor would want to stop at this crowded and characterless beach resort. One is that Alimos is the birthplace of Thucydides, the great historian of the Peloponnesian Wars. The other is that it is the site of one of the very best restaurants in all of Athens, the **Bosphorus**. Like all Greek restaurants run by Greek emigrées from Istanbul, the Bosphorus is noted for its delicious and infinitely varied *mezedes*, which combine the best of Turkish and Greek (or is it Byzantine?) cookery. Simply order hot and/or cold *mezedes* and sit back as platoons of waiters stagger to your table carrying trays freighted with little plates of fattening delicacies. Your turn to stagger will be when you are presented with the bill, but the superb food is well worth the price you pay.

Glyfada (16km from Athens). This is the most fashionable beach resort in the vicinity of Athens, with elegant villas, seaside hotels, night-clubs, restaurants, cafés, discothèques, and an eighteen-hole golf course. (Don't hit your drives too high, or they will bounce off the airliners which roar by just above tree level as they land and take off at the nearby Ellinikon Airport.) There are two score hotels of every category in Glyfada, but all of these are generally booked up solid by vacationing Greeks, who do not mind the noise of low-flying aircraft since they are making so much noise themselves. The best and most expensive place to stay in Glyfada is:

(L) Astir Bungalows, Vass. Georgiou. Tel: 8946-461. Cables: BUNGALOTEL GLYFADA. Luxurious without being elegant, this bungalow hotel is in a pleasant bay whose foreshore is lush with groves of pines and citrus trees. Each unit is air-conditioned and equipped with refrigerators, beach chairs, and so on. There are tennis courts, mini-golf, sea sports, a night-club and a restaurant. Full board usually required.
There are a great many seaside tavernas in Glyfada and the adjacent coast. Among the most famous restaurants are:
Antonopoulos. The prices reflect its fashionable location, but the seafood is undeniably excellent. The inner dining-room has bamboo chairs and a marble fireplace, though in summer one usually eats in the tree-shaded garden or at the seaside tables across the road. For *mezedes* try the shrimp salad, the *tsatsiki*, the *taramosalata*, and the aubergine salad. The swordfish (*xifias*) and the *feta spirida* are good main courses.
Asteria. Perhaps the best seafood in Glyfada, with prices to match. There is also dancing in the evening.

Vouliagmeni (26km from Athens). A superbly-situated beach resort, built on a pine-clad cape projecting out between the sea and placid Vouliagmeni Bay. Of the dozen or so hotels here by far the most outstanding is the:

(L) Astir Palace Hotel, Vouliagmeni Beach. Tel: 8960-210. Cables: BUNGOTEL VOULIAGMENI. The Astir Palace is by all standards the finest hotel in Greece. It has a palatial lobby which opens out onto an astounding marble terrace with a view of the Astir's private bay. The hotel has 147 rooms with marble bathrooms and spacious verandas. Most spectacular are the penthouse rooms and suites. Along the beach are 77 luxury bungalows with private patios and gardens. Full board is required but one can choose from three restaurants: the **Pegasus,** which opens out onto the terrace; the **Grill Room,** which has international and Greek cuisine, as well as an orchestra, and the **Club House,** which is on the small headland at the head of the beach. The **Amphitryon Taverna** serves lighter snacks and has Greek guitar music in the evening. The '37' bar serves light food and drinks. In addition to table tennis, tennis courts, a mini-golf course, and a water-skiing school, the Astir Palace also has a fully equipped yacht marina. This is where the jet set stays, and no one who sees the hotel will blame them for over-spending.

Beyond Vouliagmeni the highway winds along the rocky coast through groves of evergreens, passing the public beach at **Varkiza** (32km from Athens), and soon comes to still another fashionable resort at **Lagonissi** (40km from Athens). Here there is a self-contained tourist-resort; as at Vouliagmeni, it is situated on a verdant sea-bound cape.

(L) Xenia Lagonissi. Tel: 8958-511. Cables: LAGONISSATHINAI. The bungalows are partially air-conditioned and there is a private beach, swimming-pool, sea sports, tennis courts, mini-golf, a restaurant, and a night-club.

The corniche road continues past Lagonissi along the coast and finally brings us to Cape Sounion, a rocky headland at the extreme south-western tip of Attica. At the peak of the promontory we see the ruins of the famous **Temple of Poseidon**, one of the most photogenic ruins in Greece. The temple was completed in about 440 B.C., a decade before the Parthenon, and it is thought that it was designed by the architect who built the Hephaisteion in Athens. This is surely one of the most romantic spots in all of Greece, particularly at sunset, when the lonely columns take on the pastel colours of the western horizon, and the ruins of the temple are silhouetted against the ink-blue sky. Byron loved this place, and as a memento carved his name with great precision on one of the columns. Seeing it there, we are reminded of these lines which he wrote in Canto 3 of *Don Juan*:

> Place me on Sunium's marble steep,
> Where nothing, save the waves and I,
> May hear our mutual murmurs sweep;
> There, swan-like, let me sing and die . . .

After leaving Sounion, one will surely have had enough of the congested coastal traffic and the swarming beach resorts, and will prefer to return to Athens by another route. One can do so by continuing along the coast past Sounion, and then turning inland for the return journey.

A ten kilometre drive north of Sounion along the coast brings us to **Lavrion**, once the site of the famous silver mines which contributed so much to the wealth of Athens. Another kilometre brings us to **Thorikon**, in ancient times the site of an important Mycenaean city, of which some ruins still remain.

Once past Thorikon we turn inland through the **Mesogeia**, the loveliest and most unspoiled region of Attica. The Mesogeia is also one of the principal wine-producing regions of Greece, as evidenced by the miles of rich vineyards one passes when driving through. All of the towns of the Mesogeia are noted for their wine, particularly Markopoulo, Koropion and Peania (the birth-place of Demosthenes), and one should stop to sample them at some of the pleasant roadside tavernas along the way (best to have an abstemious chauffeur). And by this delightfully alcoholic route one returns to Athens in a resinated glow.

THE ATTIC SUBURBS

14–20km from Athens
Greece Map D4—not shown

In classical times, those who lived outside the walls of Athens were known as *perioikoi*, or dwellers-round-about. They were thus an underprivileged lot, unable to participate in the democratic life of a free city, cut off from its extraordinarily creative cultural life, and exposed to the violence of invading enemies. The situation in contemporary Athens is quite the reverse; the privileged ones are those who make a good enough living in the city and can afford a life as far away from it as possible.

The most fashionable of all the Attic suburbs is **Kifissia** (14km from central Athens). Kifissia has the best of both worlds, for it is connected to central Athens by the Underground and to the beach resorts on the Saronic Gulf by direct bus services. Nevertheless, those who really love this garden suburb have as little as possible to do with either the city or the sea, preferring to stay at home on the patios of their tree-shaded villas, enjoying the cool evening air in one of the many felicitous roadside tavernas in their neighbourhood.

For the visitor who would like to become a temporary *perioikoi*, the following are some of the better hotels in the Kifissia area:

(L) Pentelikon, 66 Deligianni. Tel: 8012-837. Restaurant on the premises.

(A) Apergi, Kefalari. Tel: 8013-537. Restaurant.

(A) Attikon, 12 Pendelis. Tel: 8013-149. Restaurant.

(A) Cecil, 7 Xenias, Kefalari. Tel: 8013-836. Restaurant. One of the grand old hotels of suburban Athens.

(A) Grand Chalet (pension), 38 Kokkinara. Tel: 8014-888. Cables: GRANCHAL. Restaurant and roof-garden.

(A) Costis Dimitracopoulos, 65 Deligianni. Tel: 8012-546. Restaurant.

(A) Palace, 1 Kolokotroni, Kefalari. Tel: 8013-577. Restaurant.

(A) Semiramis, 36 Harilaou Tricoupi and Philadelfeos, Kefalari. Tel: 8012-587. Swimming-pool, restaurant and night-club.

(A) Theoxenia, 2 Philadelfeos and Kolokotroni. Tel: 8012-751. Restaurant.

(B) Nafsika, 6 Pellis. Tel: 8013-255. Cables: NAFSIKAOTEL. Partially air-conditioned. Restaurant and roof-garden.

(C) Aegli, Platia Platanou. Tel: 8012-591.

(C) De Roses, 4 Miltiadou. Tel: 8019-952.

(C) Plaza, Platia Platanou. Tel: 8013-010.

(C) Katerina, 3 Myconou, Kefalari. Tel: 8018-495. Restaurant.

Of the many good restaurants and tavernas in Kifissia, the following are to be especially recommended:

Blue Pine Farms, 37 Tsaldari. The most distinguished of Kifissia's garden restaurants, Blue Pine has also a beautiful winter dining-room in the style of a Swiss chalet. The softly-lit garden is fragrant with the odour of pines and roses. Good hors d'oeuvres, especially the Blue Pine cheese-sticks. Specialities include *Casa Marina* (crab au gratin), chicken and asparagus au gratin, steak for two, tournedos, filet mignon, and, for dessert, pommes flambés. A good selection of domestic and imported wines. Expensive but highly recommended.

Grigoris, 6 Angiropoulou. This is a simpler garden restaurant. It is comfortably noisy and has good Greek food. The speciality of the house is *stamnaki atomiko* (veal casserole with a thick sauce). The *mezedes—ktapodi, kolokithakia tiganita* (fried baby courgettes), and *melitsanes tiganites* (fried aubergines)—are a must. The smoked pork, pigeon stew, *saganaki* (fried cheese), and grilled meats are also delicious. Reasonable.

La Belle Helene, Politea. Another expensive but excellent restaurant, with an umbrella-shaded courtyard. Specialities here are New York pepper steaks flambé, chicken a la Belle Helene, and several preparations of trout. Highly recommended.

Moustakas, Harilaou Tricoupi and 5 Kritis. Specialities in this garden restaurant are smoked pork chops, home-made sausages and stuffed aubergines. Fairly reasonable.

Mikros Boccaris, Soccratous and Acharnon. A very reasonable restaurant with good grilled meat. The artichoke *moussaka* is delicious.

Some other good restaurants in Kifissia are the **Grand Chalet,** 28 Kokkinara (rather expensive); **Le Grillons,** 12 Kolokotroni (an equally expensive restaurant with superior French food);

Salamantis, Syngrou and Anapafseas; and **Hadzakos**, Plaka Square, famous for its excellent roast chicken.

A boy and his donkey

Of course Kifissia is not the only Attic suburb of Athens, nor is everyone agreed that it is the most sybaritic. Other very pleasant spots even more remote from Athens in distance and atmosphere are **Kastri** and **Ekali**, twin towns 4km past Kifissia in a densely-wooded area fragrant with the smell of pines; **Drossia** (its name means 'cool'), another kilometre along the same road, and above all **Varibobi**, 19km from Athens on the slopes of Mount Parnes. Those who really want to escape summertime Athens would do well to stay in this delicious cool resort in the midst of an aromatic pine forest. There are two good hotels in Varibobi:

(L) Auberge Tatoi. Tel: 8013-803. Tennis courts, roof garden and night-club. The restaurant offers excellent French food at appropriate prices. Piano music in the evenings.
(B) Varibobi. Tel: 8016-305. Tennis courts, mini-golf, and restaurant.
   Besides the Auberge Tatoi, there are two other good restaurants in Varibobi:
Babis. Excellent food and service. Specialities are suckling pig and home-made sausages.
Leonidas. Another first-class restaurant with excellent food and service. In summer one can dine on the patio and command a sweeping view out over Attica, feeling well-fed and benevolent.

THE HILLS OF ATTICA

Greece Map D4—not shown

Athens is ringed by three great hills, veritable mountains in fact, whose bare slopes and peaks form the background to all views of the city to the north and west.

   The highest and most rugged of these is the **Parnes** range, which divides Attica from Boetia to the north-west. The summit of Parnes (4,635ft) can be approached quite easily, by taking the national highway north for 10km and then turning off to the left at the 'Parnis' signpost. There are also four buses to Parnes daily from Syntagma Square. The bus terminates at the pleasant little mountain resort of **Ayia Trias** (35km from Athens), where there is a comfortable hotel.

(B) Xenia. Tel: 249-101. Restaurant; full pension usually required. Open June to September.

The road continues for another 2·5km to the:

(L) Grand Hotel Mount Parnes. Tel: 249-111 (in Athens call 3229-412). Cables: PARNOTEL. This luxurious hotel has a swimming-pool, tennis courts, mini-golf, a restaurant, a night-club, and, of course, the famous Casino Mount Parnes. (The hotel can also be reached by cable-car from the foot of Mount Parnes.)

Pentelikon is the mountain range which borders Athens to the north-east. The mountain takes its name from the famous marble quarry of Pentelikon, which supplied marble for all the great temples in Athens. Pentelikon is approached by the road which passes through the suburb of Halandri. (There is also a bus service from Kaningos Square, near Omonia.) The road terminates at **Penteli** (20km from Athens, altitude 1,550ft), where there are several rustic tavernas. Close by are the sixteenth-century monastery of **Moni Pendeli** and the nineteenth-century **Palace of Rododafnis**, built for the Duchesse de Plaisance. The ancient quarries lie farther up the mountain, at altitudes of 2,300–3,300ft. From the quarries one can climb to a ridge below the summit, from where one commands the most sweeping of all views of Attica and the Saronic Gulf and out to the nearer Cyclades. Unfortunately the summit itself (3,640ft) is occupied by a radar station and is thus out of bounds.

The third of the Attic hills is **Hymettos**, which stands to the south-east near the Saronic shore. Hymettos is approached by Vass. Alexandrou and Vass. Konstandinou Aves. (Bus No. 39152 from the Royal Gardens.) Six kilometres from central Athens we come to the eleventh-century **Kaisarianis Monastery**, one of the loveliest spots in the vicinity of Athens. About four kilometres farther along we pass another and almost equally lovely monastery of the same period, **Moni Asteriou**. The road then winds up towards the summit, with panoramic views out over Attica and the sea. Unfortunately the summit itself is here again occupied by a radar station, and is thus as inaccessible as Everest.

MARATHON AND THE SEA

40km from Athens
Greece Map D4—not shown

Still more remote from Athens are the towns and villages to the north and east of Mounts Pentelikon and Hymettos. The most historic spot here is the site of the battle of **Marathon**, which took place about four kilometres south of the modern village of that name. Here on 16 August 490 B.C. Miltiades led the Athenians and their allies from Plataia to a glorious victory over the invading Persians and altered the course of European history. As Byron wrote in *Don Juan*:

> The mountains look on Marathon—
> And Marathon looks on the sea;
> And musing there an hour alone,
> I dream'd that Greece might still be free . . .

The mountain of which Byron sang was Pentelikon, and the sea upon which it and Marathon look borders the east coast of Attica, the finest and most natural stretch of seaside near Athens. All of the roads which lead from Marathon to the sea bring one to fine beaches in natural settings, most of them still unspoiled by tourism. Among these picturesque seaside villages are, starting from the south, **Loutsa**, **Rafina**, **Ayios Andrea**, **Nea Makri**, **Shinias**, **Ayii Apostoli**, and **Skala Oropou**—the port of embarkation for ferries to Eritria on the large island of Euboea. All of these villages have decent hotels and restaurants, and there is a camping site at Nea Makri. These beaches are far less crowded and unspoiled than those of the Saronic Gulf, though tourism will inevitably destroy them too.

The east coast of Attica also preserves several interesting archaeological sites. At **Vraona** (38km east of Athens) there are the remains of the **Sanctuary of Artemis Brauronia**, a fifth-century B.C. Doric temple; there is also a small museum on the site. And at **Ramnous** (14km north-east of Marathon) there are the remains of two other Doric temples of the fifth century B.C., one of them dedicated to Nemesis, goddess of divine retribution, and the other sacred to Themis, goddess of moderation and equity. This is certainly the most beautiful spot on the Attic coast, with the ruined temples of two forgotten goddesses standing serenely alone above the turquoise sea.

TOWARDS THE PELOPONNESE

10–42km west of Athens
Greece Map D3

The new superhighway from Athens to Corinth takes one through the most noxious industrial districts of Attica, obscuring to some extent the beauty and historic interest of three sites along the way.

Daphni (Dafni) (10km west of Athens). The road from Athens to Daphni follows the course and preserves the name of the Sacred Way (Iera Odos), which in ancient times led from the Dipylon Gate in the city walls to the sacred shrine of Eleusis. The name Daphni means 'Laurel', denoting the grove of laurel trees sacred to Apollo which grew in that area. The shrine of Apollo was later dedicated to the Virgin Mary, as were so many other places sacred to the worship of the ancient gods, and a church and monastery were founded there. The present church of Daphni was built in about 1180 and is one of the finest examples of Byzantine architecture that has survived in Greece. The church is famous for its superb mosaics, particularly that of Christos Pantocrator, the Byzantine Christ who looks down so sternly and majestically from the dome.

Daphni is also famous for its boisterous wine festival, held each year from mid-July to mid-September. The entrance fee is 20drs, and for another 10drs you can buy a glass which will allow you to sample any of the more than 50 varieties of Greek wine dispensed by smiling girls in archaic costumes. There are also several tavernas with music and dancing, and the whole scene is very light-hearted and gay.

Eleusis (Elefsis) (22km west of Athens). The Sacred Way terminated at the ancient shrine of Eleusis, one of the most venerated sites in all of ancient Greece, and the one most sacred to the Athenians. This shrine owed its sanctity to its association with the fertility cult of Demeter and the haunting myth of her search through the Underworld for her lost daughter, Persephone. The cult of Demeter was the most powerful in all of the ancient Greek world, and initiation into the Eleusian Mysteries was the culminating religious experience. Excavations on the site of the sanctuary have revealed that it was a sacred shrine from early Mycenaean times up through the Roman period; indeed there is a nineteenth-century church still standing there, an illustration of the continuity of religious experience in this ancient country. There is a museum on the site which exhibits the various antiquities unearthed during excavations over the past century, as well as a copy of the famous Eleusian relief now in the National Archaeological Museum.

A twenty kilometre drive past Eleusis along the highway takes us across the ancient boundaries of Attica to the town of **Megara**. In classical times Megara was often in rivalry with Athens, and it was a dispute between the two cities which was the immediate cause of the tragic Peloponnesian War.

THE SARONIC ISLANDS

Salamis (1·5km west of the Piraeus; Greece Map D,E3). Salamis is a forlorn island just off the coast of Attica; it is an illustration of the thesis that some of the most important events in world history take place on some of the least significant spots on the planet. The Battle of Salamis, fought in the narrow strait between the island and the mainland on 22 September 480 B.C., resulted in a devastating rout of the Persian fleet by the Greeks and opened the way for their final victory at Plataea the following year. Nothing much has happened on Salamis since that fateful day. Inhabited mostly by Albanian refugees for the past few centuries, it is a rocky island with undistinguished towns and a rather large naval base. The main town of Koulouri does not even have a hotel; the only hostelry in Salamis, the **Gabriel (C)**, is in the town of Eantion.

Aegina (28km from Piraeus; Greece Map E3,4). When one sails into the sleepy port of Aegina, with its blue-domed churches and pastel-coloured houses, it is difficult to believe that the island was once Athens' greatest rival. Aegina was for centuries one of the area's principal trade centres; it played a major role in the Persian Wars, and it was even the capital of modern Greece for a year, in 1828. Now it shares the fate of so many former strongholds of the Aegean: it has been reduced to a pleasant and conveniently-located resort for the Athenian bourgeoise, with the typical string of cafés and restaurants along the port and a forlorn ruined Temple of Apollo on a headland.

Aegina is so close to Athens and so accessible—there are at least ten boats a day—that it could easily have been spoiled. But if one can avoid the flabby weekend-crowds, it is still an enchanting island. The central mountains are covered with pine trees; pistachio plantations and vineyards cover the slopes which come down to the sea. The food is reputed to be better than that on most islands, and the sea is generally very clear. The good road network allows for many quick excursions between boats. **Aya Marina**, a small port on the opposite side of the island, has a sandy beach which is ideal for underwater swimming, but its real distinction is the **Temple of Aphea** (*c.* 500 B.C.), majestically perched above the town on the wooded hills. Other spots worth visiting are **Perdika**, a small fishing village, and the nearby islet of **Moni**, accessible only by caïque, where there is a beach and camping facilities, and **Palaichora**, a brooding ruin of a medieval town which comes to life once a year on the festival of the Ascension. Bicycles and horse carriages can be rented quite cheaply.

There are several good hotels on the island, among these are:

(L) **Marisa Bay**, Ayia Marina. Tel: 22-540 (in Athens call 3225-057). A luxury establishment with air-conditioning, tennis courts, mini-golf, a swimming-pool, a private beach, a restaurant, and a night-club.

(B) **Apollo**, Ayia Marina. Tel: 32-271. Cables: APOLLOTEL. Swimming-pool, private beach, sea sports, tennis courts, and restaurant.

(B) **Moondy Bay**, Aegina (town). Tel: 22-605. Cables: MOONDY AEGINA. A very well-equipped bungalow complex 6km out of town. Besides a restaurant and a roof-garden, it has a swimming-pool, sea sports, tennis courts and mini-golf.

(B) **Nausica**, 55, 21 Aprillou Blvd., Nafsika. Tel: 22-333. Another bungalow hotel with fewer facilities.

Restaurants. Madridaki in Aegina; **Stratigos** in Pharos (noted for its seafood); **Vatzoulias** in the outskirts of Aegina; **Kiriakis** and **Michalis** in Marathon.

Methana (47km from Piraeus; Greece Map E3,4). Methana is geographically part of the Peloponnese, but administratively part of the Saronic Gulf islands (though it is not *really* an island, being connected to the mainland by an insignificant isthmus). It is famous for its warm sulphur springs and for its spa, which can accommodate 3,000 people. But sulphur streams smell as well as cure, hence the nickname of Methana's port, *Vromolimni* (Foul-Smelling Harbour). The Methana area is good for fishing and hunting, and the ruined fortress and church on the nearby rocky peninsula of Nisaki are picturesque.

Hotels. Gionis (B), Pigae (B), American (C), Dima (C), Methanion (C).

Restaurants. Gigourtakis, Lekka, Nissioti; all on the waterfront.

Poros (60km from Piraeus; Greece Map E3,4). Many travellers have praised the sparkling port of Poros, calling it a miniature version of Paris or Capri.

Very popular with Greeks, foreign eccentrics and yachtsmen, Poros is actually two islands joined by an isthmus. The larger of the two is **Calavria**, which is hilly and covered with pines and lemon groves. The second island, where the town is situated, is conical and volcanic. There are many small sandy coves on both islets which are best reached by boat. Another interesting short excursion is to the **Sanctuary of Poseidon**, the former meeting-place of Greece's oldest maritime confederation, the Calavrian League, and since then a popular hiding-place for fugitives.

One of the charms of the port of Poros is its proximity to the mainland, which is at this point very colourful. Innumerable small boats ferry back and forth across the narrow strait between the island and the whitewashed Peloponnesian town of **Galata**. The countryside around Galata is extremely interesting, particularly the Lemonodassos (the Lemon Forest) and The Devil's Bridge, a single-arched span over what has been rightly called a savage gorge.

Hotels. Anessis (B). Latsi (B), Neon Aegli (B) (Askeli), **Poros (B), Saron (B), Sirene (B), Angyra (B)** (Neorion), **Stella Maris Nautical Holiday Centre (B)** (Galata).

Restaurants. Alaska, Asteria; both standard and reasonable.

Hydra (77km from Piraeus; Greece Map E4). In ancient times this island was covered with pines, but now it is dramatically bare. Its spectacular, well-enclosed harbour served for centuries as a haven for pirates and was the home of Greece's most accomplished and affluent seamen. As Antonios Kriezes once remarked: 'The island produces prickly pears in abundance, splendid sea captains, and excellent prime ministers.' This summary no longer holds for modern Hydra, but the Italianate architecture—the gabled and tiled roofs, the arches, the bell-towers, and the palazzo-like mansions—testify to a more illustrious past.

The Harbour of Hydra

Hydra went through a long stage of poverty, but a recently-established

77

artists' colony has solved its financial problems by making the island very attractive to the 'jet set' and its imitators. Now Hydra is one of the most exotic resorts in the Aegean; the cafés are filled with well-dressed and well-heeled eccentrics and the harbour is lined with yachts whose owners never cease to pop open bottle after bottle of champagne.

If one can tear oneself away from the strange parade on the waterfront, one should try to visit the old mansions of the three Koundouriati brothers and that of Boudouri. These are not museums but can be seen on request.

Most people swim off the rocks at the side of the bay, but there are adequate beaches at Kamini and Molos, both easily reached by caïque.

The discothèques on the island are mediocre, but with a good group they can be fun. The **Thalassopoula** and the **Sirocos Club** are preferable to the rest.

The best hotels in Hydra are:

(A) Miramare (pension). Tel: 52-300. Cables: MIRAMARIDRA. This hotel's bungalows are the completely remodelled lodgings of the men who worked in the old shipping yards. Very successful. Beach, sea sports and restaurant.
(A) Miranda (pension). Tel: 52-230.
(B) Amaryllis (pension). Tel: 52-249.
(B) Xenia. Tel: 52-217. Restaurant.
(C) Hydra. Tel: 52-569. An old reconstructed mansion on top of the hill; charming, but no rooms with bath.
(C) Leto. Tel: 52-280. Partially air-conditioned. Restaurant.

Restaurants. Bradley and **Archontikon** on the port; **Alkyon** at Kanoni—very good view here.

Spetsai (86km from Piraeus; Greece Map E3). Only one and a half hours from Hydra by ferry boat, Spetsai is completely different from its wild neighbour. Its hills are gentler and greener, and instead of attracting an army of safari jackets and Indian silk scarves, it is the favourite of refined Athenian society. The cobble-stoned port, Dapia, is surrounded by the whitewashed villas of the affluent. The villa courtyards overflowing with flowers and the grand terraces, which look out onto Dapia's many gentle bays, suggest an atmosphere of discreet luxury.

The principal means of transport is still the horse-drawn carriage, but walks along the coast and in the pine-clad forests are also very enjoyable. The best beach is 12km across the island at Ayii Anargyri; two other good ones are at Zogeria and Vrello. Spetsai has many other sports opportunities, such as horseback riding, bicycling, motorcycling, water-skiing, sailing, and snorkeling. For detailed information on these activities, consult Takis Pareskevas at the centrally-located Tourist Office.

There are two or more boats a day to Spetsai from the Piraeus; the journey is five hours long. Those with cars may prefer to drive down along the Peloponnesian coast and take the short car-ferry ride from the town of Kosta.

Hotels
(A) Possidonion. Tel: 72-208. Restaurant.
(A) Xenia (hotel and bungalows). Tel: 72-311 (in Athens call 636-612). Private beach, restaurant and roof-garden.
(B) Roumanis. Tel: 72-244.
(C) Ilios. Tel: 72-268. Partially air-conditioned, private beach, and roof-garden.

(C) Mirtoon. Tel: 72-555. Restaurant and roof-garden.
(C) Star. Tel: 72-219.

Restaurants. Haralambos, on the old port; **Gregos**, above the Tourist Office (juke box and Greek dancing, bad service but lively atmosphere); **Tzortzis** at Aya Marina (more expensive but with excellent bouzoukia music).

Bus terminals for Athenian suburbs and towns in Attica

A (Athens Map C3). No. 70: Omonia—Piraeus. No. 165: Syntagma—Piraeus—Kalithea—Neon Faliron.
B (Athens Map C4). No. 15: Psihikon. No. 24: Filothei.
C (Athens Map D4). No. 1: Paleon Faliron—Ag. Kosmas.
D (Athens Map E4). No. 184: East Air Terminal.
E (Athens Map E4). No. 30: Glyfada. No. 84: Voula. No. 89: Vouliagmeni. No. 90: Varkiza.
F (Athens Map E5). No. 42: Palini.
G (Athens Map C3). No. 18: Kifissia—Kefalari. No. 138: Varibobi.
H (Athens Map B3). No. 121: Amaroussion.
I (Athens Map B4). Nos. 105, 106: Penteli.
J (Athens Map D2). No. 44: Peania. No. 46: Koropion. No. 96: Loutsa.
K (Athens Map D2). No. 68: Eleusis. No. 88: Perama. No. 100: Daphni.
L (Athens Map B3). No. 116: Parnes.

Souvlaki is as popular with Greek families as it is with starvation budget travellers

The Peloponnese

The Peloponnese, or the 'Isle of Pelops', is a huge peninsula connected to mainland Greece only by the slim isthmus at Corinth. It is mountainous for the most part, and even on the level stretches along the sea coast there are always lofty crags and peaks looming in the background of every view. The Peloponnese is a land deeply steeped in history and rich in antiquities from every period in Greek civilization. The modern political boundaries of the peninsula correspond almost exactly to its divisions in ancient times, divisions which the land itself imposed.

The north-east corner of the Peloponnese comprises the Argolid, a country of fertile fields and green rolling hills. To the south of this lies Laconia in the south-east, once the dominions of the Spartans, a land as remote and rugged as the men who dominated it. The centre of the Peloponnese is ancient Arcadia, completely girded by harsh and forbidding mountains, a region which has always been somewhat isolated from the rest of Greece. The south-western corner of the peninsula is Messeni, a lush and fertile region which the ancients called 'The Happy Land'. Even more verdant is Elis, which comprises the north-west corner of the Peloponnese, so rich and so abundant that the Crusaders called it 'The Milk Cow of the Morea', using the name by which the peninsula was known in medieval times. Then finally there is Achaia, that smiling land which rolls down from the mountains of the northern Peloponnese to the Gulf of Corinth, to a seashore indented with pleasant ports and sandy coves. And so the Peloponnese is really a country in itself, so different is it from the rest of Greece, and so various are the characters of its ancient regions.

Most visitors who tour the Peloponnese begin at Corinth, crossing the famous Corinth Canal; from there one can drive around most of the peninsula, with excursions into the interior.

CORINTH (KORINTHOS)
86km from Athens
Greece Map D3

Modern Corinth is a busy, small provincial town, with little to interest the tourist. It is principally important as the starting-point for excursions to ancient Corinth, which lies about 6km to the south-west.

The ruins of ancient Corinth are spread across a plateau at the foot of

The Temple of Apollo, Corinth

Acrocorinth, a lofty acropolis which once served as the citadel of the town below. The most imposing monument on the site is the ruined Temple of Apollo, one of the oldest in Greece; though only seven of its original thirty-eight columns remain standing, it is a grand and noble sight, silhouetted against the blue sky and water and the mountains beyond. From the temple steps one can survey the extensive ruins of what was once the wealthiest city in Greece, now an historic junkyard of massive stones scattered across the landscape.

There is a museum on the site which is particularly noted for its collection of painted vases, an art form in which the ancient Corinthians excelled.

From the museum a road mounts to the summit of Acrocorinth at an altitude of 1,890ft, one of the great natural fortresses of Europe. One can still see the massive remains of the great wall which once ringed the citadel; in its time this was occupied by Greeks, Romans, Byzantines, Franks, Venetians and Turks, each of whom contributed to the construction of its ramparts and towers. Not a trace remains of the famous Temple of Aphrodite which once stood there, served by a thousand sacred prostitutes.

Hotels. There is an excellent hotel with a restaurant at the site of ancient Corinth; this is the **Xenia (A)**. There are also several hotels in the modern town of Corinth; among them are: the **Bellevue (B)**, **Kypselos (B)**, **Acropolis (C)**, and the **Ephira (C)**. In addition there is a good motel near the Corinth Canal, just 2km out of town; this is the **Isthmia (B)**, with restaurant, swimming-pool and night-club.

EXCURSIONS. The ancient city of **Nemea**, 36km to the south-west of Corinth; this was the site of the Nemean Games, one of the four great Panhellenic festivals.

After leaving Corinth one can proceed either westward along the shore of the Gulf, or south through the Argolid plain. The latter route is generally preferred, for it takes one directly to some of the most interesting and historic sites in Greece.

MYCENAE (MYKNAI)
131km from Athens
Greece Map E3

The site of ancient Mycenae is 3km off the main road, 37km south of Corinth. As we approach it we begin to appreciate why the Mycenaean kings chose such rocky eminences for their palaces, for the site commands the whole plain around and is itself secure from assault. This is the mighty city which Homer describes as being 'well-built', 'broad-streeted', and 'rich in gold', and whose King Agamemnon led the Greeks in their long siege of Troy. Until a century ago Mycenae and the shades of its departed rulers were the subject of myth and tragic drama. But in 1874–6 Heinrich Schlieman's excavations on this site revealed that the Homeric epics were based on historic fact, and Mycenae has since given its name to an entire civilization, one of the cultural ancestors of the ancient Greeks. The ruins at Mycenae are extremely impressive and evoke the heroic age of which Homer wrote, especially if one recalls the bloody tragedies which the great Greek dramatists placed here. As Sophocles has one of his characters conclude sadly in *Electra*: 'A house of death if there ever was one.'

Hotels. There is a **Xenia (B)** near the site. In the nearby village there are two others, the **Agamemnon (B)**, and the venerable **Hotel de la Helene et de Menelas (E)**, a famous little inn which for many years was the only hostelry near the site.

ARGOS
137km from Athens
Greece Map E3

A pleasant market town near the southern end of the Argolid plain. The modern town occupies the site of the ancient city of Argos, one of the most important in the Greek world. Ruins from various periods in the city's history are scattered throughout the town and its environs, the most important of which is the **Sanctuary of Apollo and Hera**. There is also an excellent museum, whose most unique exhibit is a bronze helmet and cuirass from the eighth century B.C. Above the town are its two ancient citadels, **Larissa** and **Aspid**, the first of which is crowned with a very impressive medieval fortress.

Hotels. Mycenae (C), Telessila (C).

EXCURSION. Eight kilometres out of Argos on the way to Nauplia the road passes the site of ancient **Tiryns**, the second of the two great Mycenaean palaces in the Argolid. Although not as striking in its location or structure as Mycenae itself, Tiryns is nevertheless an impressive and important sight and is well worth a visit.

NAUPLIA
146km from Athens
Greece Map E3

Nauplia is a photogenic port superbly situated at the head of the Argolic Gulf; from 1824 to 1834 this little town was the capital of Greece. The town clusters picturesquely on the slopes of a rocky headland surmounted by an old Turkish fortress. Above the town on a precipitous rock perches the eighteenth-century fortress of **Palamidi**, from where one commands a widespread view of the surrounding area. Out in the harbour one can see the romantic islet of Bourdzi with its tiny **Castello Pasqualigo**, once a hostel for retired hangmen. The town has also a very interesting little museum whose most important exhibits are Bronze Age pottery from the Argolid and a complete suit of Mycenaean armour, the only one of its kind in existence. Nauplia is an ideal base from which to make excursions to the various sites in the Argolid or to Epidauros; in fact it is so pleasant that one might decide to pass up the excursions and just wander around the town itself.

Hotels
(L) Xenia's Palace. A luxurious establishment perched on the Acronafplia Hill overlooking the sea, with a swimming-pool and restaurant.
(A) Xenia. Private beach and restaurant.
(B) Agamemnon. Swimming-pool, sea sports, restaurant and roof-garden.

Other hotels. Alkyon (C), Dioskouri (C), Galini (C), Nafplia (C), Parartima (C), Hotel de Rose (C), Park (C), Rex (C), Victoria (C), Argolis (D), Lito (D), Tiryins (D).

Restaurants. Glaros, Hellas, Fikos (in a shady garden), and the **Grill Room of the Hotel Grande Bretagne** (despite its prestigious name, this is merely the street-side taverna of a simple D class hotel, nevertheless it enjoys a pleasant view across the bay to Bourdzi islet).

EXCURSIONS. There are good beaches nearby at **Arvanatia**, **Karathona**, and **Banieres**. **Tolo**, 12km along the coast, is a picturesque fishing village with a beautiful beach; there are several hotels in the village and a camping ground nearby.

EPIDAUROS (EPIDAVROS)
29km from Nauplia and 186km from Athens
Greece Map E3

Epidauros is the site of the Sanctuary of Ascelepius, the god of medicine, the most famous shrine of healing in ancient Greece. Unlike modern Lourdes, the curing and healing here were not brought about just by religious faith, but also by medicine and therapy administered by the physician-priests of the shrine. Epidauros was very much a spa in the nineteenth-century sense, for while the patients awaited their recovery they were entertained by athletic events in the stadium and by performances of drama in the theatre. The **Theatre of Epidauros** is the best-preserved ancient theatre in Greece, and in recent years it has been judiciously restored so that it is now in virtually the same state as when it was first built in the fourth century B.C. The theatre can accommodate 14,000 spectators, and its acoustics are so perfect that the slightest sound uttered on stage is clearly audible throughout the audience. The theatre is now the site of the annual Epidavria Drama Festival, during which the National Theatre of Greece presents performances of ancient Greek drama.

Performances are given every Saturday and Sunday evening from late June until mid-August. (Tickets may be obtained at the box-office of the National Theatre in Athens, Aghiou Konstantinou and Menandriou Sts., Tel: 523-242.) On days when performances are being given there is a direct bus service from Athens to Epidauros. There is also a boat service from the Piraeus to Palia Epidavros, a nearby port, from whence a bus takes one to the theatre. Either way the return journey takes one back to Athens about 3 a.m. Or one might decide to while away a day or two at Palia Epidavros

The majority of beaches have simple tavernas, so one can get a tan and a fat stomach at the same time

itself, where there is a good beach with hotels and restaurants. There is also a hotel near the archaeological site, the **Xenia II (B)**.

After visiting Epidauros, one returns to Argos to continue the tour around the Peloponnese. From Argos the road goes south beside the hills that border the Argolid plain, and soon after heads up and inland into the mountains of the central Peloponnese, into the ancient lands of Arcadia.

TRIPOLIS
195km from Athens
Greece Map E3

Tripolis is the capital of the modern district of Arcadia and is its only large town, for almost all of the other settlements in this mountainous region are small villages inhabited principally by farmers and goat-herders. The town, pleasant and lively and with a bracing climate, is an excellent base for excursions into the central Peloponnese, a land rich in history and magnificent mountain landscapes.

Hotels. Menalon (A), Arcadia (B), Semiramis (B), Alex (C), Anaktorikon (C), Artemis (C), Galaxy (C). There is also a camp-site at **Campos Milias.**

Restaurants. The best is **Kipos Sosoli**, an excellent garden restaurant; others: **Ethnikon, Mainalon,** and **Kipos**, also with a garden.

MOUNTAINEERING AND SKIING. There are opportunities for climbing and skiing on Mount Mainalon, where there is a shelter and a ski-lift. For details contact the Tourist Police.

EXCURSIONS. Two important archaeological sites in the immediate vicinity of Tripolis are **Tegea** (10km SE) and **Mantineia** (13km N). In classical times these were two of the key cities in Arcadia, and were continually at war with one another, as well as being caught up on one side or another in the Peloponnesian Wars. At Tegea one can still see the ruins of the great **Temple of Athena Alea**, as well as a museum containing finds from all over Arcadia. And at Mantineia there are some scattered remains of the agora, the theatre and a few temples. Mantineia is famous as the site of the battle where the Thebans under Epaminondas routed the Spartans, their first great defeat.

Megalopolis (34km SW of Tripolis). The city founded in 370 B.C. by Epaminondas as the capital of the Arcadian League, an alliance against Sparta. The most impressive of the extensive ruins of the ancient city is the theatre, the largest in ancient Greece, with a capacity of 20,000 spectators.

Karytaina (16km NW of Megalopolis). A pretty little village built on the slopes of a dramatic eminence surmounted by a Crusader castle.

Andritsaina (45km NW of Megalopolis). A tiny mountain village which serves as a base for visiting the temple at **Bassae** (10km away); there is a **Xenia (B)** hotel in the village with a sweeping view of the surrounding mountains. The **Temple of Apollo Epicourios** at Bassae is one of the most impressive monuments in the Peloponnese, and its setting is absolutely unsurpassed, a magnificent Doric temple of grey limestone standing all by itself on a stark and lonely mountain top, far away from the rest of civilization.

The temple was built in about 450 B.C. by Iktinos, the architect of the Parthenon.

From Andritsaina one can return to Tripolis by a northern route, thus making a circular tour around the mountains of Arcadia. En route we pass some of the most characteristic villages of the central Peloponnese, poor but picturesque hamlets clinging to the mountain sides like goats; the largest and most interesting is **Dimitsania** (46km from Tripolis). At **Vitina** (46km NW of Tripolis, altitude 3500ft) there is a mountain resort noted for its marvellous climate and its magnificent scenery. There are four hotels in Vitina: **Villa Valos (B)**, **Xenia (B)** (Motel), **Aegli (C)**, and **Menalon (C)**; there is also a camp-site nearby.

From Tripolis the highway heads south across the plain of Tegea and then begins to wind downwards into the plain of Lacedaemon, the ancient home of the Spartans.

SPARTA (SPARTI)
253km from Athens
Greece Map E3

Sparta stands in an impressive setting in the centre of a broad highland plain ringed by the lofty Taygetus and Parnon ranges, both snow-capped for half the year. The town itself dates only from 1834, when King Otho grouped together the inhabitants of the surrounding villages in a new settlement near the site of ancient Sparta, the scant remains of which can be seen to the north of the modern town. The very paucity of ancient monuments here is a testimony to the hard character of the Spartans; they depended on discipline and valour rather than on fortresses, and they were too busy with war to waste their resources on theatres and temples.

Hotels. **Xenia (A)**, **Menelaion (B)**, **Apollo (C)**, **Dioskouri (C)**, **Lakonia (C)**, **Mystras (C)**.

Restaurants. **Diethnes**, **Kali Kardia** (The Good Heart), and **Semiramis**.

MOUNTAINEERING. There are many opportunities for climbing on both Mount Taygetus and Mount Parnon; for information contact the local Tourist Police.

MISTRA
6km west of Sparta
Greece Map E3

Mistra is the most bewitching sight in Greece, a medieval ghost-town perched on the slope of a conical hill overlooking the Lacedaemonia plain. The town originally grew up under the protection of a fortress built there in 1249 by William de Villehardouin, the Frankish Prince of Achaia. During the following century Mistra was fought over by the Franks and the Byzantines, with the latter finally victorious in 1349. Thereafter Mistra served as the capital of Byzantine Morea, governed by a despot who was usually the heir-apparent of the Byzantine Emperor in Constantinople. This was the most glorious period in the history of Mistra, when it became one of the cultural centres of the Byzantine Empire during its last renaissance. A visit to Mistra is especially poignant to those who have studied Byzantine history, for Constantine XI Dragases, the last Emperor of Byzantium, was crowned here in 1448 in the beautiful little church of **Ayios Dimitrios**. And here the Byzantine Empire ended its thousand-year history in 1460, seven years after the fall of Constantinople, when the fortress at Mistra was finally taken by the Turks. Today the town is a virtual museum of Byzantine architecture and art, with a dozen lovely churches decorated with superb frescoes, as well as the splendid and unique **Palace of the Despots** and the **Fortress of Villehardouin**, which still broods above the ruined streets of this deserted town.

The tourist authorities have recently instituted an annual festival here, the Palaiologhia, a pageant designed to dramatize the past history of Mistra, complete with *son et lumière*.

The pleasant modern village of Mistra is a short distance away from the archaeological site. There is a good hotel there, the **Vyzantion (B)**; it has a restaurant and the rooms have views out over the archaeological site and the plain of Lacedaemon.

From Sparta there is a choice of three routes, each of which leads to one of the three great peninsulas of the southern Peloponnese.

MONEMVASSIA

360km from Athens
Greece Map F3

Monemvassia is one of the most spectacularly-situated towns in the country, perched perilously on a huge rock high above the sea, a situation which has led to its being described as the Gibraltar of Greece. Because of its strategic location, dominating the south-eastern peninsula of the Peloponnese, Monemvassia has been fought over by every army which has invaded the Morea. The old fortress, which is a virtual palimpsest of the military architecture of its various owners, Normans, Byzantines, Venetians and Turks, crowns the great rock which rises sheer nearly a thousand feet above the sea, connected to the mainland only by a narrow stone bridge. The remains of the old town of Monemvassia lie on a narrow ledge at the south side of the rock. It is wildly picturesque, with silent, narrow lanes winding through a maze of abandoned medieval houses. But the old town has all but lost its life, and it will soon be just a museum-piece for the modern village on the mainland, whose sandy beach is now being developed into a tourist resort.

There is a hotel in the mainland village, the **Monemvassia (B)**. There is also a charming little hostelry in the old town, and rooms can be rented in the local houses.

Although one can drive down from Sparta, the easiest way to get to Monemvassia is by sea, with two boats a week from the Piraeus. The voyage takes seven hours to Monemvassia, after which the boat rounds the infamous

Cape Malea at the extreme south-eastern tip of Greece, and then sails on to the lonely isle of **Kithira**, the birthplace of Aphrodite. If you really want to get away from it all, this is the place to go, for the island is said to be quite beautiful, but terribly lonely, for many of its residents have emigrated and are now far away in Australia.

THE MANI
Greece Map E, F3

The Mani is the central and southernmost of the three Peloponnesian peninsulas. It is the remotest region of Greece, surrounded on three sides by the sea and cut off by mountains to the north. Its remoteness has isolated the Mani from change and protected it from the armies which have swept over the Peloponnese. This was the only part of Greece which the Turks failed to conquer, and even today the Maniotes preserve traditions which have all but vanished elsewhere in Greece.

The best approach to the Mani is from **Githion**, a very pretty little port on the upper end of the peninsula. One can either drive down to Githion from Sparta, or else come by the same boat that calls at Monemvassia and Kithira. Githion has a good hotel, the **Lakonis (A)**, as well as several simpler but decent hostelries. There is a magnificent sandy beach near the town.

From Githion a road cuts across the peninsula to the town of **Areopolis** on the western side. Areopolis is on the edge of the Deep Mani and is its administrative centre; the remoteness of this region can be gauged by the fact that the town has a population of only 700 souls and has only a single hotel, the **Taygetus (E)**, which has only four rooms with eight beds.

From Areopolis a road runs south into the Deep Mani, through a region bristling with the fortified tower-houses from which the Maniotes have fought off not only foreign invaders but their neighbours as well, for the Mani has been bloodied for centuries by murderous vendettas between warring clans. The landscape is fierce too, the last spurs of the Taygetus which run down the peninsula here are called Kakovounia, the Evil Mountains.

Just south of Areopolis are the famous **Diros Caves**, which the authorities hope to develop into a tourist attraction.

The road continues from Areopolis up the west coast of the Outer Mani to **Kalamata**. One can also reach Kalamata directly from Sparta, driving over the awesome Langada Pass, where one sees some of the wildest mountain scenery in Greece. And then the road winds down into Messeni, the lush and fertile land which the Crusaders called the 'Paradise of the Morea'.

KALAMATA
287km from Athens
Greece Map E2, 3

Kalamata is the capital of Messenia, famous for its figs, its huge black olives, and for its lively local dance, the *Malamatianos*. The town is framed in a splendid setting, fronted by miles of white sandy beach, surrounded by olive fields and groves of citrus trees, with the peaks of Mount Taygetus rising majestically in the background. Above the town stands its ancient citadel, fortified since Mycenaean times; the fortress which we see today was built in 1208 by Geoffrey de Villehardouin.

Hotels. Rex (A), Xenia (B) (on the sea 2km out of town), **America (C), Taygetus Beach (C)** (on the sea 8km from town). Camp-site at **Aghiaso**.

Restaurants. There are a number of tavernas along the seafront, of which the **Aegli** is perhaps the best. In town: **Gallia, Koilakos**, and **Moustakis**.

EXCURSION. The site of ancient **Messene** (30km from Kalamata) can be reached by taking the road towards Pylos and then turning right at the modern town of Messini. Ancient Messene was founded in 369 B.C. by Epaminondas after his victory over the Spartans. The most impressive part of the ruins are the defence-walls, almost six miles in length, built to defend the Messenians from their ancient enemies, the Spartans.

CORONI and METHONI
335 and 348km from Athens
Greece Map F2

The main highway from Kalamata can be taken directly to Pylos, cutting across the last of the three Peloponnesian peninsulas. But if there is time it

A decaying but beautiful Venetian house—a remnant of the past

89

D

is preferable to take the longer route down around the peninsula, for it is a very pleasant ride beside the sea and takes one past two of the most romantic-looking spots in the southern Peloponnese. These are the twin villages of **Coroni** and **Methoni**, which stand on either side of the peninsula at its very tip, Coroni to the east and Methoni to the west. They are both tiny villages which cling, as if for protection, to two mighty Venetian fortresses jutting out into the sea. In Crusading days these fortresses were called Coron and Modon and the Venetians referred to them proudly as the 'Two Eyes of the Republic', because their guns literally looked down on all shipping passing this way to and from the Levant. Koroni has only a single modest hotel, the **Xenon Koronis (C)**, but rooms can also be rented in the village houses. At Methoni there is an excellent hotel which stands right on the white sand beach beneath the sea-walls of the fortress; this is the **Methoni Beach (B)**; when you look out from your balcony in the morning you will see the Lion of St. Mark staring at you from the fortress wall across the moat.

At Methoni half the tour round the Peloponnese has been completed, and the road now heads north along the western coast.

PYLOS

324km from Athens
Greece Map E2

Pylos is a little seaport nestling in one corner of a magnificent natural harbour, its stacked rows of pastel houses looking as if they had been built for dolls. The harbour is the famous Bay of Navarino, where on 20 October 1827 Admiral Cordington and the Allied fleets of Great Britain, France and Russia literally destroyed the Turkish navy and effectively liberated the Peloponnese. The bay is closed on its seaward side by the long and narrow isle of Sphacteria, the scene of a climactic Athenian victory over the Spartans in the summer of 427 B.C. Two historic battles fought in the same place more than twenty-two centuries apart in time—such is the great span of history in this ancient country. Above the town there is still another Venetian fortress.

Hotels. The Castle (B), and the **Xenia (B)**.

Restaurants. There are several adequate restaurants on the quay, all of them with fine views of this beautiful and historic bay.

EXCURSION. 18km north from Pylos the road passes the archaeological site known as **Nestor's Palace**. This is the Mycenaean palace which some scholars have identified with Homer's 'sandy Pylos', where Telemachus was royally entertained by King Nestor. The remains of the palace are not nearly as impressive as those at Mycenae and Tiryns, but they do give one an excellent idea of how a royal Mycenaean residence was laid out. It was the collection of inscribed clay tablets from this site which revealed that the script used by the Minoans and Mycenaeans was a form of archaic Greek, establishing the fact that these peoples were truly the cultural ancestors of the Greeks of the classic age.

PYLOS to PYRGOS
Greece Map E2

The west coast of the Peloponnese is markedly different from the rest of the peninsula. The rugged mountains which dominate the scenery elsewhere are here muted to gentle pine-clad slopes and hillsides silver-green with olive groves, seen through a green frieze of cypress trees. The shore itself is fringed with a succession of fine beaches, interspersed with headlands verdant with evergreens. Few of the beaches are developed for tourism, fortunately, so that if you are driving along you can simply stop when you see a likely spot and just plunge in.

As we drive farther north, we pass from Messini into the ancient district of Elis, which is so lush and verdant that it seems part of the off-shore Ionian isles than of the harsh and sear Peloponnese. Elis was always a land of peace and plenty, and was free from much of the struggle and contention that perpetually troubled the rest of the Greek world.

The largest town in Elis is **Pyrgos** (319km from Athens); it is of interest to tourists only as the turning-off point for Olympia, which is 22km inland.

OLYMPIA
325km from Athens
Greece Map E2

Perhaps it was the peaceful character of Elis that led the Greeks to establish their greatest Panhellenic festival in Olympia, where men from all over Hellas could find a common social and religious meeting-ground. According to tradition, the first Olympic games were held here in 776 B.C., and thereafter every four years during the full moon period following the summer solstice. Such importance did the Greeks attach to this festival that a Sacred Truce was declared during the celebration of the Olympic Games, and peace was the symbol of the Games themselves.

Olympia today ranks with the Athenian Acropolis and Delphi as the three greatest survivals from the world of classical Greece. Its importance comes partly from the historic monuments standing in the **Altis**, or Sacred Precinct, particularly the great **Temple of Zeus**, the holiest edifice in the sanctuary and the largest temple in mainland Greece; and the **Heraeum**, the oldest temple in the country. It stems also from the great works of art gathered in Olympia's two museums, most notably the beautiful relief sculptures from the pediments and metopes of the Temple of Zeus, and the famous Hermes of Praxiteles. But perhaps the most profound significance of Olympia is the extent to which it conveys the Greek spirit at its best, the striving for excellence and perfection in all things, in sport as well as in architecture and art, the desire, however often frustrated, to form a peaceful union of enlightened human beings; and the sense of communion which they felt between themselves and their gods, who made their lordly presence felt in such majestic shrines as this.

The site of Olympia is pastoral and serene, and the ruins seem almost a part of the soft Elian landscape, so long have they stood there now. Fallen column-drums lie half-buried in the ground, covered over with a mantle of grass and garlanded with wild flowers. The ancient stadium, where the Games themselves took place, is just a long, sandy field flanked by grassy embankments where the spectators sat, just as they do today at a country cricket-match or football game.

(Opening hours. The archaeological site is open in summer daily from 7.30 a.m. till sunset; Sundays and holidays 10 a.m. to 1 p.m. and 3 p.m. to 7 p.m. In winter it is open daily from 9 a.m. till sunset; Sundays and holidays 10 a.m. to 1 p.m. and 2.30 p.m. to 5 p.m. The Museums are open in summer daily from 7.30 a.m. to sunset; Sundays and holidays 10 a.m. to 1 p.m. and 3 p.m. to 6 p.m. In winter they are open from 9 a.m. to 1 p.m. and 2.30 p.m. to 5 p.m.; Sundays and holidays 10 a.m. to 1 p.m. and 2.30 p.m. to 5 p.m. The Museums are closed on Mondays all year-round.)

Hotels. The oldest and best hotel at Olympia is the **S.P.A.P. (A)**; it has a restaurant and roof-garden and many of the rooms have a view of the archaeological site. Other hotels (all with restaurants and private baths): **Apollo (B)**, **Leonidion (B)**, **Neda (B)**, **Neon Olympia (B)**, **Xenia (B)**, **Xenios Zeus (B)** (Motel), **Ilis (C)**, **Alexandros (D)**, **Cronion (D)**, **Pelops (D)**, **Praxiteles (D)**.

PYRGOS to PATRAS

Greece Map E2–D2

The northern part of Elis, between Pyrgos and Patras, is a flat and tree-less plain, the best agricultural land in the Peloponnese. This was the part of Greece which the Crusaders coveted most, for it reminded many of them of their native countryside in Champagne and Flanders. Many of the Frankish nobles settled here, their ruler calling himself 'Prince of all Achaia', and built powerful fortresses and castles to defend the dominions which they had taken from the Greeks. The greatest of all these Crusader fortresses is **Castel Tornese**, a mighty bastion whose ruins stand by the sea just south of the little village of **Killini**, 47km north of Pyrgos. Killini itself stands on the site of medieval Glarentza, once the busiest port in all of Frankish Morea.

There are some excellent beach hotels along the coast between Pyrgos and Patras; all of them have bungalows on private beaches and are equipped with sports facilities, restaurants and night-clubs. The best hotels of this type are:

(A) **Miramare Olympia Beach,** Skafidia (just north of Pyrgos).
(A) **Killini Golden Beach,** Killini (turn off from Andravida).
(B) **Kalogria Beach,** Metohi (34km south of Patras).
There are also camp-sites by the sea at **Kourouta** (turn off 14km north of Pyrgos), **Loutra Killini** (turn off at Gastouni), and at **Kato Achaia** (23km south of Patras).

PATRAS

219km from Athens
Greece Map D2

Patras is the most important city in the Peloponnese and the fourth largest in Greece, with a population of 120,000. It is also an international harbour and is the port of embarkation for the car-ferries to Italy. If you have a few hours to spare you might look into the rather interesting museum in Platia Olgas or climb to the Kastro, the old fortress above the town, where there is a superb view of the entrance to the Gulf of Corinth.

Hotels. The best hotel in town is the newly-opened **Astir (A)**, on the waterfront. This is the most handsome and well-appointed hotel of its class in Greece, and at the moment it is a bargain because its prices are being kept low to attract visitors. Other hotels: **Galaxy (B)**, 8 Agiou Nicolaou. **Majestic (B)**, 67 Agiou Andreou. **Delfini (C)**, Terpsithea 102, 21 Aprilliou. **El Greco (C)**, 145 Agiou Andrea. **Mediterranee (C)**, 18 Agiou Nikolaou. **Metropolis (C)**, Platia Trion Symmachon.

Restaurants. The best restaurant in Patras is probably **Kotopoula**, on the outskirts of town. There are also a number of adequate restaurants along the quay.

THE GULF OF CORINTH
Greece Map D2, 3

Travellers from Patras to Athens usually take the super highway. However, if one has time to spare, it is perhaps pleasanter to drive along the old shore road at a more leisurely pace, for then one has the opportunity to swim or eat along the way.

6km from Patras the old road passes **Rion**, the embarkation-point for the car-ferries across to **Antirion** on the other side of the Gulf. This is the best point to cross the Gulf, for the service is very frequent and takes only about fifteen minutes. Near the ferry-landing there is a quaint little Turkish fortress, the **Castle of the Morea**, built by Sultan Beyazit II in 1499. Beyazit also built an exact replica, the Castle of Rumelia, on the other side thus controlling the entrance to the Gulf.

A 10km drive past Rion brings one to the fishing village of **Psathopyrgos**, where there is a bungalow hotel, the **Florida (B)**, with a private beach and swimming-pool.

At **Lambiri** (27km from Patras) there is an establishment of the Club Mediterranee, as well as a simpler hotel, the **Avra (C)**, which also has a private beach.

10km farther on we come to the industrial town of **Egion**, the largest on the Gulf; this is the embarkation-point for the ferry across to **Galaxidi** and **Itea**, the port of Delphi. The boats leave about every two hours and the ride is long, three and a half hours; in summer there is usually a long waiting line. Therefore one might be well advised to cross at Rion instead.

At **Diakofton**, 14km past Egion, there is a miniature railway which makes its way up the Buraicos Gorge into the mountains of the northern Peloponnese to the famous shrine of **Megaspileon** and to the monastery of **Ayia Lavra**.

Just over 100km beyond Patras we come to **Xylokastron**, the most popular summer resort on the Peloponnesian shore of the Gulf, with a superb beach backed by a pine forest.

There are about a dozen hotels near the sea, the best of which are the **Apollo (A)**, **Arion (A)**, and **Miramare (B)**, all with restaurants and private beaches. There is also a tourist complex here, the **Pefkias (C)**, which rents a large number of straw huts and wooden bungalows.

Central Greece

Central Greece has a totally different character and appearance to Attica or the Peloponnese. One sees this difference as soon as one has driven an hour or so out of Athens, when the austere hills of Attica give way to the fertile farms and pasture lands of Boetia, the country which Hesiod describes so lyrically in his *Works and Days.* Beyond Boetia to the north-west lie the ancient districts of Phocis, Locris, Aetolia and Acarnia, mountainous regions which are nearly as harsh and forbidding as Arcadia or Laconia in the Peloponnese. Epirus, in the north-western corner of Greece, is dominated by the majestic Pindus range, the most beautiful mountains in the country. Although the peaks of the Pindus are as high as those of the Taygetus, its flanks are not at all sear and bare, but are covered with forests of oak, beech and pine, and the mountain scenery is relieved here and there with highland meadows bright with patches of waving grain and sprinkled with wild flowers. All this is just a geographical prelude to the heart of central Greece, the great plain of Thessaly, the granary of Hellas since Homeric times, a region as rich in history and mythology as it is in the products of its fertile soil. Here we have left the Mediterranean far behind; gone are the olive groves and fishing villages and temples of Athena and Apollo, for one is now in an older and more pastoral land through which the remote ancestors of the classic Greeks moved long before they reached Attica and the Peloponnese.

The Pindus Mountains divide central Greece into two quite separate regions, Epirus to the west and Thessaly to the east, connected by only one or two difficult mountain roads. Consequently, one must plan two separate itineraries to see the whole of central Greece. The western route follows the old highway north-west to Thebes, where it turns westward to follow the northern shore of the Saronic Gulf; there it turns northward and goes through Aetolia and Epirus as far as Ioannina, and then westward again to the Ionian coast at Igoumenitsa. The other route follows the new super highway out of Athens and along the eastern seaboard as far as the slopes of Mount Olympus, with excursions east and west along the way.

THEBES (THIVAI)
73km from Athens
Greece Map D3

Thebes was the leading city of Boetia and a perpetual rival of Athens. It is a town of great antiquity, the legendary birthplace of the gods Heracles and

Dionysus, the tragic hero Oedipus, the great Theban general Epaminondas, and the lyric poet Pindar. But Thebes stands on one of the great invasion routes through Greece and has suffered at the hands of virtually every invading army which has passed through. Consequently there are almost no monuments of the ancient past to be found in modern Thebes except some fragments of the almost mythical Palace of Cadmus, parts of which one sees in excavations scattered around the town. There is, however, a small but very interesting museum, important for the large number of Mycenaean antiquities which it preserves from sites all over Boetia. The best time to visit Thebes is on the first Monday of Lent, when the town celebrates the Vlach Wedding Festival with revels which are positively Dionysian.

Hotels. Dionyssion Melathron (B), Niobe (B).

EXCURSION. 13km back along the road to Athens and then another 5km to the right brings one to the village of **Erythrai**, on the foothills of Mount Kitharion. On the plain below we can see the site of the historic battle of **Plataea**, where in 379 B.C. the Greek allies under Pausanius decisively defeated the Persian army, ending forever their hopes of conquering Hellas.

LIVADIA
118km from Athens
Greece Map D3

Livadia is a pleasant and prosperous trading town, the capital of modern Boetia. In ancient times its prosperity came from its proximity to the Oracle of Trophonios, one of the most popular in the Greek world. A two-hour walk into the hills above the town takes one to what is probably the site of the oracle, an underground chasm beside the springs of Memory (*Mnemosyne*) and Forgetfulness (*Lethe*). Another quarter-mile climb brings one to the **Castro**, a ruined fortress built by the Grand Army of Catalans, Spanish soldiers-of-fortune who ruled large areas of Greece in the fourteenth century.

Hotels. Helikon (C), Midia (C).

EXCURSIONS. **Orchomenos** (13km NE of Livadia), one of the most important and interesting Mycenaean sites in Greece.

    Chaeroneia (14km from Livadia along the road to Lamia), the site of the historic battle where Philip of Macedon decisively defeated the Athenians and Thebans and thus established the power of Macedonia over all of Greece. The great marble Lion of Chaeroneia, which we see in an olive grove on the site, stands on the common grave of the Theban Sacred Band, which perished to a man in the battle.

    Osios Loukas (37km to the SW of Livadia), an eleventh-century monastery dedicated to St. Luke. It is one of the most interesting Byzantine church complexes in Greece and is decorated with mosaics which are comparable in quality to those at Daphni.

Returning from Osios Loukas to the main road, we continue on towards Delphi, approaching the great massif of Mount Parnassos. We soon pass the pretty village of **Arahova**, its main street lined with shops selling garishly-coloured home-made rugs and carpets. Arahova is the best base from which to ascend Mount Parnassos, a climb of six hours. The view from the summit is reputed to be the most panoramic in all of Greece.

DELPHI
178km from Athens
Greece Map D3

After the Athenian Acropolis, Delphi is the single most important ancient site in Greece. In classical times it surpassed even the Acropolis in its importance, for while the Parthenon was sacred to the Athenians, Delphi was a shrine holy to all Greeks, the centre of their religion. The very 'navel of the world' some called it, and Pindar in his Pythian Odes sang of Delphi as 'The shrine that is the centre of the loudly echoing earth.' The site owed its sanctity to the presence there of the Oracle of Pythian Apollo, which was consulted for advice by everyone from simple peasants to the governments of city-states. The shrine really began to flourish in the sixth century B.C., when the various city-states of Greece began building treasuries there to house their gifts to the shrine and to erect monuments celebrating triumphs and other fortunate events, all of which were attributed to the divinely-inspired advice of the oracle. The great **Temple of Apollo**, whose ruins we see today, was erected in 548 B.C., replacing an even older one which had been destroyed by fire. This period also witnessed the institution of the Pythian Games, second in importance only to those at Olympia.

The ruins at Delphi are located just outside the modern village, standing at either side of the road from Livadia. Above the road we enter the **Pythian Sanctuary of Apollo**, and climb uphill along the Sacred Way, passing on the way the ruined treasuries of the various city-states of ancient Greece. This brings us to the great **Temple of Apollo**, dominating the sanctuary even in its ruins. Above the Temple is the **Theatre** and still farther up the **Stadium**, the site of the Pythian Games.

Beside the sanctuary is the **Museum** where some of the works of art, with which the shrine was once adorned, are exhibited. Some of the antiquities exhibited here are: the Frieze from the Siphynian Treasury, the Naxian Sphinx, the famous Bronze Charioteer, and the marble statue of the youth Antinous, as well as numerous other works of art, all admirably displayed.

Continuing on the road past the entrance to the sanctuary we see the **Castillian Spring**, where Aphrodite bathed to renew her virginity after each act of love. Farther up and on the other side of the road we descend to the precinct called the **Marmaria**, where two temples sacred to Athena stand serenely in the midst of an olive grove. This is a pleasant spot to pause and rest, sitting in the shade of a gnarled olive tree, undisturbed by the crowds of tourists who swarm over the ruins above. From here one has a full view of the incomparable site on which the sanctuary stands, with the ruins sprawling up the steep south slope of Parnassos to the base of a thousand-foot precipice, which the ancients called **Phaedrides**, the Shining Rocks. The twin cliffs of this eminence bear the names *Rhodini* (Roseate) and *Phleboukos* (Flamboyant) because of the colours they assume in the light of late afternoon. And when the sun is about to set, one walks back to the village and looks down upon the **Sacred Plain**, a silver-green sea of olive trees rippling from the slopes of Parnassos to the true blue sea at the bay of Itea. One then knows that Apollo himself must have chosen the site.

(Opening hours. The archaeological site is open in summer daily from 7.30 a.m. till sunset; Sundays and holidays 10 a.m. to 1 p.m. and 3 p.m. to 7 p.m. In winter it is open daily from 9 a.m. till sunset; Sundays and holidays 10 a.m. till 1 p.m. and 2.30 p.m. to 5 p.m. The Museum is open in summer daily from 8 a.m. to 1 p.m. and 3 p.m. to 6 p.m.; Sundays and holidays 10 a.m. to 1 p.m. and 3 p.m. to 6 p.m.; Mondays 11.30 a.m. to 1 p.m. and 2.30 p.m. to 5 p.m. In winter it is open daily from 9 a.m. to 1 p.m. and 2.30 a.m. to 5 p.m.; Sundays and holidays 10 a.m. to 1 p.m. and 2.30 p.m. to 5 p.m.)

Hotels. The best hotel in Delphi is undoubtedly the **Amalia (A)**. Superbly designed in harmony with its setting, its rooms all have views out over the Sacred Plain to the Gulf of Corinth and the mountains of the Peloponnese beyond, and its excellent restaurant opens onto a deliciously cool garden-terrace. It is expensive for its class but well worth the price, if you can afford it. Other hotels: **Xenia (A)**, **Vouzas (A)**, **Europe (B)**, **Kastalia (B)**, **Hermes (C)**, **Phaeton (C)**, **Greca (C)**, **Oracle (C)**, **Parnassos (C)**, **Pythia (C)**, **Stadion (C)**, **Phoebos (D)**, **Iniohos (D)**, **Kastri (D)**, **Lefas (D)**, **Sivylla (D)**, **Varonos (D)**.

EXCURSIONS. **Itea** (17km) and **Galaxidi** (21km) are two little villages on the gulf below Delphi. In ancient times Itea was the port of Delphi and is today the terminus of the ferry from Egion. Galaxidi was formerly a busy shipping-centre and is now a village of caïque-builders. There are pleasant hotels and tavernas in both villages, where one might while away an hour or a day after visiting Delphi.

From Delphi the highway crosses the Sacred Plain and skirts its western side as far as the town of **Amfissa**. From there it follows a tortuous path across the Locrian hills and finally reaches the sea at **Naupactos**, at the western end of the Gulf of Corinth.

NAUPACTOS
248km from Athens
Greece Map D2

Naupactos was known in the Middle Ages as Lepanto, and gave its name to the famous battle fought in the straits nearby, where the Turkish navy was destroyed by Don Juan of Austria, commanding the allied fleet of Mediterranean Europe. The town is charming and picturesque, with a tiny harbour enclosed by a miniature Venetian fortress—altogether it is the prettiest port on either side of the Gulf. There are several hotels near the town beach, the best of which is the **Amaryllis (B)**. There are also a number of tavernas along the seaside; the best of them by far is the **Delfini** (The Dolphin), run by our dear friend Petros Psani.

The road continues past Naupactos along the Gulf to **Antirion**, the mainland terminus of the ferry from Rion in the Peloponnese. Beside the ferry-landing we see the **Castle of Roumelia**, the twin to the fortress which Sultan Beyazit built across the straits. The road then veers inland for a bit and then passes the town of **Mesolongi**, near the western end of the Gulf. Philhellenes will always honour this town as the place where Byron died, on 19 April 1824, striving to the end for the cause of Greek liberty; his heart is buried in a little park just inside the town gate.

After Mesolongi the highway turns north through the ancient region of Acarnia, skirting lakes, lagoons and land-locked bays until it passes into Epirus.

ARTA
380km from Athens
Greece Map C2

Arta is the oldest city in Epirus and has a long and distinguished history. In ancient times it was the capital of the Molossian kingdom, whose most famous ruler was King Pyrrhus. In the third century B.C. Pyrrhus won several brilliant victories over the Romans and the Carthaginians, but eventually succumbed to the rising power of Rome. Arta again came into

The bridge at Arta

prominence in the thirteenth century, when for two hundred years it was the capital of the autonomous Despotate of Epirus. Ruins of the great days of Arta survive in the **Frourion**, a thirteenth-century fortress, and in three Byzantine churches, one of which, the thirteenth-century church of Panayia Paragoritissa, now serves as the **Museum of Christian Antiquities**. The town stands on a loop of the Arakhthos River, crossed by a quaint old Turkish bridge which has been made the subject of legends and folksongs.

Hotels. The best hotel in Arta is the **Xenia (B)**, which stands on the beautifully landscaped grounds of the Frourion fortress, on the site of the medieval Palace of the Despots.

Restaurants. The best restaurant is the **Amvrakikon**, noted for its *avgotaracho*—smoked fish roe packed in wax.

From Arta the highway runs up the Louros valley through the Pindus Mountains, whose slopes are covered with pines and dwarf cypresses. This is some of the most beautiful mountain scenery in Greece, with none of the harshness of the Peloponnesian ranges. The road brings us finally to the city of Ioannina, the capital of modern Epirus.

IOANNINA

459km from Athens
Greece Map C2

There are many who say that Ioannina is the most beautiful and fascinating city in all of Greece.

The city stands on the shore of lovely Lake Pambotis, on the edge of a highland plain ringed by ridges of the Pindus Mountains. The oldest part of the city is contained within the medieval citadel, which stands on a rocky promontory jutting out into the lake; the domes and minarets of its two old mosques giving the town an oriental silhouette. Most of the houses within the citadel date from the early nineteenth century or before, and the atmosphere is reminiscent of an older and more colourful Greece, that of which Byron wrote. The poet stayed here for several weeks at the time of his first visit to Greece in 1809 and was tremendously impressed by Ioannina and the magnificent mountains of Epirus. While here he was a guest of Ali Pasha, the Lion of Tebelini, the fabulous character who for half a century ruled most of Epirus almost independently of the Sublime Porte, and kept its people in terror from his murderous outrages. Ali Pasha's mark is still upon the town, for most of the ruination which we see in the citadel was brought about during his last stand against a besieging Turkish army in the autumn and winter of 1821–22. The old Lion's headless body is buried near the ruins of his palace on the citadel. (The head itself was sent to Stamboul, where it was displayed on a pike outside the Saray gate as proof that Ali Pasha was truly dead.)

From the ramparts of the citadel there is a splendid view of the old town and the lake. The citadel dates from the eleventh century; in its north-west corner is the former **mosque of Aslan Pasha** (1618), now a local museum; and in the south-east corner is the **Fethiye Mosque**, built at the time of the Turkish conquest of Ioannina in 1430.

Across the lake we see the lush little island which is one of the great charms of Ioannina; hidden away there are two Byzantine churches and the eighteenth-century monastery where Ali Pasha met his end. One can reach the island by boats which leave from the pier just outside the city gates. One lands at a little hamlet at the far side of the island, where there is an extremely pleasant outdoor taverna shaded by a four-hundred-year-old plane tree. There one can drink a few bottles of the local sparkling Zitsa wine and dine on the famous eels of Lake Pambotis.

The modern town of Ioannina is not without its charm, and there are many picturesque old streets and colourful market squares. Ioannina is especially noted for its exceptionally fine jewellery and the beautiful handicrafts produced by its many goldsmiths, silversmiths, wood-carvers and weavers—altogether an extraordinary town, and one which no visitor to Greece should miss.

Hotels. Xenia (B), 33 Vass. Georgiou. **Acropole (B)**, 3 Vass. Georgiou. **Palladion (B)**, 1 Pan. Scoumbourdi. **Astoria (C)**, 8 Paraskevopoulou. **Bretannia (C)**, 11 Kentriki Platia. **Dioni (C)**, 10 Tsirigota. **Egnatia (C)**, 20 Aravantinou. **Esperia (C)**, 3 Kaplani.

Restaurants. There are several good restaurants along the lake shore, particularly the **Pharos**, and several others on the island. In addition to eels, Ioannina is also noted for its frogs' legs and lake carp.

EXCURSIONS. **Metsovo** (62km NW of Ioannina). The drive to Metsovo takes one into the heart of the Pindus, through the most magnificent mountain scenery in Greece. Metsovo is the largest and most distinguished of all the mountain villages in Epirus. The village houses are very attractive, particularly the striking handsome **Tositsa Mansion**, which has been superbly restored and now serves as a museum for exhibiting the beautiful handicrafts of the region.

Dodona (20km S of Ioannina). This is the site of the oldest oracle in Greece. The most important monument which survives on the site today is the magnificent **Theatre**, built by King Prusias in the third century B.C. The Theatre, which seats 20,000 spectators, has been superbly restored in recent years. It is now the site of the **Dodona Festival**, held annually in August. The Festival includes performances of classical drama by the National Theatre of Greece, and also performances of local folk-songs and dances sponsored by the Society for Epirote Studies.

After leaving Ioannina the road crosses the Pindus westward to the Adriatic, bringing one to **Igoumenitsa**, the port of embarkation for Corfu and Italy. One can also board a car-ferry here for Patras, which is about 200km away. From Igoumenitsa one can drive down the coast of Epirus to two of the most charming seaside towns in Greece.

PARGA

500km from Athens
Greece Map C1

A very picturesque little town sprawling over the flanks of a rocky promontory and surrounded by a forest of aromatic pines. The promontory ends in an equally picturesque Venetian fortress, which gives a medieval flavour to the little port. The shore nearby is a succession of secluded coves with pink and white sand, absolutely ideal for swimming or underwater fishing.

Hotels. Hellas (B) (Furnished apartments), Kryoneri. **Lichnou Beach (B)** (Hotel and bungalows). **Parga Beach (B)** (Bungalows), Chryssoyali. **Arra (C)**, 3 Agiou Athanassiou. **Paradissos (D)**, Platia Ayiou Nicolaou. There is also a camp-site nearby.

Restaurants. There are several tavernas on the waterfront, the best of which is **Sostis**.

PREVEZA
420km from Athens
Greece Map C2

This charming little port, surmounted by the inevitable Venetian fortress, has an unrivalled view out over the Ionian Sea. The town stands on the north shore of a narrow strait, the entrance to the Ambracian Gulf. Here, on 2 September 31 B.C. the famous Battle of Actium was fought, in which the fleet of Octavian, commanded by his admiral Agrippa, completely routed the combined navies of Antony and Cleopatra and so changed the course of Roman history. Just north of the modern town are the ruins of the Roman city of **Nikopolis**, founded by Octavian after his victory.

Hotels. Aktaeon (C) (no rooms with bath), Venizelon Ave. **Almini (C)** (two-thirds of the rooms have private baths). **Metropolis (C)** (no rooms with bath).

There is a car-ferry at Preveza which provides a frequent service across the strait. From there one can take the new coastal highway through ancient Acarnia, one of the least-known regions of Greece. This road then brings one to Antirion, where it is advisable to cross the strait and take the Peloponnesian coastal highway back to Athens.

The second itinerary through central Greece begins with the super highway leading north from Athens. After leaving Attica, the road for the most part follows the strait which separates the mainland and the long island of **Euboea**, whose blue mountains we see just across the way. There are several pleasant resort towns along the shore, most notably **Agios Konstantinos** and **Kammena Vourla**, the latter noted for its radioactive hot springs (which are reputed to cure a host of nineteenth-century ailments, but which might cause some twentieth-century ones).

A short distance beyond Kammena Vourla brings us to the famous **Pass of Thermopylae**, where Leonidas and his band of 300 Spartans held off the entire Persian army of King Xerxes until all but two of them had fallen. The common grave of the Greek warriors is now marked by a white marble monument surmounted by a bronze statue of Leonidas; on the facade are inscribed three epigrams written by the poet Simonides of Keos, including this laconic tribute to the Spartan dead: 'Passerby, tell them in Lacedaemon that we lie here obedient to their command.'

Beyond Thermopylae the highway bears inland and rounds the end of the gulf, bypassing the town of **Lamia**; it then turns northward along the coast of the Pagasetic Gulf, with a turn-off to the right leading to the town of **Volos**.

VOLOS
321km from Athens
Greece Map C3

Volos is a pleasant town at the head of the Pagasetic Gulf; since antiquity it has been the principal seaport of Thessaly. In ancient times it was known as Iolkos, and it was from here, according to tradition, that Jason and the Argonauts set sail in search of the Golden Fleece. In recent times Volos has been destroyed twice by earthquakes, in 1954 and 1955, and so there are no ancient monuments to be seen in the town. Nevertheless, the town does have a very interesting museum, the most important exhibit being painted funerary stelai from ancient **Demetrias**, one of the predecessors of modern Volos. The modern town is a confused jumble, with a railway line running down its main street, but the broad seaside promenade is very lively and attractive, and the harbour is filled with picturesque old caïques and the ferries coming and going to the Northern Sporades islands.

Hotels. Aegli (A), 17 Argonafton. **Pallas (A)**, 44 Iassonos. **Argo (B)**, 135 Vass. Konstantinou. **Xenia (B)**, 2 N. Plastira. **Admitos (C)**, 43 Vass. Konstantinou. **Alexandros (C)**, Topali 3. **Avra (C)**, 5 Solonos. **Galaxy (C)**, 3 Agiou Nicolaou. **Kypseli (C)**, 1 Agiou Nicolaou. **Ariston (D)**, 40 Makedonias. **Thessaloniki (D)**, 17 S. Spyridi.

Restaurants. All of the good restaurants are along the seaside promenade; some of the best are: **Athinaiki Taverna, Boheme, Kalyvia, Kentrikon.**

ENTERTAINMENT. **Metaxi Mas** (night-club with orchestra and disco-thèque). **Volos Yacht Club** (orchestra). **Majorca** (*bouzoukia*). **Astir** (*bouzoukia*).

BEACHES. The best beach nearby is at **Neae Pagasae**, 5km from town; there are also several restaurants and night-clubs.

THE PELION
Greece Map C3

Mount Pelion is the long mountain range which extends down the peninsula enclosing the Pagasetic Gulf to the west. This is one of the most delightful regions in Greece, for the mountains are heavily wooded and covered with lush vegetation, and the climate is superb the whole year round. The Pelion villages are among the most attractive in Greece, rivalled only by the island towns, and the houses are extremely attractive, framed in timber and with their upper floors extending out on graceful wooden corbels, with latticed windows and balconies festooned with flowering vines, slate roofs shining in the sun. Some of the most beautiful villages are: **Ano Volos** (4km from Volos), **Portaria** (13km), **Makrynitsa** (16km), **Hania** (27km, a wintersports centre with a ski-lift), **Zagora** (47km), and **Tsangarada**. Many of the Pelion villages have small hotels and one can always rent rooms in the local houses. On the Aegean coast below the mountain there are several villages blessed with some of the best beaches in Greece, particularly at **Agios Ioannis** (72km from Volos); there are also several hotels here, the best of which is the **Aloe (B)**.

Leaving Volos, we drive westward to regain the main highway, which now heads north-west across the great plain of Thessaly.

LARISSA
361km from Athens
Greece Map C3

Larissa is a large and busy agricultural town in the centre of the Thessalian plain. Though it has been the capital of Thessaly since earliest times, there are almost no ancient monuments in the town, other than the scanty remains of a classical temple, a Byzantine fortress, and a former Turkish mosque, which now serves as the local museum. For the visitor, Larissa is important mainly as a stopping-place on the way to central and northern Greece. Nevertheless, one ought to sit for a few hours at a café table in the main square, to see just how lively and animated life can be in a Greek market town.

Hotels. Motel Xenia (B), **Melathron (B)**, 20 Kouma. **Olympion (B)**, 1 Megalou Alexandrou. **Achilion (C)**, 10 Kentavron. **Acropole (C)**, 142 El. Venizelou. **Adonis (C)**, 8 Vass. Konstantinou. **Anessis (C)**, 25 Megalon Alexandrou. **Aegli (C)**, 5 Ossis. **El-Greco (C)**, 8 M. Alexandrou. **Helena (C)**, Kouma and 28 Octovriou. **Galaxy (C)**, 23 Vass. Konstantinou. **Kentrikon (C)**, 17 Roosevelt. **Metropole (C)**, 8 Roosevelt. **Pella (C)**, 1 Vass. Frederikis.

Restaurants. Arxos, Averoff, Dio Fengaria, Elatos, Frourio, Hawaii, Hermes.

ENTERTAINMENT. **Hayati** (*bouzoukia*).

Larissa is one of the great crossroads in Greece, and from there one can drive in one of several directions. The two most interesting routes are west, which takes one across the Thessalian plain to **Trikala**, **Kalambaka** and the **Meteora**, and north, which brings one through the **Vale of Tempe** and out to the seacoast below **Mount Olympus**.

TRIKALA
333km from Athens
Greece Map C2

Trikala is a very lively and attractive farming town, standing astride the

Lethaios River. According to mythology, this was the birthplace of Asclepios, the god of medicine, and was the site of the first *Asclepieion*, or shrine of healing. The region around Trikala was also the abode of the Centaurs, half man–half horse and more lascivious than either. The town is also the centre of the Vlach country, the semi-nomadic people who herd their flocks in the mountains north and west of Thessaly. The best time to visit Trikala is mid-September, when the **Pazari**, or market festival is held. This is one of the most interesting festivals in Greece, when the Vlachs come down from the hills in their thousands, their women dressed in local costume and jewellery, to shop and drink and dance at the fair. (The last time we went to the fair there was a ten-piece band with a ginger-haired lady from Alexandria who sang in Greek, Vlach, Turkish and Arabic, while a troupe of off-duty circus acrobats took turns throwing one another out of sight through the vines which covered the outdoor taverna.)

The old quarter of the town sprawls down the hillside below the Byzantine fortress; one sees here some very picturesque old houses in the Turkish style.

Hotels. Achilion (B), 1 Platia Vass. Georgiou. **Divani (B)**, 11 Kitrilaki. **Dina (C)**, 40 Asklepion. **Rex (C)**, 1 Apollonos.

Restaurants. There are several very good restaurants along the river embankment in the centre of town.

THE METEORA
355km from Athens
Greece Map B, C2

Driving north-west from Trikala for half an hour or so one reaches the most spectacular sight in all of Greece, a series of extraordinary rock formations rising precipitously straight up out of the valley floor to heights of several hundred feet, each of them crowned with a medieval-looking monastery. These are the famous **Meteora** (literally 'The Hanging Rocks'), which geologists tell us were formed by erosion in earliest times when the Thessalian plain was still an inland sea. The first monasteries were established on the Meteora in the mid-fourteenth century; many were completely cut off from the valley below, and the monks generally pulled one another up in rope baskets (although one shudders to think how the first monk got up). There are twenty-five monasteries and convents in all, dating from the fourteenth to the seventeenth century, of which only five are now inhabited. Nearly all of the monasteries are decorated with highly original paintings in fresco, and together they constitute a veritable museum of religious art of the late Byzantine and post-Byzantine periods. The largest and loftiest of the monasteries is the **Grand Meteoron**, a fourteenth-century monastery perched 1,725ft high in the air. The most beautiful frescoes are found in the **Monastery of Varlaam**, established in 1566. The best base for visiting the Meteora is the village of **Kalambaka**, which cowers on the edge of the Thessalian plain just under the hanging rocks.

Varlaam Monastery which is situated high on the rugged Meteora cliffs

Hotels. (Kalambaka): **Motel Divani (A)**, **Xenia (A)** (Motel), **Aeolikos Astir (C)**, **Odyssion (C)**, **Rex (D)**.

THE VALE OF TEMPE
Greece Map C3

A half-hour's drive north of Larissa the road turns north-west towards the sea and passes through the beautiful Vale of Tempe. This is a gorge 6 miles long and only 100–150 feet wide through which the Peneios River makes its way to the sea. In ancient times the Vale was sacred to Apollo, for it was here that he cleansed and purified himself in the Peneios after having slain the serpent Python at Delphi. There are several lovely spots within the Vale where one might while away an hour or two, particularly at the **Spring of Venus**, or at the medieval **Kastro tis Oraias** (the Castle of the Beautiful Maiden).

THE THERMAIKOS GULF
Greece Map B3

Once past the glen one soon sights the sea again on the shore of the Thermaikos Gulf. The first village one comes to is **Platamon**, where there is a magnificent castle built by the Crusaders in the early thirteenth century; below there is an excellent beach, one of the many which fringe the shore of the Gulf. And all along the shore there are pleasant hotels, from which one can look out on one side to the sea and on the other to Mount Olympus, whose majestic peaks dominate the western horizon.

Hotels along the Thermaikos shore. Platamon: **Platamon Beach (B)**, **Xenia (B)** (Motel), **Olympos (C)**, **Diana (D)**. There is also a camp-site in Platamon. Leptokaria: **Galaxy (C)**. Methoni: **Arion (C)**. Litohoron: **Leto (B)**, **Olympios Zeus (B)** (Bungalows).

MOUNT OLYMPUS
Greece Map B3

Olympus, the mythological home of the gods, is the highest mountain range in Greece, with half-a-dozen peaks over 9,000ft and the highest of all, the Pantheon, at 9,570ft. The ascent is most conveniently made from the pleasant town of **Litohoron**, just 5km from the Gulf. The Greek Alpine Club has an office here, where one can obtain information and hire guides. The ascent is arduous but not difficult, and the climb takes two days up and down, spending one night in a shelter on the mountain.

Northern Greece

Having passed Mount Olympus one enters northern Greece; for Olympus forms the natural boundary between Thessaly and the northern province of Macedonia, the threshold to the Balkans. The difference is imperceptible at first, but soon the changes in the face of the countryside and of the people make one realize that one has left old Greece behind and entered the provinces. And as one continues into north-western Greece, into the province of Thrace, the change becomes even more pronounced. Even on the shore highway the Balkan mountains are sometimes only a dozen miles away, and one begins to see minarets in farm villages and old-fashioned Turkish costumes along the road.

Northern Greece was a frontier country in the days of the Roman Empire and it has been a battlefield ever since, more recently in the Balkan Wars and World War I. The region suffered terribly in World War II and the wounds have hardly healed; one still sees ugly pillboxes at river-crossings, and there are villages where the entire male population was executed by the Germans. Much of the region became part of Greece only early in the present

There are supermarkets in Greece, but small stores do most of the business

century, other parts not until after World War I, and so Macedonia and
Thrace have not yet had time to catch up with the rest of the country culturally
and economically, although the gap is closing fast.

Macedonia and Thrace have relatively few monuments of the past, since
they lay outside the world of classical Greece. (But Aristotle was a Macedonian,
and Democritus was a Thracian.) The monuments which survive are Macedonian, such as at Pella, its ancient capital; or Roman, as at Phillipi; or
Byzantine, as in the churches of Salonica. But the region nevertheless has a
great deal to offer in other ways, particularly in the variety of its towns and
cities, some of which are unlike any others in Greece. They range from the
sprawling industrial metropolis of Salonica to the sleepy Turkish farming
town of Komotini; with absolutely unique places such as Edessa with its
dozen waterfalls and Kastoria with half-a-hundred Byzantine churches;
startling contrasts as between the almost-Balkan mountain town of Florina
and the white Aegean port of Kavalla, and, most extraordinary of all, the
medieval theocratic world of Athos, the Holy Mountain. And so one will
not have seen Greece in its entirety until one has seen Macedonia and Thrace,
the northern provinces.

SALONICA (THESSALONIKI)
539km from Athens
Greece Map B3

Salonica is the capital of Macedonia and the second largest city in Greece,
with a population of 300,000. The city was almost totally destroyed by fire in
1917, and has since been completely rebuilt; consequently there is very little
left of the old town, except in the neighbourhoods near the Byzantine ramparts. Fortunately the fire spared most of the city's antiquities, and the
majority of these have now been restored. There are a dozen Byzantine
churches in the city, ranging over a thousand-year period from the fourth
to the fourteenth centuries, so that Salonica is second only to Istanbul as a
museum of Byzantine architecture. There are also other monuments from all
periods of the city's past: a Roman Forum and the Triumphal Arch of
Galerius; the Byzantine walls and defence-towers; the famous White Tower,
a landmark on the city's waterfront, built in about 1430 by either the Turks
or the Venetians; and several Turkish mosques and public baths. There are
also monuments of the more recent past of Salonica: The Statue of Prince
Constantine, who led the Greek forces in the re-conquest of Salonica on 26
October 1913, thus ending five centuries of Turkish rule; the British military
cemeteries in the suburbs, where more than four thousand British soldiers,
who died on the Macedonian front in 1916–18, are buried and the Memorial.
to the fifty thousand Salonican Jews who perished in the gas-chambers of
Auschwitz during World War II—one wound which will never heal.

But modern Salonica seems to pay little heed to its painful past. It is an
industrial and commercial city, the fastest-developing and most vigorous
in Greece. The city is unreservedly boisterous and working-class. Its streets

and squares are lively and its crowds animated, and one sees far fewer of the portly, briefcase-carrying bourgeoise than one does in Athens, but far more high-spirited young people rushing from shops and factories to get dressed to the nines for an evening in a taverna or a discothèque.

Salonica is particularly crowded during the annual International Fair, in which firms from all over the world exhibit their wares. During the Fair two Film Festivals are held, one for foreign films and a second for recently-released Greek films. There is still another festival in October, the 'Demetria', a pageant designed to dramatize Salonica's rich heritage of Byzantine culture and history.

SIGHTSEEING. Salonica's most important Byzantine church is **Ayios Demetrius**, a basilica originally built in the fifth century and dedicated to St. Demetrius, the patron-saint and protector of the city. The church was gutted by fire in 1917, but has since been reconstructed according to the original plan. It is the grandest and most impressive of the churches in the city, and still preserves some of its medieval mosaic decoration.

The oldest of the city's churches is **Ayios Yeoryios** (St. George) which dates from the early fourth century. In form it is a Roman rotunda, apparently intended (but never used) as a mausoleum for the Emperor Galerius, later converted into a church and still later as a mosque—an architectural palimpsest of Salonica's long history. Near the church, on the Odos Egnatia, we see the **Arch of Galerius**, erected by him in A.D.297 to commemorate his victory over the Persians. And just around the corner from the Arch is the pretty little church of **St. Pandeleimnos**, which dates back to 1169, or earlier.

Excavations in the Platia Dikastirion, the main square of Salonica, a decade ago unearthed the foundations of the **Imperial Roman Forum**; to one side of the archaeological site one sees the **Cifte Hamam**, a fourteenth-century Turkish bath, and to the other side the dainty little church of **Panayia Khalkeon**, Our Lady of the Coppersmiths, founded in 1028. Like so many of the churches of Salonica, this was converted into a mosque after the Turkish conquest, and for five centuries it was known as *Kazanciler Camii*, the Mosque of the Coppersmiths, a poignant illustration of the continuity of life in this ancient city.

Other Byzantine churches which one comes across in strolling through the streets of Salonica are: the **Panayia Akheiropoietos**, a church founded in the fifth century and still in use today; **Ayia Sophia**, an eighth-century sanctuary with mosaics of the ninth and tenth centuries; the thirteenth-century church of **Ayia Katerini**; and the fourteenth-century churches of **Ayios Nikolaos Orfanos**, **Moni Vlataion**, and **Agii Apostoli**. Altogether they constitute a textbook study of the development of Byzantine architecture and a living link to Salonica's historic past.

The **Archaeological Museum** preserves relics of an even more remote past, with antiquities ranging in time from the Neolithic period and the Early Iron Age up to early Byzantine times. The most interesting exhibits are from the nearby site of Dherveni, excavated only in 1962, including iron and bronze weapons, silverware and jewellery, the magnificent bronze Dherveni Krater, and the oldest-known papyrus in Greece.

(Opening hours: In summer daily from 8 a.m. to 1 p.m. and 3 p.m. to 6 p.m.; Sundays and holidays 10 a.m. to 1 p.m. and 3 p.m. to 6 p.m. In winter daily from 9 a.m. to 1 p.m. and 2.30 p.m. to 5 p.m.; Sundays and holidays 10 a.m. to 1 p.m. and 2.30 p.m. to 5 p.m. Closed on Mondays .the whole year.)

Finally, one should not fail to stroll on and around the ancient ramparts of the city, built towards the end of the fourth century A.D. by the Emperor Theodosius the Great. The contrast with the modern town below, with its broad squares and busy boulevards, could not possibly be greater, for here life is slowed to an almost oriental pace along narrow, winding lanes lined with picturesque old houses adorned with corbelled balconies and latticed windows in the old-fashioned Turkish style. On one such street one can find the birthplace of Atatürk, the father of modern Turkey and the man who changed the course of Greek and Turkish history. Atatürk was born as Mustapha Kemal, the son of a government clerk, in a neighbourhood which was then the Jewish quarter of old Salonica.

Hotels
Makedonia Palace (L), Kennedy Ave. Tel: 837-521. Cables: MACEPAL. Air-conditioned, with restaurant and roof-garden.
Mediterranean Palace (L), 9 Vass. Konstantinou. Tel: 228-521. Cables: OLYMPIC. One of the grand old hotels of Greece, in an exceptionally handsome building (literally a palace) right on the esplanade. It is air-conditioned and has a roof-garden; its restaurant is by far the best in Salonica, as is its cosy bar, presided over by the charming Marilena, a lady of most devastating wit. For a luxury hotel it is completely unpretentious and is a bargain considering what one gets in service and comfort.
Capital (A), 8 Monastiriou. Tel: 516-221. Cables: CAPITOTEL. Air-conditioned, with restaurant.
Electra Palace (A), 5A Platia Aristotelous. Tel: 235-739. Cables: ELECTRA PALACE. Air-conditioned, with restaurant.
Aegeon (B), 19 Egnatia. Tel: 522-921.
Ariston (B), 5 Diikitiriou. Tel: 519-630. Cables: HOTEL ARISTON. No rooms with private bath.
Athos (B) (Pension), 20 Dangli. Tel: 232-652. Night-club.
Capsis (B), 28 Monastiriou. Tel: 521-421. Cables: CAPSIOTEL. Partially air-conditioned. Restaurant, roof-garden, night-club and swimming-pool.
City (B), 17 Comninion. Tel: 69-421. Cables: CITY. Partially air-conditioned, with restaurant.
Cosmopolit (B), 23 Hermou. Tel: 75-245. Cables: COSMOPOLIT.
Egnatia (B), 11 Leontos Sofou. Tel: 536-320. Cables: EGNATIOTEL. Partially air-conditioned, with restaurant.
El Greco (B), 23 Egnatia. Tel: 520-620. Cables: GRECOTEL. Air-conditioned, with restaurant.
Elisabeth (B) (Motel), 283 Monastirious. Tel: 515-712. Partially air-conditioned, with restaurant and night-club.
Emborikon (B), 14 Syngrou. Tel: 525-560.
Metropolitan (B), 65 Vass. Olgas. Tel: 824-221. Cables: METROTEL. Restaurant and roof-garden.
Olympic (B), 25 Egnatia. Tel: 522-131. Cables: OLYMPICHOTEL. Roof-garden.
Palace (B), 12 M. Alexandrou. Tel: 70-505. Restaurant.
Philippion (B), Asvestohori. Tel: 23-983. Tennis courts, swimming-pool, restaurant and roof-garden.
Rotonda (B), 97 Monastiriou. Tel: 517-121. Cables: HOTELROTONDA. Restaurant and roof-garden.
Queen Olga (B), 44 Vass. Olgas. Tel: 824-621. Restaurant.
Victoria (B), 13 Lagada. Tel: 522-421. Partially air-conditioned, with restaurant.
A.B.C. (C), 41 Agelaki. Tel: 21-761. Cables: HOTELABC. Restaurant.
Amalia (C), 33 Hermou. Tel: 68-321. Cables: AMALIAHOTEL. Air-conditioned.
Anessis (C), 20 Octovriou 26. Tel: 515-505.
Delta (C), 13 Egnatia. Tel: 516-321. Cables: DELTAHOTEL. Partially air-conditioned, with restaurant, roof-garden and swimming-pool.

Egli (C), 111 Egnatia. Tel: 77-589.
Esperia (C), 58 Olympou. Tel: 69-321. Cables: ESPERIHOTEL. Air-conditioned, with restaurant.
Mandrino (C), 2 Antigonidon and Egnatia. Tel: 526-321. Cables: MANDRINO. Roof-garden.
Olympia (C), 65 Olympou. Tel: 35-421. Cables: OLYMPOTEL. Partially air-conditioned, with restaurant.
Park (C), 81 I. Oragoumi. Tel: 524-121. Air-conditioned, with restaurant.
Pella (C), 65 I. Dragoumi. Tel: 524-221. Air-conditioned.
Rea (C), 6 Comninon. Tel: 78-449. Night-club.
Rex (C), 39 Monastiriou. Tel: 517-051. Roof-garden.
   There are also hotels in the suburbs of Salonica; at **Panorama**, in the hills 10km west of town; and at **Aghia Trias**, on the seashore 15km to the south.
Sun Beach (B), Aghia Trias. Tel: 52-21. Air-conditioned. Sea sports, restaurant and night-club.
Galaxy (C), Akti Aghias Triados, Aghia Trias. Tel: 22-291. Cables: GALAXIASHOTEL. Partially air-conditioned. Sea sports, restaurant, roof-garden and night-club.
Nephele (A), Panorama. Tel: 841-393. Cables: NEFELHOTEL. Partially air-conditioned. Restaurant, roof-garden and night-club.
Panorama (A), Panorama. Tel: 841-123. Restaurant and roof-garden.
Pefka (C), 9 Aprilliou 21, Panorama. Tel: 841-153. Restaurant and roof-garden.

Restaurants. The most popular restaurant in town is the **Olympos-Naoussa**, on the esplanade next to the Mediterranean Palace Hotel, a huge, barn-like establishment with the most extensive menu in town. The food is mediocre and rather expensive, the service slap-dash.
Stratis, 19 Vass. Georgiou, a pavement restaurant, very popular with tourists.
Tambakio, on the waterfront by the old fishing port, an informal taverna which serves the best seafood in Salonica.
Krikellis, 284 Vass. Olgas Ave., about 5km from the centre of town, a charming taverna with excellent food at very reasonable prices.
Ta Kastra, up by the old Byzantine ramparts, with a superb view. The food and service are good but it is quite expensive.
Soudzoukakia, 3 Rongoti St.

Night-clubs. Barbarella, Mitropoleos and Gounari Sts., **Can-Can**, Terma Neapoleos. **Deilina**, Terma Neapolis.

BEACHES. There are good beaches at **Aretsa** and **Aghia Triada**, both about 15km from town. There is a camp-site at Aghia Triada.

Leaving Salonica we follow in turn two separate itineraries in order to see the most interesting and scenic regions of Macedonia, first westwards toward the borders of Yugoslavia and Bulgaria, then eastwards towards Thrace.

PELLA

38km west of Salonica
Greece Map A3

The highway west from Salonica brings us past the site of ancient Pella, the birthplace of Alexander the Great and the capital of the Macedonian kingdom at the height of its power. The site was excavated only in 1957, and revealed the existence of a palatial residence whose floors were paved with beautiful mosaics made from naturally-coloured stones. The mosaics are now on exhibit *in situ* and in the little museum on the site.

EDESSA

89km west of Salonica
Greece Map A2, 3

Edessa is beautifully situated on a steep bluff at the eastern end of the Salonican plain, with a view out over the whole of central Macedonia. The waters of the Vermion Mountains pour through the town and over the bluff in a series of spectacular waterfalls. There is a beautiful park at the edge of the bluff with rustic bridges over the rushing streams and paths leading around and under the cataracts themselves. There are also two restaurants in the park where one can spend a deliciously cool afternoon, listening to the sound of falling water and watching transient rainbows.

Hotels. Xenia (B), 41 Philippou. Restaurant on the premises.

NAOUSSA

94km from Salonica
Greece Map B2, 3

Naoussa, situated at the foot of Mount Vermion, is the centre of one of the great wine-producing regions of Greece and is famous for its red *brousco*. The town stands in the midst of acres of peach and apple orchards and vineyards, a landscape quite unlike any other in Greece. At the nearby village of **Seli** (18km, altitude 4,700ft) there is a lift which takes skiers another thousand feet up Mount Vermion.

Hotels. Hellas (C), 14 M. Alexandrou. **Olympia (D)**, 14 Zafiraki. Rooms can also be rented at Seli in various guest-houses in the village.

FLORINA

161km west of Salonica
Greece Map A2

Florina is a quaint mountain town reminiscent of villages in the lower Italian Alps, but with an indefinable Balkan flavour, and it is located near the mountain lakes of Great and Little Prespa, at the junction of Greece, Yugoslavia and Albania. There are splendid locations for skiing and climbing in the surrounding mountains.

KASTORIA

206km from Salonica, 512km from Athens
Greece Map B2

Kastoria is without question the most beautiful and interesting town in

Macedonia. The town is situated on a promontory jutting out into lovely Lake Orestios, more than 2,000 feet above sea level, and is set in a ring of heavily wooded mountains. There are no less than fifty-four old churches in the town, seven from Byzantine times and most of the others from the post-Byzantine period, many of them decorated inside and out with highly original frescoes. Kastoria is also noted for its many *arkhontika* houses, handsome mansions of brick and stone dating from the seventeenth and eighteenth centuries. The town owes its wealth to the fur trade, established there by Jewish traders in the eighteenth century.

Hotels. Xenia du Lac (A), Acropolis (C), Kastoria (C), Orestion (C).

Restaurants. Acropolis, Karania, Klimateria, Oraia Kastoria, all in the lower town. There are several other good but unfortunately nameless little tavernas in the quieter and more picturesque upper town.

CHALCIDICE
Greece Map B3, 4

Chalcidice is the huge peninsula which protrudes out into the Aegean west of Salonica. Chalcidice is bounded to the north by Lakes Koronia and Volvi,

A typical fishing village in the Chalcidice

which almost separate it from the rest of Macedonia, and to the south it narrows out into three long and narrow secondary peninsulas; the eastern one is called **Kassandra**, the central **Sithonia**, and the eastern **Agion Oros**, or

113

the Holy Mountain. This region, which is given over principally to farming and mining, has recently been developed for tourism, and a large number of really beautiful beach resorts have been built there, principally on or near the Kassandra peninsula. For those who would rather go it on their own, there are whole stretches of the Chalcidice coast which are still untouched.

The main highway, which leads south from Salonica, soon turns west and crosses the centre of the Chalcidice peninsula. Half way across (58km from Salonica) a branch to the south leads to **Polygiros**, the capital of the region, and then continues on to Kassandra and Sithonia. The main road from Salonica continues on to the east coast of the Chalcidice and then turns south to the town of **Ouranoupolis** at the base of Agion Oros (entry to the peninsula itself is restricted).

Hotels

Akti Gerakinas (B) (Bungalows) (at **Gerakinis**, on the coast south of Polygiros). Tel: 474 (in Athens call 736-743). Cables: ARGOTEL. Private beach, swimming-pool, sea sports, tennis courts, mini-golf, restaurant, roof-garden and night-club.

Pallini Beach (A) (Hotel and Bungalows), Kalithea (Kassandra). Tel: 21-480 (in Athens call 716-730). Cables: PALLINI BEACH. Air-conditioned, private beach, swimming-pool, sea sports, tennis court, mini-golf, restaurant, roof-garden and night-club.

Ammon Zeus (B), Kalithea (Kassandra). Tel: 21-356 (in Salonica call 416-009). Cables: AMON-OTEL. Sea sports, restaurant and night-club.

Vassos (B), Kryopigi (Kassandra). Tel: 21-342. Private beach, restaurant and roof-garden.

Kalithea-Belvedere (C), Kalithea (Kassandra). Tel: 21-352.

Mendi (A), Kalandra (Kassandra). Tel: 21-470. Partially air-conditioned, private beach, swimming-pool, sea sports, tennis courts, mini-golf, restaurant and night-club.

Xenia (A) (Motel), Paliouri (Kassandra). Tel: 2. Private beach, tennis courts and restaurant.

King's Palace (A), Ouranoupolis (Mount Athos). Tel: 228-521 in Salonica. Private beach, sea sports, restaurant, taverna and night-club.

Xenia (A) (Motel and bungalows), Ouranoupolis (Mount Athos). Tel: 2. Private beach, tennis courts and restaurant.

Mount Athos (B), Ierissos (Mount Athos). Tel: 225. Private beach, sea sports, tennis courts and restaurant.

MOUNT ATHOS (AGION OROS)
Greece Map B4

Agion Oros (the Holy Mountain) is the easternmost of the three peninsulas of the Chalcidice. In the west it is better known as Mount Athos after the peak which stands at the tip of the peninsula. Mount Athos is a semi-autonomous theocratic state, and to enter it one must have permission from the civic and religious authorities. (Enquire at the NTOG offices in Athens or Salonica for details.) Women are not permitted to enter its precincts (although people still talk about a scandal involving Vlach shepherdesses on the mountain in the late Middle Ages), nor are beardless youths under the age of twenty-one. Such dependents are to be left behind in one of the hotels at **Ouranopoulis**, at the base of the peninsula, from where one can catch a caïque for **Daphni** the port of entry of the Holy Mountain. There one boards a bus (driven by a monk) and rides up to **Kariai**, the administrative centre of the Mountain, and obtains a permit which allows a three-day stay. This permit should be presented at any of the monasteries one visits, and it entitles one to free food and lodging for the night. One is expected to leave a gratuity compensating for this hospitality, for the monasteries are very poor these days, since the demise of their royal benefactors in Russia and Byzantium.

Formalities aside, a visit to the Holy Mountain can be an extraordinarily moving experience, for one literally steps back a thousand years in time, into the theocentric world of the Middle Ages. The first monastery was founded here in the year 963 and over the following centuries two score more were established on Athos. The community reached its zenith in the fifteenth century, when more than 20,000 monks inhabited the forty monasteries, but today there are fewer than 2,000, and only twenty monasteries are still functioning, some of them with only a handful of monks. Still, the spirit of the mountain seems much the same as it was a thousand years ago.

It is impossible to see more than a few of the more important monasteries in the allotted three days. The best itinerary is perhaps the following: walk over the hills from Kariai to the monastery of **Vatopedi** and spend the night there. In the morning one can catch a caïque to the port of the **Grand Lavra**, near the tip of the peninsula and under the shadow of the Holy Mountain itself. The Grand Lavra is the oldest and most important of the monasteries, founded in 963 by the Byzantine Emperor Nicephorus Phocas. Its church and monastic buildings form the loveliest cloister on the peninsula, its refectory has some of the most beautiful frescoes, and its library has the most interesting books and manuscripts. One can spend the second night at the Grand Lavra and then embark on the caïque once again to round the tip of the peninsula for the eastern side; while rounding the tip one sees some of the *sketes*, or isolated houses of two or three monks loosely connected with some monastic establishment, and high on the cliff face one spies the caves of the real loners, hermits whose only connection with the outside world is a rope and pulley with which they haul up their supplies from the world below. If one has the time to walk around the tip of the peninsula one will encounter some of the vagabond or mendicant monks, highly original characters who are more truly hippies than the long-haired youths one sees outside the American Express in Athens. One can then spend the third night at one of the cliff-hanging monasteries on the eastern coast, **Pavlou**, **Dionysiou**, **Grigoriou**, or **Simon Petra**. When one embarks from Daphni the following day, one will surely have been touched by the medieval spirit of the Holy Mountain.

From Ouranoupolis one usually returns by the same route to Salonica, and from there resumes the tour of northern Greece. (There is a road directly north over the mountain to **Stavros**, on the Strimonikos Gulf.)

Leaving Salonica once again and heading eastward, one passes along the shore of **Lakes Koronia** and **Volvi** (a poet friend of ours, who has passed these insipid ponds a hundred times, calls them Lake Weary and Lake Dreary). This brings us out through a beautiful glen to the town of **Stavros** on the Strimonikos Gulf. After a few hot days tramping around on the Holy Mountain one might be in the mood to rest and swim here, for the coast is one long and continuous beach of white sand, along which there are several pleasant little hotels and camp-sites.

Hotels. At Stavros: **Possidonian (C)**, **Aktaeon (D)**. There are camp-sites at **Asprovalta** and farther up the coast towards **Amfipoleos**.

The road turns inland at the estuary of the Strimon River, which it crosses a little farther on. The river crossing is guarded by the colossal stone **Lion of Amphipolis**, erected in the late fourth or early third century B.C. It surmounts a tomb which is thought to be that of Laodemon, a mariner from Lesbos who became Governor of Syria.

The road returns briefly to the coast and then turns inland again, crossing a very pleasant countryside of rolling hills and tobacco farms. The road passes through the town of **Eleftheroupolis**, a good base for climbing the nearby Mount Pangaion (6,400ft). Sixteen kilometres past Eleftheroupolis we climb up into the hills and then down again till we are suddenly presented with a magnificent view of Kavalla and its harbour.

KAVALLA
170km from Salonica; 685km from Athens
Greece Map A4

Kavalla, a beautiful pastel town reminiscent of those on the Aegean islands, is superbly situated at the end of a large and sparkling bay, its houses sprawling picturesquely around the natural amphitheatre formed by the outlying slopes of Mandra Kari. The lively port is filled with colourful caïques and old lumbering wooden frigates, and the waterfront is lined with cafés and tavernas which serve some of the best seafood in the Aegean. Behind the port is the picturesque old Turkish quarter, surmounted by the medieval Byzantine ramparts, the most perfectly-preserved in Greece. Here we find the handsome old Turkish mansion which was the birthplace of Mehmet Ali, the founder of the last Egyptian dynasty. Nor far away is one of the most interesting of all the Turkish antiquities in Greece, the **imaret**, or public kitchen and lodging house which Mehmet Ali built for the indigent Turks of Kavalla; in its day it was known as **Tempel Hane**, which in either Greek or Turkish means the Lazy Mens' Home. Striding grandly across the valley between the main town and the old citadel is the handsome aqueduct built in the mid-sixteenth century by Sultan Süleyman the Magnificent. Then finally there is the local museum, which houses some interesting finds from local and nearby archaeological sites.

The waterfront of Kavalla is especially animated in summer, with crowds of tourists being ferried out to the off-shore island of Thassos, and with others bound for the cultural festival at nearby Philippi.

Hotels. Tosca Beach (A) (Hotel and bungalows on a private beach). Tel: 24-754. Cables: TOSCA. **Galaxy (B)**, 51 El. Venizelou. Tel: 24-521. Cables: GALAXY. **Olympion (B)**. Tel: 22-037. **Philippi (B)**, 3 Filellinon. Tel: 22-856. Cables: PHILIPPI. **Nefeli (C)**, 50 Erithrou Stavrou. Tel: 27-441. Cables: NEFELI. **Panorama (C)**, 32 El. Venizelou. Tel: 24-205.

Restaurants. Belvedere, superbly situated, with a panoramic view of the town and the harbour. **Oraia Mytilini**, an outdoor restaurant just beside the fish-market at the end of the harbour; excellent squid and lobster at very reasonable prices. Other restaurants: **Morais**, **Palladion** and **Kyriakos** (in the quarter known as Peryali).

ENTERTAINMENT. The **Kavalla Yacht Club**, situated on a jetty in the harbour, offers excellent food and dance music nightly during the summer. **Michalis**, an old Kavalla institution which offers good food and dance music all year round. **La Nuit** and the **Jockey Club** are popular cabarets.

BEACHES. **Batis beach**, just outside the town, a large installation well-run by the NTOG, with a large and well-appointed camp-site. **Tosca beach**, at Myrmingia bay, 6km from town, a tourist complex with bungalows on a private beach (in Athens Tel: 340-592). There are also good beaches without organized facilities at the following locations in the immediate vicinity of Kavalla: **Irakleitsa**, **Kalamitsa**, and **Palia Peramos**.

EXCURSION. **Philippi** (15km NW of Kavalla). Together with Pella, this is one of the most important archaeological sites in Macedonia. It is famous as the site of the two battles of Philippi, which took place in October of the year 42 B.C., when the army of Antony and Octavian routed that of Brutus and Cassius, both of whom committed suicide after their defeat.

THRACE
Greece Map A4, 5

Leaving Kavalla and continuing westward, we soon leave Macedonia and enter the ancient province of Thrace, in the extreme north-western corner of Greece. The scene changes completely now, for we are seldom more than a dozen miles or so from the mountainous Bulgarian border, and the proximity of Turkey is evidenced by the increasing number of village mosques one sees, and by the obviously Turkish peasants who wave to one along the way, often dressed in old-fashioned costumes now no longer worn in Turkey itself. One drives through corridors of stately elms past miles of tobacco plantations, with Turkish farmers and their wives labouring in the fields with ancient farm implements and ox-drawn ploughs and wagons. Only the occasional olive grove or glimpse of the still-blue sea reminds one that one is still in Greece.

The first large town to which we come is **Xanthi** (219km from Salonica), the most important tobacco-processing centre in Thrace. The tobacco produced here is far better than that produced elsewhere in Greece, or in Turkey for that matter. On the Aegean coast at a distance of 26km from Xanthi are the ruins of ancient **Abdera**. In ancient times Abdera was the butt of jokes about the stupidity of its citizens; nonetheless it is the birthplace of Democritus, one of the originators of the atomic theory, and of Protagoras, one of the most gifted and original of the early Greek natural philosophers.

Hotels. **Xenia (B)**, 9 Vass. Sophias. **Sissi (C)**, 14 Lephkipon. Both hotels have restaurants and there are several other plain but good ones on and around the town square.

After Xanthi the road heads south-east and reaches the sea at **Porto Lagos**, a unique and picturesque little village on a lagoon. Just beyond Porto Lagos there is a turn-off to the sea at **Fanarion**, where there is a long but somewhat stony beach.

The road then turns inland once again and soon brings one to **Komotini** (276km from Salonica), the capital of western Thrace and its most important commercial centre. The strong Turkish element makes this the most interesting and colourful town in Thrace, though it has lost much of its charm since the construction of the new highway and civic square which resulted in the destruction of some picturesque old Turkish houses. The local museum, which houses antiquities from all over Thrace, is quite interesting; its most important exhibit is a unique gold bust of a Roman Emperor, thought to be Marcus Aurelius.

Hotels. Xenia (B), 43 Sismanoglu (means the Son of the Fat Man). **Astoria (C)**, 28 Platia Vass. Konstantinou. **Democritus (C)**, 8 Platia Vyzlinou.

Restaurants. Another sign of the nearness of Turkey is that the food gets generally better as one approaches the border. There is a humble little restaurant in the square in Komotini, the **Klimateria**, which serves roast chicken as good as one could get in the best restaurants in Athens, and at a third of the price.

Leaving Komotini we pass down a long and particularly handsome corridor of giant elms. Within a few miles we are out in a great open plain covered with tobacco plantations, then we climb up into a series of brush-covered hills, before we finally come back to the Aegean for the last time, to the port-city of Alexandroupolis.

Alexandroupolis is the last town of any size on the Greek side of the Thracian border. A dozen years ago, when we first passed through, Alexandroupolis was a sleepy little frontier town of old wooden houses with a single ramshackle hotel. But in the last decade the town has developed dramatically, with brand-new shops, cinemas, banks, hotels and even a night-club. The seafront is quite handsome, with a broad esplanade and an enormous and strikingly handsome lighthouse. There is a very colourful fish market around the quay, where ferries leave for the off-shore island of **Samothrace**.

Hotels. There are two excellent motels just outside of town on the road from Komotini, standing in a pine grove beside the sea.
Motel Astir (A). Tel: 26-448. Cables: ASTIROTEL. Private beach, swimming-pool, sea sports, and restaurant.
Egnatia (B). Tel: 28-661. Private beach, tennis court (usually inoperative and used for stringing linen out to dry), and restaurant.
Other hotels in town (all on the main street): **Alex (C)**, **Galaxias (C)**.

Restaurants. There are a number of good restaurants in the old town square and one or two along the sea-front. The best of all of these is the **Taverna Pharos**, a very cheerful little place with tables on the esplanade just beside the lighthouse. Its charming owner, our old friend Demitrios Kanakis, will see that you are well-fed before you face the long ride to Istanbul, the next stop after Alexandroupolis.

The Ionian Islands

In order to love the Ionian islands, one has to imagine what they must have been like half a century ago, and then search for the vestiges of that romantic past. At the time, *cantades*—Italianate love songs—were at their most popular. Groups of young men would gather under balconies, and, using the young lady perched primly and breathlessly above as an excuse, serenade each other throughout the night, continually straining to bring guitars, basses, tenors, and drunken smiles into a more poignant harmony than before. Now, as the islands slowly modernize, *cantades* are infrequently heard, and most of the beautiful Venetian streets, where the wistful lovers sang, have been destroyed by earthquakes and German bombers. Still, the whole tradition of *cantades* continues to symbolize the difference between the Ionian islands and the rest of Greece. Life here is softer, more romantic, and deeply influenced by Italy.

Of course, Italy is not the only western country to have influenced the Ionians, but the length and the success of the Venetian occupation make the Italian influence the most obvious. At the end of the Byzantine era, the Venetians took over the islands for roughly five centuries.

When Venetian rule disintegrated, the islands passed to the French for a few years; this occupation was followed by a brief and atrociously unsuccessful attempt at self-government. The English finally took over and made the island group a British Protectorate. Although colonialism was more successful here than in most places, England handed the islands over to the Republic of Greece in 1864 (a birthday present from Queen Victoria!).

Even though Ionian history is only a footnote to that of Western Europe, it is unique and therefore fascinating. Arthur Foss, in his excellent book, *The Ionian Islands*, feels that the islands were actually a bridge, or a stepping-stone, between the opposing influences of east and west: 'Lying between the ancient Greek city states and Magna Graecia, between Rome and Athens, between Christendom and Islam, between East and West, the Ionian islands have always acted as a bridge over which both armies and ideas have moved back and forth. . . . Out of this, the islands have developed their own identity, a harmonious amalgamation of Byzantium and Venice—admittedly on a small scale—which can be enjoyed in the various island capitals, villages, churches, monasteries, and country houses, when these have been spared by earthquakes and human destructiveness.'

Several of the most beautiful buildings in the Ionian islands have been destroyed during the last twenty-five years. In addition to bombing and related atrocities during the last war, a tremendous earthquake in 1953,

A street scene in Corfu, where Greek, French, Italian and even British architectural styles mix and mingle

followed by various fires, completely destroyed the exquisite Venetian towns in all the islands but Corfu. Fortunately, the natural beauty of the islands makes up for much of the loss. The Ionians are extremely green, and their hills are covered with the most surprising combinations of plants and trees. Few people will forget the experience of sailing past a wooded coast which is 400 metres away and being bombarded by the aroma of pine trees.

Despite their common history, the islands each have their own ambiance. Corfu, which is often said to be the most beautiful and is beyond all doubt the most popular, has a cosmopolitan flavour. Lefkas, on the other hand, is wild and remote, while the large Cefalonia is, for all its luxuriance, melancholic. The nearby island of Ithaca is primitive and enchanted—a perfect illustration of the mythical mood. Zakinthos, which falls short of being grand, has a very tame beauty. Paxos is a tiny lump of olive groves. These islands should ideally be seen one after another, since their underlying similarities make their differences all the more striking. Those without yachts may have

Visitors to Athens will immediately recognize the celebrated Parthenon, sited high on the Acropolis, which is first glimpsed across a field strewn with column drums and fragments of scattered marble

The hustle and bustle of a market in Athens where the rich colour of the wares contrasts strongly with the drabness of the clothes

The beautiful porch in the Stoa of Attalos, Athens; built in the second century A.D. and destroyed during the Herculian sack, the Stoa was reconstructed on its original foundations in the 1950s by the American School of Classical Studies

The ruins of Olympia where the famous Games were originally held so many centuries ago—such importance was attached to this quadrennial festival that their symbol was peace

Dramatically framed against a deep blue sky, the Temple of Poseidon stands on the top of Cape Sounion—reputed to be one of the most romantic spots in Greece when visited at sunset

A side-view of the picturesque Church of Daphni—one of the finest surviving examples of Byzantine architecture in Greece

*The great Temple of Apollo at Delphi, which was erected in
548 B.C., even in ruins dominates the site of the most sacred
shrine in ancient Greece*

*A scene of peaceful activity on the quay at Nauplia with the
Bourdzi fortress, once a hostel for retired hangmen, in the
background*

difficulty following such an itinerary, because steam-ship services between the islands are infrequent. Of course, renting an occasional caïque can solve this problem; one can obtain a more intimate impression of the Ionians from these fishing boats. And if the sea is rough, one will also quickly acquire a deep appreciation of life.

CORFU (KERKIRA)
Greece Map B, C1.

The scythe shaped island of Corfu has enchanted more than one poet, but Homer captures its soft, regenerative beauty better than any of his countless successors:

> Here great trees cool-shades grow, pear, pomegranate, rich apple, honeysweet fig and blossoming olive, forever bearing fruit, winter and summer never stripped, but ever blowing the western wind brings fruit to birth and ripens other. Pear follows pear, apple after apple grow, fig after fig, and grape yields grape again.

Corfu combines the best qualities of Greece—clear blue water, excellent beaches, and ample sunshine—with the lushness of a subtropical isle. Of course this communion of green land and blue sea, and the continual changes of light in the olive groves have been somewhat marred by the ubiquitous and unsightly luxury hotels which have sprung up everywhere. Nonetheless, Corfu town has retained all of its old grandeur and variety. A walk through Corfu will take one past sedate Georgian houses, tennis clubs, arcaded streets and imposing Venetian mansions, through hidden squares hung with laundry, down narrow alleys filled with cavernous tavernas and overshadowed by perilous balconies. And then from the slums of a decaying Italian city, one bursts out on to the Esplanade, the enormous plaza lined on one side by grand arcaded buildings, designed by the French in imitation of the Rue de Rivoli. The sparkling arcades are taken up by Corfu's most popular cafés. Locals and tourists alike sit under the ornate lanterns for hours on end, talking very happily about nothing and watching the well-dressed crowds stroll by. It is not noisy here at night, but a brilliant buzz filters out across the wide Esplanade, making it seem more than ever like an Italian piazza.

The most dramatic entrance to the town is from the wide Garitsa Bay. As you walk along the sweeping waterfront road, the **Old Fortress** comes completely into view. Its heavily fortified walls cover a large hilly promontory. Inside are various buildings and clusters of bright green trees. When the Venetians took over Corfu, they decided to make it the headquarters of their Greek possessions, and the fortified headland proved impregnable during more than one battle. The Old Fortress now houses a military training school and is seldom open to the public.

Continuing in the same direction, one passes through the enormous Esplanade. The first half of this park contains a bandstand and a rotunda in commemoration of Corfu's first Lord High Commissioner, the controversial

Maitland. The second half is a gravel field which has a dual role as a car park and a cricket field. Then, near the entrance to the Old Fortress, is the **Royal Palace**, appropriately grand, which now houses the public library and a collection of Oriental art. Walking past the palace, one comes to a downward spiralling road, suspended over the sea, which is lined with the most charming Venetian mansions. At the end of this road is the Old Port with its smaller park, and on the hill above is the sombre **New Fort**. Although it is less impressive than the older one, it undoubtedly dominates that side of town.

Other things to see are the **Museum**, whose Gorgon pediment from the temple of Artemis is as frightening as it is famous; the **Church of St. Spiridon**, Corfu's patron saint, who has often saved the island from plagues and other evils; and the **Town Hall**, formerly the Venetian Loggia.

Corfu is the best equipped town for tourists in the Ionian islands. It has a large number of good hotels, and the food in the restaurants is notably better than most parts of Greece. (Try the Corfiot specialities—*sofrito*, *pastitsada*, and *bourdeto*—they will be a welcome change from roast lamb.) The town is terribly crowded with foreigners, but one does not seem to notice; the towering Venetian mansions are impressive enough to make one forget about the bald heads and sunburnt noses which glisten below. And those who do not wish to be confined to the town during the day will have no trouble getting around. One can rent cars, motor scooters, and bicycles for minimal prices.

There are a good number of interesting spots to the south of the main town. The **Palace of Mon Repos**, a sturdy mansion hidden from the public by massive trees, was the birthplace of Prince Philip and a favourite hiding-place for many of his relatives. Four kilometres farther on is **Kanoni**, a tired beauty spot. From the Tourist Pavilion one can see a small chapel at the end of a narrow pier, and **Mouse Island** (Pontikonissi), which springs up from the sea like a small shock of hair. Unfortunately, this view has been marred by the landing-strip extending out into the sea. No observer can be poetic to the sound of landing aircraft. Across the lagoon, a narrow coastal road winds around the hills past innumerable villa gates and overflowing gardens. Approximately 7km from Corfu town, a steep and twisting road turning inland leads up to the lofty **Achillion**. This was originally built for the beautiful and mysterious Empress Elizabeth of Austria, who had an overwhelming personal style but no architectural taste whatsoever. The grotesque mansion is filled with stormy murals, important relics, and classical statues striking romantic poses. Its multi-level gardens are beautifully arranged and have a panoramic view of the island. Achillion has now very appropriately become a casino, with a daytime role as a museum. There is a modest hotel in the grounds. If one descends to the coast again, one can drive through the fishing town of **Benitses**, once picturesque but now affected and overloaded with cheap souvenir shops; **Moraitika**, where Corfu's best hotel, the Miramare Beach, is located; and finally to **Messonghi**, which is surrounded by Corfu's finest olive groves.

To the north of Corfu town is the stone beach of **Dassia**, where the Club Mediterranee has one of its most popular holiday villages. **Nissaki** has pretty villas and an excellent taverna right over the sea (those who know come from

Pontikonnissi, or Mouse Island

town expressly to eat the delicious fish here). Nearby are the two adequate beaches of **Ipsos** and **Pirgi**. The small fishing village of **Kassiopi** is more remote, but since such distinguished guests as Cicero, Nero, and Casanova have stayed there, it is worth trying to visit. The most celebrated spot on the coast facing Italy is **Paleokastritsa** (25km from the town). Lavish descriptions of its spectacular bay and high, rocky headlands abound in famous books, and although the water is still crystal clear, the bay is so packed with boats, sunbathers, and construction workers, that it is perhaps advisable to close one's eyes and recite Durrell in an attempt to recreate Paleokastritsa's tranquil past: 'Drenched in a silver of olives . . . the little bay lies in a trance drugged with its own extraordinary perfection—a conspiracy of light, air, blue sea, and cypresses.' Nevermore.

Behind Paleokastritsa is **Lakones**, a typical village; from here one can visit **Angelokastro**, which hangs on the cliffs over the beauty spot, where there is an underground cistern and a small chapel. The coast facing Italy has several excellent and remote beaches—**Ermones** (where Odysseus met Navsica), **Myrtiotissa**, **Glifada**, and **Aghios Gordis**—although these are being built up, and will soon be very crowded. **Sidari** is another beach with strange limestone formations. When the sea is calm one can swim through the most interesting of these—the Canal d'Amour.

Finally there is **Pelekas**, a high point in the centre of the island famous for its panoramic view. A huge fleet of buses brings people up from town every day at sunset, which is Pelekas' most glorious hour.

Hotels (Recommended)
(L) **Corfu Palace,** Vass. Constantinou. Tel: 29-485. Cables: GAUERHOTEL. On the lovely Garitsa Bay, presently being renovated. Swimming-pool, tennis courts, and sea sports.
(A) **Astron,** 15 Donzelotou. Tel: 29-505. Overlooking the old port. Simple but elegant décor; high ceilings.
(A) **Cavalieri,** 4 Kapodistriou. Tel: 29-091. Cables: CAVALIERICORFU. Completely renovated Venetian nobleman's mansion, on the far end of the Esplanade. Elegant and unique. Many rooms have a sitting room on one level and the bedrooms on the other; a charming arrangement, but perilous if one has had too much *retsina*.
(B) **King Alkinoos,** 29 Panou Zafiropoulou. Tel: 23-900. In a residential area; modern with roof-garden.
(B) **Olympiakon,** 4 Doukissis Marias. Tel: 28-532. Cables: OLYMPIC. A modern hotel with large public rooms decorated primarily in marble; in a very agreeable neighbourhood.
(C) **Arcadion,** 44 Kapodistriou. Tel: 22-670. Cables: ARCADIONCORFU. Rather drab but comfortable hotel, ideally situated near the middle of the Esplanade. Sad restaurant.
(C) **Suisse,** 13 Kapodistriou. Tel: 29-815. Old but charming hotel on the Esplanade overlooking the most popular cafés. No rooms with bath, but still preferable to some of the colourless modern hotels.
(D) **Constantinople,** 11 Zavitsianou. Tel: 22-569. On the old port. High walls, arched doors, balconies, statues, and potted plants. Clean and very cheap.

Other hotels. Bretagnia (C), 27 Ethnikon Stadion. Tel: 28-724, Cables: HOTELBRETAGNE. **Calypso (C)**, 4 Vraila. Tel: 24-747. **Hermes (C)**, 12 G. Markora. Tel: 29-268. **Ilios (C)**, 4 G. Markora. Tel: 28-265. **Ionion (C)**, 100 X. Stratigou. Tel: 29-915. **Splendid (C)**, 39 E. Voulgareos. Tel: 29-867. **Acropole (D)**. Tel: 29-569. **New York (D)**, 21 Ypapantis. Tel: 24-695.

Hotels outside the main town. There are 36 hotels outside the main town in Corfu; most of them are comfortable and work almost exclusively with package tours. Here are a few exceptional ones.
(L) **Miramare Beach Hotel,** Moraika. Tel: 28-183. Cables: MIRAMARE. Bungalows, excellent beach, tennis, mini-golf, restaurant, sea sports.
(L) **Castello,** Dassia. Tel: 93-201. Formerly a medieval castle; magnificent grounds, staid atmosphere.
(A) **Corcyra Beach,** Gouvia. Tel: 28-770. Cables: GREKAMER. Bungalows, swimming-pool, tennis, sea sports, restaurant, night-club.
(B) **Tourist Pavilion (Xenia),** Palaeokastritsa. Tel: 4-208. The only picturesque hotel in the village; good restaurant.
(B) **Xenia,** Kanoni. Tel: 28-041. Cables: XENIAPALACE. Beautifully situated with private beach; very near town.
(C) **Mega,** Ypsos. Tel: 93-208. A modest hotel over an excellent restaurant. Beach nearby.

Restaurants
Ragnatella Bar, Aspioti St. Reputed to be the only restaurant in town with a truly sophisticated atmosphere and clientele. Plausible Venetian décor. Prone to close mysteriously for days. Expensive.
Aegli, Kapodistriou. On the Esplanade. Tables outside and inside. Noisy service but good Corfiot food.
Rex, Kapodistriou. Inside tables only. Reasonable prices and amazingly organized kitchen. The swordfish and the *bourdeto* are excellent.
Aktaion, Esplanade. Overlooking the sea, the Aktaion affords an excellent view of the Old Fortress and the moon. Elegant, subdued atmosphere. Corfiot specialities; take note of the special dishes of the day. Extensive list of Greek wines. Reasonable to expensive.
Averof, near the Old Port. Brightly coloured tables and awnings in a quiet alley with a Venetian portal at the end. Reasonably priced *sofrito, pastitsada*, veal *stamnas, bourdeto*.
Mavronas, Esplanade. Well run, tables set under huge trees. The food—*moussaka, pastitsada*, etc.—simple but good.
Yioyas, Gilford St. A tiny taverna in the back streets behind the Esplanade. Extremely picturesque, authentic, and cheap. Eccentric management. Wine only from the barrel. One can sometimes hear excellent *cantades* music, but this occurs more commonly during the off-season months.

Xenichtis, near Plathera Monastery. Located on the outskirts of town, this is a very special place for people who want to hear *cantades* music. Tables are set under a grape arbour; when most people are gone, the musicians leave their platform and play for their friends at the tables. Excellent singing. Frequented almost exclusively by locals. Food is simple and cheap; meals are eaten late.

Navsica, on the road to Kanoni. Charming garden-restaurant where the menu is a mixture of Greek, French, and Italian dishes.

George Kaiser Restaurant, Perama. Two-level garden restaurant overlooking the coastal road, with a jetty on the sea. Vines, nets, lanterns, and twisted olive trees create pleasant atmosphere. Specialities are *moshari kapama* and *moshari lagoto* (two variations of stew) but everything is good. A simple hotel upstairs.

Lucciola (Firefly) Inn. Half way between the main town and Paleokastritsa, the inn is famous not only for its teas but for its excellent and original Greek cuisine. Small hotel attached.

Paleokastritsa, Corfu

PAXOS
Greece Map C1

Paxos is a tiny rocky island situated ten miles away from the southernmost tip of Corfu. Unlike the rest of the Ionians, it has hardly any historical or mythical significance, but it is charming in its own unimportant way. Whereas the surrounding islands live under the cloud of their former glory, Paxos is an unpretentious mass of olive groves.

In fact, the olive oil from Paxos, which is very light and golden, is about the best in Greece. Since the olive trees far outnumber the 3,000 inhabitants, Paxos has to hire armies of field workers from Corfu at harvest time. Apart from harvest time and the Festival of the Virgin Mary on 15 August, which attracts thousands of pilgrims, Paxos is left sleeping in the middle of the Ionian Sea. One small steamer comes from Corfu daily, and two buses service the entire island.

The tiny villages along the coast, with their boxlike white houses, are very cheerful. **Lekka** has an almost perfect harbour, which is ideal for swimming, and is surrounded by terraced olive groves and clumps of cypresses. **Gaios**, on the other side of the island, is small and placid. The same white houses line the shore, facing the remarkable rocky green islet which blocks Gaios from the open sea and makes its harbour seem more like a channel. Next to Gaios is the dependent island of **Antipaxos**, where the wealthier of the Paxiots have vineyards. These produce a sweet sparkling wine which is the pride of Paxos. One can visit Antipaxos easily by caïque and afterwards explore the beautiful deserted coves and grottoes along the Paxos shore. It is a good idea to avoid the Paxos road network as much as possible; pencil-thin dirt tracks often disappear into fern-covered fields. These idiosyncrasies are being corrected but only very slowly.

Hotels. (B) Paxos Beach. This is a charming bungalow-hotel which provides all comforts while still preserving the island's primitive atmosphere. Bungalows overlook the swimming coves from terraced fields still filled with olive trees. Excellent restaurant; night-club, sea sports, table tennis.

Restaurants. O Kaklis Taverna. In the back streets of Lekka. Simple food and good local wine. Very friendly owner. Teddy Kennedy ate here in 1968 and his letter of thanks is framed on the wall.

LEFKAS

Greece Map C, D1

The narrow channel which separates Lefkas from the mainland has not always existed, and the appearance as well as the customs of the inhabitants suggest that culturally it is a peninsula of Epirus instead of an Ionian island. Its history is also distinct; it was a Turkish possession for two centuries, only passing to the Venetians in 1684. And although Lefkas has its fair share of pine trees, it has a landscape which differs dramatically from that of its neighbours. A disturbingly high mountain ridge serves as the backbone to the island, and towards the shore there are shallow lagoons and dismal salt marshes.

The main town of **Lefkas** is sited at the far end of the channel on a very large lagoon. It was almost completely destroyed by an earthquake in 1948, and the houses, turned away from the water, look grey and temporary. Fortunately, the townspeople do not fit in with this sad tableau; they are lively to the point of being boisterous, especially when they flood the cobblestoned streets for their evening stroll.

In addition to the **Fortress of Santa Mavra**, directly opposite Lefkas on the mainland, one should see the church of **Aghios Dimitrios**, which contains paintings by P. Doxaras, and also the small museum of post-Byzantine art. Two miles away from town, on the limestone hills, is the monastery of **Phaneromene**. Completely rebuilt after 1948, the monastery itself is very routine, but the view of the fortress and the mainland, the lagoon and the olive fields below, is incomparable.

Those who arrive with the infrequent ferry will disembark at the small port of **Nydri**. Near here are the Mycenaean ruins which Dorpfeld, an obstinate and inspired scholar, claims are the ruins of Odysseus' real home. Just off the port are a number of small islands; one of them, the pine-covered **Madouri**, was the home of Valaorites, a nineteenth-century poet, but Onassis' private island, **Skorpios**, is more famous.

Another interesting, and very remote, part of the island is **Cape Ducato**, to the extreme south. This is a white and treacherous promontory which rises 300 feet above the sea. The poetess Sappho is supposed to have flung herself off these cliffs because of her desperate love for Phaon. According to the story, the inhabitants of Lefkas then established an annual tradition of cliff-leaping. The victim would be a criminal decked in a grotesque array of bird feathers, his death-dive serving as a sacrifice to Apollo.

Lefkas is most easily approached from the mainland. There are three buses and one plane flight daily from Athens. The best time to visit the island is in August, when there is a rather good arts festival.

Hotels. (C) Santa Mavra, Lefkas town.

CEFALONIA (KEFALLINIA)
Greece Map D1

Cefalonia, the largest of the Ionians, has a melancholic splendour of its own. The mountains, which are covered with fir trees, olive groves, cacti, strange flowers, and precarious roads, take one's breath away. The surrounding sea is deep blue—even black, during the all too frequent thunderstorms. The characterless modern towns, which replaced those totally destroyed in 1953, remind one constantly of the tragedies Cefalonians have suffered during the last war and the subsequent earthquake.

After walking through some of the blinding white avenues of a Cefalonian town, one might be very surprised to hear that the islanders are reputed to be the most enterprising people in Greece. In past centuries, Cefalonia was famous for its excellent doctors, who practised not only in Greece but in Asia Minor. And today, the island produces shipowners and university professors. Those who have come to know the islanders claim that they have an 'Irish wit'. The only way one can reconcile these well-documented and cheerful facts with the oppressive atmosphere is to assume that all enterprising people leave the island at the earliest possible age.

Argostoli is the capital of the island. Although it was once very beautiful, it is now a series of wide, haunted avenues and concrete whitewashed houses. The great square, with its cafés, oaks, and palms, is pleasant, but does little to cheer up the town. It is not even pleasant to stroll along the sea and look at the sweeping gulf of Argostoli: the water smells. Fortunately, there are excellent beaches nearby. **Platys Yalos** is a small but fully-equipped beach with an admission fee. Nearby is **Makri Yalo**, which is free but still provides excellent swimming. Another interesting excursion from this depressing town is to visit the two water mills, which operate mysteriously because of an inrush of the sea down a hundred-metre pipe. No one knows exactly where this water goes, but there is now evidence to the effect that it surfaces on the other side of the mountain in the beautiful Melissani caves. If one wants to see the countryside starting from the capital, one can try either of two very traditional itineraries. The first is called **mikros giros** and is a 7km tour around the peninsula of Lassis to the fertile plain of Livatho. Longer and much more interesting is the **megalos giros** (the big tour), which is 25km long. Starting from town, one goes to the Kountavos Lagoon, the Kraneri plain, and to Kastro. Near Kastro is **Aghios Georgos**, the site of the island's medieval capital, with the ruins of a castle, a church, a drawbridge, and moat, etc. From here one continues to **Mazarakata**, which has an interesting Mycenaean necropolis, to **Metaxata**, where Byron lived for a few months (one can still see his house), and to **Lakithra**, which has antique grain silos.

A drive to the south-west will take one through many beautiful villages to the town of **Poros**. Here, as usual, the view of the mountains, the deserted islets, Ithaca, the gentle beach, and the sea, is slightly marred by the ugly concrete houses. The same is true of **Sami**, the island's principal port on the Ithaca Channel. The majestic fir trees on the surrounding hills make the façade of houses on the coast seem even cheaper. **Fiscardo**, a tiny port on the northernmost tip of Cefalonia, is about the only village which still retains a Venetian flavour. Its pastel-coloured houses and its luminescent harbour make it an attractive place at which to stay. But the most strikingly beautiful town is **Assos**, also in the north, which is built on the thin neck of land between the island and a rocky promontory. A Venetian castle stands on the promontory overlooking the two harbours. Most foreigners who come to Cefalonia admit that they made their decision after seeing the ubiquitous travel poster of Assos.

Hotels (Recommended)
(B) Xenia. The best hotel in Argostoli; modern and conveniently removed from the centre of town.
(C) Aegli. 3, 23 Martiou. Homelike, cool, and small, no rooms with bath.
(C) Dido, Plat. Valianou. Very near the square, pleasant, cool, with high ceilings.

Other hotels. Armonia (C), 1 Geroulianou. **Phocas (C),** 3 Geroulianou. **Tourist (C),** 94 J. Metaxa. **Emborikon (D),** 2 L. Mitaki.

Restaurants
Demosthenis. This is a good garden-taverna near Metaxas Square. The owner is gruff but capable. Try the local island wine, *robola*.
Antonelou. Adjacent to the Rex Cinema and the square, this restaurant is popular with Greeks, which accounts for the indecipherable menu. Choose dishes in the kitchen.

ITHACA (ITHAKI)
Greece Map D1, 2

Even those who ridicule old-fashioned Homer-quoting classicists, and who mock their nostalgic longing for the vanished Heroic Age, will be completely taken aback by the classical simplicity of Ithaca, Odysseus' home. It embodies the concept of every Greek island; a glorification of the basic elements— mountains, sea, wind, and sunlight. Looking at the coast from the steamer which connects Cefalonia to Ithaca, one begins to understand what an appropriate place Ithaca is for the home of a legendary hero. The boat circles around the southern coastal mountains; they are covered with limestone boulders and low green shrubs, and disappear abruptly into the sea. The boat then enters the wide Gulf of Molos (which nearly cuts the island into two), and heads towards the great Mount Aenos at the end of the gulf. Suddenly the boat makes a sharp turn left and sails between two large headlands into a long, narrow bay, which is completely sheltered from the sea, and is so deep that its water is almost as dark as ink, or wine. At the end of the bay is **Vathi** itself, a tiny town of red-roofed houses spread like a 'U' along the shore and rising into the steep hills on all sides. The town, with its cobblestoned streets, tiny gardens, and clumps of olive trees, is simple without being typical, beautiful without being hackneyed.

Those who know the *Odyssey* well are disappointed by the paucity of landmarks. Apart from the **Grotto of the Nymphs** (now called Marmarospilia) and the **Spring of Arethusa**, there are few readily identifiable Homeric sites. The Venetian fortress at **Pelikata**, the lofty monastery of **Moni Panayia Kathariotissa**, and perhaps the bay of **Poros**, thought by some to be the site of Odysseus' home, are the only other spots of historic interest. However, one should not approach Ithaca as a museum, but as one of the few places in Greece where one can still let the imagination loose and relive the mythical world of Homer.

This spiritual adventure cannot be conducted in the greatest luxury. Vathi's hotels are modest and usually booked up, so one normally stays in rented rooms. Sweet-shops far outnumber the restaurants, and the few that do exist serve a limited selection of food. Still, these shortcomings have kept the island from being overrun with tourists. And even if the main dish at dinner is boring, one will enjoy the well-water—by far the best in Greece— and the excellent local dry wine.

Services between Vathi and Cefalonia and Patras operate three times a week.

Hotels. Mentor (B), Odysseus (B).

Restaurants
Thiaki. The more prominent of the town's two restaurants; on the waterfront, passable food for reasonable prices.
Zambelis. A taverna in the back streets; smaller and cheaper. Menu changes daily. Dishes are well prepared: try the *marida tiganito*, small fried fish; *Vakalaos skordelia*, codfish cooked in a garlic sauce; *moshari katsarolas*; and *kreatopita*, meat pie.

ZANTE (ZAKINTHOS)
Greece Map D, E1, 2

Before the infamous earthquake, the town of Zakinthos, with its arcaded streets, palazzi, baroque churches, ornate stone buildings, and its opera house, rivalled Corfu as the most beautiful town in the Ionian Sea. In 1953, however, the island was the hardest hit of the group. Tremors continued over an entire week; the major one came on a Sunday noon, when all the stoves were lit for the midday meal, and the resulting fire demolished the town.

Although the new Zakinthos is completely modern, it is infinitely more graceful than the rebuilt Argostoli. The wide, crescent-shaped bay alone, surrounded by graceful mountains, is more pleasing to the eye. Those in charge of reconstruction decided to follow Venetian lines, and many streets, including the one along the waterfront, are arcaded. The overall atmosphere is very cheerful. In the evenings, Solomos Square fills up with mothers, their children, and an unwarranted number of smirking youths. The whole waterfront becomes a madhouse of bicycles, monocycles, and very strange pedal carriages for two.

The golden age of Zakinthos took place during the Venetian occupation. The island operated under the feudal system, and the local nobility had a marvellous life both in their country estates and in their town mansions. The trading guilds, which developed, competed with each other to patronize the island's most beautiful church. In this way they encouraged the arts, and a minor school of religious painting developed. P. Doxaras is the most distinguished painter of this school. Zakinthos is also the birthplace of an Italian poet, Ugo Foscolo, and two Greek poets, Solomos and Kalvos.

There are understandably few remains of the past in Zakinthos. The **Church of St. Nicholas**, on Solomos Square, is one of the remaining Venetian buildings. The nearby museum contains those art treasures which were salvaged. The Roma mansion is so exquisite and complete that it seems almost an anachronism in modern Zakinthos.

The island is rough and rocky in the north, but the southern plains are beautifully fertile—ideal for bicycling. The beaches are gentle with very fine sand. **Alikies** is 17km from town and is large enough for one to escape the noisy crowds which arrive on the midday buses. **Porto Roma** is remote but spectacular. **Laganas**, with its long beach and shallow sea, used to be beautiful but is now taken over by lazy Athenian families who virtually dive into the water from their cars and eat huge meals immediately afterwards in the loud tavernas which line the beach. **Tsilivi**, Zakinthos' most accessible beach, has suffered an even worse fate.

To obtain a marvellous view of the town, one can go up to **Akrotiri**, where there is a fortress. Strani Hill, which is nearby, is the place where Solomos would go for inspiration; he wrote *Hymn to Liberty*, which later became the national anthem, while watching the siege of Messolongi from this hill. Another unique spot is **Keri**, which has pitch wells which have been used for boat bottoms since Homeric times.

The food in Zakinthos is surprisingly good with a slight Italian influence.

The local Verdea wine is interesting but rather heavy. And finally Zakinthos is famous for its singers. They don't often sing in the tavernas any more, but when they do, they are phenomenal.

There are at least two boat-buses from Athens daily and three flights a week.

Hotels (Recommended)
(B) Strada Marina, 16 K. Lomvardou. More elegant than its category would suggest. Spacious and carefully furnished public rooms. The bedrooms have huge balconies and a marvellous view of the harbour. The roof-garden has a café-restaurant with a view from all sides.
(B) Xenia, 66 D. Roma. Modern, with a pleasant café in front and a jetty from which to dive into the sea. Restaurant.
(C) Phoenix, 2 Plat. Solomou. On the main square, rather garish, but comfortable. An enormous bird-cage in front of the hotel.

Other hotels. Diana (C), 11 Kapodistriou. **Ionion (D),** 18 A. Roma. **Rezenta (D),** 36 A. Roma.

Restaurants
Ximeronata, 22 Desida. A charming roof-garden restaurant with *cantades* music playing in the background. Very graceful service. Grilled food and chicken on the spit.
Psitaria. On the right end of the harbour as one faces the sea, this is a typical but cheerful place to eat. Mostly grilled foods, but also serve *moussaka*, baked fish, and *briami*, a Greek variation on *ratatouille*.
Zohios, 9 Psaron. Small, simple taverna. Food cooked on the old charcoal stoves. Try the fried sardines.
Boukios, behind Solomos Square. This is the best restaurant in Zakinthos and is reputed to be the town's social centre. The speciality is *zakinthino*, which bears some resemblance to goulash but has a different and delicious sauce. Excellent *sofrito*, meat in a heavy garlic sauce; *bene ala bolonesa*, a special spaghetti with meat sauce; *kouneli*, rabbit stew; and *pastitsio*. Completely staffed with wits, and the owner, Boukios, is the wittiest.

Two impish children pretend they haven't seen the camera

The Aegean Islands

The isles of Greece, the isles of Greece!
Where burning Sappho loved and sung,
Where grew the arts of war and peace,
Where Delos rose, and Phoebus sprung,
Eternal summer gilds them yet . . .

So wrote Byron in *Don Juan*, giving voice to his own and everyone else's romantic ideal of the Greek islands. Although a century and a half have passed since he wrote those lines the ideal remains, for the Aegean islands are Greece par excellence. Their barren mountains, cubist architecture, blinding white alleyways, and sandy coves seem exhilaratingly primitive to the modern Byron. Seen from the sea, they appear to be the perfect place for the poet, who works all day at his simple wooden table, stopping only to take a dip in the blue sea, eat bread and cheese, or gaze at the moon.

Then the inevitable occurs: the ship docks. The pier becomes a madhouse of porters carrying everything from potatoes to apricot jam, grandmothers dragging baskets of cheese, children running around in circles, and sleek youths flexing their muscles. The Aegean islanders are hardly the pensive and resigned farmers of the poetic utopia; they are industrious, intelligent, egotistical, and noisy; well acquainted with poverty but not oppressed by it.

The actual number of islands in the Aegean is an astounding 1,425— only 166 of these are actually inhabited. In the middle of the sea are the classically barren Cyclades, scattered around the 'sacred centre' of ancient times, Delos. The Northern Sporades, Euboea, and the Northern Aegean islands, which are relatively fertile and often thickly wooded with pine trees, lie between mainland Greece and the Turkish coast. The Dodecanese and the Eastern Aegean islands are spread out along the coast of Asia Minor; their splendid mountains and fertile plains—not to mention their cultural heritage—make these last islands more a part of Anatolia than of the distant Greek mainland.

Most of the islands are extremely poor and depend on the sea for their livelihood. Those islands which are not pure rock usually manage to produce one or two 'special crops', e.g. potatoes, almonds, melons, or the usual olives. Although tourism has brought a lot more money to the islands during the last few years, life, especially in the winter, is still very hard. But the islanders continue to make the most out of nothing with their own brand of romanticism. They break the monotony of long winter nights in the coffee house by telling tall tales, gambling, and involving themselves in silly intrigues with their neighbours; and whenever there is a village festival, they sing and dance as if their drunken dreams had come true:

Play the *tzabouna* loud
Add the sound of the *doubi*
And if we dance, maybe
The dark-eyed one will come.
Your face is like the lemon flower,
Your eyes flash like shining orbs,
Your mouth is sweet as sugar and your cheek's an apple,
Your breasts are paradise, your body is a lily.

Where else in the world could one see a man seriously addressing this song to his grim, fat wife, as she circles around the dance floor with frightening determination?

Beautiful island chapels are to be found all over the Aegean

Although most tourists appreciate the beauty of the port towns and are quick to discover the fine beaches, very few become acquainted with the marvellous life of the back streets. You need not go far to find out what it is like; just leave the tourist restaurants along the quay and stroll through the arcaded alleyways until you hear the sound of a few fishermen singing island songs. Enter the taverna quietly, order a flagon of wine, and wait. Within half an hour you will be at their table or they at yours, and before the evening is out you will leave with your head full of wine and song, having made a few friends whose fond memory will ease out a cold winter in London or New York. Or take a bus out into the inland villages early one morning, and climb up to one of the white villages which are perched like eagles on the barren mountains. When you get there sit at a *kafenion* in the village square and bear the clear blue-eyed inspection of the ageing locals, as they come

133

stamping in in their knickers and cockaded hats, pounding on the marble pavement with their staves. They will address you clearly in demotic Greek, assuming that you understand perfectly what they are saying, for one who cannot is a barbarian. But their faces are so open and their gestures so dramatic that you cannot help but understand them and answer with your broken Greek, complemented by nods and signs. 'Who are you?' 'What country do you come from?' 'What work do you do?' 'Are you married?' 'How many children do you have?' (By now there are three generations of your interrogator's family looking on.) 'How much do you earn?' (Make up a much lower figure than you actually earn, no matter how little that is, for whatever it is it will be beyond their ken and you will be considered an idle boaster.) Once your interrogation is over, you will know that you have passed the test when the old man smiles broadly and slaps you on the back, nearly knocking you to the ground, and orders a couple of deadly *strofilias* at his expense. If you pass that test, then your only problem will be how to survive an afternoon of matching wits and *strofilias* with your eighty-five year old friend.

THE CYCLADES

Andros, Kea, and Kithnos

(Greece Map D, E4) These are the Cycladic islands closest to Attica. All of them are relatively dull and mountainous and have dwindling populations. They also have innumerable isolated sandy coves, which are ideal for those who want absolutely nothing except sea, stone, and sky.

Syros

(Greece Map E4; 130km from Piraeus) This small, barren island, the most densely populated of the Cyclades, had its heyday during the nineteenth century, when its large natural harbour was one of the most important ports in the Aegean. The stately neoclassical buildings which line the waterfront at **Ermoupolis**, and the colonnades, cafés, and bandstand in Miaoulis Square remind one of Syros' more glorious past. The atmosphere is not at all sad, however; the twenty thousand inhabitants of Ermoupolis are more prosperous than those in the neighbouring islands. A large part of the population is, in fact, Roman Catholic—descendants of the Venetian and Genoese merchants who settled there in the wake of the Crusaders—although the commerce of the island is largely in the hands of the Psariots and Chiots who came to Syros en masse as refugees during the War of Independence.

There are numerous villages on the island. **Dellagrazia Bay** and **Finikas** are two popular summer resorts with fine old villas. But one will probably go to Syros primarily to make inter-island connections. There are three boats from Piraeus daily and one from Rafina, as well as numerous boats going to all points in the Aegean.

Hotels. Hermes (B), Plat. Kanari. **Europe (C)**, 72 Stam. Proeou. **Cycladikon (C)**, Plat. Miaouli. **Nissaki (C)**, Ep. Papadam.

Syros—capital of the Cyclades—a view from the Catholic quarter inhabited by the descendants of Venetians and Genoans

Tinos

(Greece Map E4, 5; 140km from Piraeus) Tinos is a tamely pretty island which is often called the 'Lourdes of Greece' because of its popularity among pilgrims. Its wonder-working icon of Our Lady attracts cripples and people with incurable diseases from all over Greece twice a year, on 25 March and 15 August. On these days, the icon is carried through the streets for all to see. Non-believers would be well advised to avoid the island at these times, because it becomes hopelessly packed, and the crowd of invalids is disheartening.

The main town, dominated by the church of Our Lady, is lovely but inconsequential. Much more spectacular are the old Venetian capital, **Borgo,**

135

perched in the mountains; the village of **Lutra**, which used to be the summer residence of the local Venetian merchants; and **Pyrgos**, which has marble quarries and an attendant School of Fine Arts for sculptors. The entire island has a pronounced Venetian flavour, and here as in Syros, most of the population is Roman Catholic.

There are at least three boats a day from Piraeus.

Hotels. Tinos Beach (A). Bungalows, restaurant, swimming-pool, sea sports, tennis courts, sauna, night-club. **Favie Souzane (B)**, **Theoxenia (B)**, **Tinion (B)**, **Avra (C)**, **Delfinia (C)**, **Flisvos (C)**, **Galini (C)**, **Oceanis (C)**, **Poseidonion (C)**, **Aeglie (D)**.

Mykonos

(Greece Map E5; 160km) The picturesque whitewashed town of Mykonos, its inoperative wind-mills, and its resident pelican are hardly mysteries to the civilized world. This formerly beautiful village has become a complex of refined handicraft shops during the day and an amusement park by night.

But it is an excellent amusement park; the procession of American beauty queens, other queens, and yachtsmen in loud outfits is far from boring, and the atmosphere in the discothèques—the **Remezzo**, **Mykonos Dancing**, **Windmill**, **Nine Muses**—is appropriately wicked. The food in the restaurants is good and surprisingly cheap, and the town stays open until very late.

The simpler beach people will prefer the opposite side of the island where there are a series of makeshift nudist colonies. The first beach, **Platys Yalos**, accessible by bus, is for conformists, and the true nudists are forty-five minutes away on **Paradise Beach**. They are very friendly to newcomers and give out free blankets for the night—a mixed blessing.

There are three boats and eight flights daily to Mykonos from Athens, so in August the number of tourists on the island is more than double the number of available beds.

Hotels. Leto (A), **Aphrodite (B)**, **Alkistis (B)**, **Kouneni (B)**, **Rhenia (B)**, **Xenia (B)**, **Manto (C)**, **Apollo (D)**, **Delos (D)**. Rented rooms are plentiful.

Restaurants. Antonini's, **Madoupas**, and **Alefkantra** (with the pelican) all serve traditional food, the first one having perhaps the highest quality.

Delos

(Greece Map E5; 160km) Legend has it that Leto, one of Zeus' many mistresses, who had recently been turned into a quail, flew to the barren island of Delos to give birth to the divine twins, Artemis and Apollo. It is said that immediately after the birth, the island was suddenly filled with trees, flowers, and singing birds. Partly because of its mythological importance, and partly because it is a very logical stopping-off point for many trade routes, this tiny island soon developed into a religious, cultural, and trading centre. Peisastratus in the sixth century B.C., decided to purify the island and decreed that no one should be born or die there thenceforth. He immediately had all the graves removed, and subsequently all pregnant

Peaceful charm radiates from this harbour on the island of Zante

The medieval Street of the Knights, Rhodes

Domed roofs and turrets contribute to the quaintness of the Monastery of Panteleimon on Mount Athos

An old woman, deep in her own thoughts, takes a rest in a quiet back street of Lindos

The peaceful serenity of Heracleion

A world of wisdom is reflected in the lined features of this holy visionary from Mount Athos

One of the five remaining lions of Delos, crouched tautly on his pedestal, guards the remains of the sacred city

The portico at the North entrance of the famous Palace of Knossos

mothers and invalids were ferried over to neighbouring Rhenia.

Every four years, a fantastic festival, **Delia**, took place in honour of Apollo. Special delegations would come from Athens and proceed in processional form to the Temple chanting a hymn in honour of the goddess and her twins. After a solemn tour of the sanctuary, there would be a sacrifice, followed by games, which included horse-racing, athletic sports, and musical contests. There would also be a sacred dance in front of Apollo's altar, and the festival would end with plays and great banquets.

The daily boats from nearby Mykonos sail into the Sacred Harbour. To the left are the sanctuaries and major public buildings. The sanctuary of Apollo, formerly graced with a colossal statue of the god and a huge bronze palm tree, now leaves most details to the imagination. Farther on is the Sacred Lake, now dry, which used to hold the swans and geese of Apollo. Beyond this are the eerie archaic lions—the five which are left of the original nine set a unique mood for the ruined city as they crouch tautly on their pedestals. Here also is the museum, which contains a fine collection of archaic sculpture, figurines, masks, vases, and so on. To the right of the Sacred Harbour is the theatre, now mostly ruined but affording a good view of the area from the top, and the ancient town, which is compact with winding streets. Many of the houses here—those of Dionysus, Cleopatra, the Trident, the Dolphins, and the Masks, to name a few, have fascinating mosaics of gods and animals on their floors. There are innumerable other buildings on the site of equal interest, but after one has seen enough of the sacred town, one should climb up to the top of Mount Kynthos, which has an absolutely magnificent view of the area, especially at sunset.

Hotels. Xenia (B). Four rooms.

Paros

(Greece Map E4, 5; 160km) Paros is one of the blander of the Cycladic islands; it is oval in shape with few dramatic indentations and its central mountains, though faithfully terraced, are a boring brown. Nevertheless, it has developed a tremendous following of Americans, Europeans, and Greeks. The main town of **Paroika** is rather pleasant, although it has far too many souvenir shops with identical souvenirs, and is in danger of being permanently ruined by the mountains of orange rucksacks which invariably appear a few hours before a boat is due to leave. The pretty village of **Naoussa** is a better place to stay as it is near some good beaches, but probably the best way to enjoy the island is to rent (or buy) one of the many converted farmhouses on the hills.

Paros is famous for the church of **Panayia Katapoliani** (Our Lady of the 100 Gates, reputedly founded by St. Helena herself) which attracts enormous numbers of pilgrims on the fifteenth of August. For the past few years, groups of foreign musicians have been giving concerts outside, and this has been very well received by all.

Hotels. Hippocampus (B). Bungalows, roof-garden. **Xenia (B), Paros (C), Kontes (D), Kypreou (D), Oassis (D), Pandrossos (D)**.

F

Naxos

(Greece Map E5; 175km) Naxos is the largest and the most beautiful of the Cyclades. The port town is not as obviously pretty as Paros nor as perfectly Cycladic in its architecture as Mykonos, but it has an appealing charm which is quite its own, with its labyrinthian alleyways leading through a maze of Venetian arches and chock-a-block houses, redolent with the smell of bread, cheese, wine, food, whitewash, donkey dung, and incense. The Castro in the upper town is still inhabited by the descendants of the Venetians who followed after Marco Sanudo when he conquered the island in 1205; proud but fading old families with resonant names like Sommaripa, Barozzi, and Della Rocca. The interior of the island has a majesty and a fascination unequalled by any other in the Aegean isles, with high mountains and lush valleys adorned with white villages glimpsed here and there in the midst of the olive groves, tiny Byzantine churches nearly a thousand years old sitting serenely in a farmer's field, Venetian castles still lording over remote villages, Hellenistic towers guarding coasts where no corsair has set foot for centuries.

Naxos is famous for its numerous folk-poets, musicians, and singers. The villagers of **Apiranthos**, who, according to their traditions, came to Naxos from Crete in the Middle Ages, are famous for their *katzakia*, the extemporaneous poems which they recite at weddings, baptisms, and funerals, expressing all of their deepest feelings in simple verses of quite moving beauty. In **Komiaki**, every man and boy plays the fiddle or the guitar, and in **Halki**, every farmer's son is a doctor or a lawyer or a university professor. (And the men of **Filoti** are said to be sheep-stealers, but there they will tell you that the libel is put out by the men of Apiranthos, who are liars and bandits . . .) And so it goes on this beautiful and extraordinary island.

Hotels. Ariadne (B), Apollo (C), Coronis (C), Hermes (C), Dionysus (D), Oceanis (D), Pantheon (D), To Proto (D).

Restaurants. Nereide and **Antonios** are the most popular restaurants among tourists, and **Lucullus** in the back streets also caters for foreigners. One can get excellent grilled meats in the nameless restaurant exactly half way down the waterfront road. Near Lucullus there are two excellent little tavernas, both known as **Vasilis**, and which have a marvellous atmosphere. There are also a few tavernas along Aghios Georgos beach.

Ios

(Greece Map F5; 170km) Ios has all the necessary qualities of an *ideal* Greek island: a long sheltered harbour, barren mountains set against a vivid blue sky, a crooked cobble-stoned path, filled with donkeys carrying picturesque loads, leading up to an immaculate whitewashed village whose ageing inhabitants smile with unfailing and unappreciated hospitality. Ios is still astoundingly picturesque, but the great influx of young travellers, who climb up from the beach in the evening in their expensive peasant outfits to buy bread, wine, and cheese, has turned it from an everyday Aegean island town into a rather overworked cinema set.

Nevertheless, the islanders have bravely carried on some of their more cherished customs. Old men still haunt their favourite coffee houses, the tavernas are still modest, with a very small variety of well-cooked food and good barrel retsina, fishermen occasionally use their nets, and the bank is safely hidden in the back of a clothing store.

The beach behind the village, at **Mylopotas**, is still one of the finest in the Aegean.

Ios has no important archaeological site, although the 400-odd chapels scattered among the hills create a singular impression. It is reputed to be the burial place of Homer.

There is a daily service from Piraeus, and the journey is about eight hours.

Hotels. Chryssi Akti (B), **Psathy Beach (B)** (Bungalows), **Armadoros (C)**, **Actaeon (D)**.

Sikinos

(Greece Map F5; 150km) One of the smallest of the inhabited Cyclades, this bleak island has at various points in history served as a place to keep political prisoners. It has nothing more than a few olive groves, fig trees, wheat fields, and a vaguely picturesque town. There are two or three steamers from Piraeus weekly.

Santorini (Thera)

(Greece Map F5; 215km) This island, which is actually the outer rim of a sunken volcano, has often been described as 'fairy-tale like'. But when one first sees the multi-coloured cliffs, the whitewashed village of **Fira** perched dangerously on the rim of the island, nine hundred feet above the sea, and the smouldering volcanic islets in the middle of the dark, dark bay, the word 'fairy-tale' seems very flimsy. Those who arrive by small ships will take a donkey from **Skala Fira** up the five hundred steps to the town; those who come to **Athinon** with the larger car-ferries will reach town via a breathtaking cliff road which passes nothing but dwarfed, whitewashed trees and domed 'earthquake proof' houses.

The outer half of the island slopes gently down to the sea, and despite the rocky appearance of the land, it produces excellent tomatoes and choice grapes. The sweet light wines of Santorini have been famous since the Middle Ages. The beaches are black and stinging hot on summer days, but those who are dying for a swim can go to **Kameni** or **Perissa**, where conditions are adequate. Instead of sunbathing, one would probably benefit more from seeing the ruins of ancient **Thera**, the numerous monasteries and forts, walking about the haunting town of **Oia**, sited at the northern edge of the island, or taking the three-and-a-half hour excursion to the volcanic islets in the bay. The museum in town is also quite interesting. The one truly unforgettable experience is to walk along the edge of the cliff at Fira when the sun is beginning

Santorini: View to the sea

to set. As one strolls between white chapels and skeletons of houses destroyed during one of the innumerable earthquakes, the cliffs take on an orange glow, and the wind competes with silence. Santorini is frightening but spectacular.

There is at least one boat a day from Piraeus.

Hotels. Atlantis (B), Kamari (C), Kostas (D), Panorama (D).

Restaurants. Babys for grills. The other tavernas are also adequate.

Serifos

(Greece Map E4; 120km) Serifos once derived some income from its ore and copper mines, but even these yield virtually nothing now. The island is mountainous and barren with two fertile valleys in the interior. The beautiful landlocked harbour would remind one of a Norwegian fjord if it were not for the ruthless sunlight and the classic white village perched three hundred feet above. There are steamers from Piraeus five times a week.

Hotels. Perseus (B).

Sifnos

(Greece Map E4; 130km) Boats dock mostly on the ugly side of Sifnos, in **Kamares Bay**, so one's first impression is of an oppressively barren island.

But even this unattractive bay will astound one in the evening, when the whole village, instead of taking the typical evening stroll along the waterfront, takes an evening row in the harbour. One wonders why this custom is not more widespread. On the other, infinitely more fertile, side of the island is the dilapidated medieval town of **Castro**. Situated on a conical hill overlooking the sea, Castro is rightly considered one of the most remarkable villages in the Aegean. Houses are built into the fortified walls of a Venetian castle, and many have enclosed wooden balconies which are seen nowhere else in the vicinity. In the old days, Sifnos was famous for its gold mines; now it is known for its pottery and its good cooks. There is a daily steamer service from Piraeus.

Hotels. Apollonia (D), Artemon (C), Xenia (B).

Milos

(Greece Map F4; 150km) A volcanic and barren island with a huge natural harbour, a few early Christian catacombs, and hot springs. Its greatest asset, the famous Venus de Milo, is in the Louvre.

Amorgos

(Greece Map E, F5; 220km) The long-narrow island of Amorgos, with its huge cliffs, is one of the Aegean's most dramatically isolated islands. The main town, 6km up from the little port, has a marvellous view of the sea on both sides of the island. The most unforgettable sight in Amorgos is the **Monastery of the Panayia of the Presentation**, which hangs precariously to the side of orange cliffs falling sheer into the sea. The hike to this monastery is breath-taking in more than one way. Amorgos is an ideal place for those who want solitude and spartan conditions. There is a steamer from Piraeus twice weekly.

Hotels. Mike (C).

THE DODECANESE

Rhodes (Rodos)

(Greece Map F6, 7; 450km) The 126-foot Colossus of Rhodes, one of the seven wonders of the ancient world, once stood astride the harbour of Mandraki. But the bronze statue of Apollo toppled over during an earthquake and was eventually carted away by some Syrian merchants. Unlike many islands, whose entire historical importance is based upon a monument or statue which has since disappeared, Rhodes continued to be a strategic and desirable island—for the Knights of St. John, the Turks and the Italians in this century. The first two of these powers, at least, left behind an impressive number of houses and monuments, and somehow, the blending of distinct styles does not give an impression of a vaudeville stage set but one of grandeur. There are now twenty-two de luxe and A class hotels.

The most spectacular part of Rhodes is the medieval city of the Knights. It is surrounded by huge ramparts and the interior is a labyrinth of narrow alleys and colonnaded courtyards. The main thoroughfare is the **Street of the Knights**, along which one can see the various Inns, each with its own coat of arms and architectural style. This very strict chivalric order was divided into different 'tongues' or languages—Provence, France, Aragon, Castile, Auvergne, England, Germany, and Italy—and each group belonged to one of these Inns. At the end of this remarkable street is the imposing **Palace of the Grand Masters**; the Turks used it as a prison. The museum is sited in the fifteenth-century hospital. The old city also became the Turkish quarter after Süleyman the Magnificent deprived the knights of their prized island. They added mosques, minarets, hamams, a clock tower, and houses with the characteristic enclosed latticed balconies. But the most lively reminder of the Turkish occupation is the **Old Market**, which, with its tiny shops, aggressive shopkeepers, and coffee houses, looks very much like an eastern bazaar.

Modern Rhodes was built up primarily by the Italians, but in the last ten years, great modern hotels, restaurants, and cafés have sprung up beside the pretentious Italian monuments. Here, as in the old part of town, one is hard pressed to believe that Rhodes is in Greece.

The rest of the island should not be ignored, as it has remarkable ruins, villages, and beauty spots. **Ancient Rhodes** (2km from town) has temples of Zeus and Athena, of which little remains, as well as a restored temple of Apollo and a small theatre.

Rodini (2km) is a garden suburb, where the Rhodes Wine Festival is held from 15 July to 30 September. **Ialisos** (9km) has a fifteenth-century monastery with a panoramic view. **Kamiros** (34km) has extensive ruins of an ancient city—one can still see arcades, cisterns, houses, streets, and a temple. **Lindos** (55km) is justifiably the most celebrated Rhodian village. The **Temple of Athena**, perched above the village over the sea, is one of the most intrinsically beautiful temples in Greece. Below is a Genoese fortress with the white town spread around it. Lindos has a good number of restored fifteenth-century houses, some of them with lovely courtyards paved in mosaics of naturally-coloured pebbles. Finally, one can go to the **Valley of the Butterflies** (26km), a thickly-wooded gorge filled with streams and bridges and, in the spring, butterflies.

Rhodes is well connected with Piraeus by steamer, to Italy and France by car-ferry, to Athens (five flights daily), Crete, England, Germany, and Scandinavia by air.

HOTELS. Those without reservations will have trouble finding accommodation in Rhodes. The Tourist Police at 5 Koundouriotous Square, are very helpful in this case.

(L) Grand Hotel Summer Palace, Akti Miaouli. Home of one of Greece's three casinos, this hotel is appropriately sumptuous. Facilities include a private beach, air-conditioning, restaurant, swimming-pool, sea sports, tennis courts, and a night-club, 'Isabella'.

(L) Miramare Beach Hotel, Ixia Rodos. Under the same management as the Miramare in Corfu. Luxury bungalows, a private beach, a restaurant, swimming-pool, sea sports, and tennis courts. Run with absolute efficiency.

(L) Hotel des Roses, 8 Vass. Constantinou. An extravagant relic from the Italian occupation, this has a private beach, a swimming-pool, tennis courts, sea sports, and a restaurant.

Most A class hotels have swimming-pools; many have tennis courts. All A and B hotels have restaurants, and most work almost exclusively with package tours.

A class hotels. Avra Beach, Bel Air, Belvedere, Blue Sky, Castos, Cairon Palace, Chevaliers Palace, Dionysos, Eden Roc, Golden Beach, Hibiscos, Imperial, Kamiros, Mediterranean, Metropolitan, Capsis, Oceanis, Park, Regina, Riviera, Rhodos Bay, Siravast, Thermae.

B class hotels. Acandia, Alexia, Amphitron, Angela, Athina, Constantinos, Delfini, Despo, Esperia, Europa, Korali, Lite, Manoussis, Monte Carlo, Olympic, Phoenix, Plaza, Posseidon, Solemar, Spartalis.

Recommended C class hotels (there are 55 in all). **Achillion, Karpathos, Marie, Royal.**

Restaurants
Kontiki. An elaborate variation on the original Kontiki, this is a luxurious floating restaurant in Mandraki harbour. Excellent international cuisine.
De Loucas, Kos St. on beach. Typical food in pleasant surroundings.
Dionysos, nr. Sokratos St. in old town. Beautiful soft décor, limited menu of well-made foods.
13, Kos St. Extensive, if conventional menu.

NIGHT LIFE. In addition to the casino at the Grand Hotel, there is a sound and light show in the park near the Palace of the Grand Masters. Good night-clubs include the **Rodini** and the **Tivoli** in Rodini, the **Romatica**, and the **Rhodian Cellar** in the Park Hotel.

Cos (Kos)

(Greece Map E, F6; 340km) 'Cos,' wrote Lawrence Durrell, 'is the spoiled child of the group. You know it at once, without even going ashore. It is green, luxuriant, and a little dishevelled. An island which does not bother to comb its hair.'

The fertile hills of Kos are covered with fruits and plants exotic to Greece— bananas, figs, pomegranates, mulberries, and cacti—and its avenues are lined with luxuriant palm trees. But far from being dishevelled it is a very tame resort for Athenian families who want an inexpensive holiday in subtropical surroundings. The atmosphere is light and unsophisticated, and though it is packed in the summer, it does not give the impression of being spoiled.

Kos has the distinction of being the birthplace of Hippocrates, the 'father of medicine', and an old plane tree is very implausibly pointed out as the place where he habitually cured and taught. Four kilometres out of town is the three-terraced **Asclepieion,** the sanctuary of the god of medicine. The **Odeum,** in town, is a Roman villa with remarkable mosaics. One will have to make no extra effort to see Kos' most striking monument, the **Crusader's fort**, because it guards the harbour most imperiously.

Excursions into the island are well worth-while. There is an exceptional beach at **Cardamena**, which has equally exceptional fish tavernas. Another enjoyable day trip is to visit **Bodrum**, a beautiful village on the Turkish coast.

Kos is very well connected to Piraeus, Rhodes, Kalymnos, and Mykonos by sea, and to Athens by air (one or two flights daily).

Hotels. Alexandria (B), restaurant, night-club, roof-garden, sea sports. **Kos (B), Theoxenia (B), Acropole (C), Christina (C), Doris (C), Ekaterini (C), Elli (C), Elizavet (C), Koulias (C), Milva (C), Veroniki (C), Zefiros (C).**

Restaurants. Miramare and **Erotokritos**.

Karpathos

(Greece Map G6; 390km) The remote and rarely-visited island of Karpathos still retains some of the primitive mystery which once surrounded all the Aegean islands. Whereas the southern half of the island (European Karpathos) is fertile and typical, the inhabitants of the northern half still live according to archaic customs. At **Olimbos**, especially, one sees houses following the ancient designs, and a lock-and-key pattern dating from Homeric times; the people wear elaborate traditional costumes for everyday work, and their speech contains many ancient Doric words.

Simi

(Greece Map F6, 7; 425km) Very close to the Turkish coast, this island is both rocky and fertile, but most of the males prefer to sponge-dive rather than farm. The boats are passed along from father to son, but the women inherit the houses—an interesting and reasonable division of wealth. The town is dominated by the typical **Castle of the Knights**, but it is slightly defaced by the plastic sea-water conversion plant in the main square. Nevertheless, the island has an unspoiled charm, and well repays the visit.

Astipalaea

(Greece Map F5, 6; 310km) As there is only one boat a week to Astipalaea from Piraeus, this island, though spectacular, is virtually unspoiled. It was known in ancient times as 'The Table of the Gods' because of its fertility, but none of that remains. But it is the barren cliffs which make the approach to Astipalaea dramatic, as well as the crumbling **Castello** which dominates the town. The island is primitive but not typically Greek; the Italians, who held Astipalaea throughout the Middle Ages, returned in this century between the two wars and renewed their influence. Most of the 1,500 inhabitants still speak Italian.

Kalymnos
(Greece Map E6; 335km)

> Sea, seafarer's sea, my sea,
> Don't lash them with your waves,
> Because of you I watch till dawn,
> Be like rosewater, sprinkle calm, my sea
> and bring my love.
> Sea, salt-water sea, I can't forget.
> Sea, you have drowned them,
> taken men from their girls—
> bring my love.
> A girl is small, black doesn't suit her,
> My sea, bring my love.
> Sea, salt-water sea, I can't forget.

This folk-song is still very real to most of the women of Kalymnos. After Easter, their men leave the island for five months to go sponge-diving off the coast of Africa, and the occupational hazards are diver's palsy, nitrogen saturation, loss of limbs, or death. Despite these frequent tragedies, the island has a cheerful atmosphere throughout the year, and a euphoric one at the end of the summer when the divers return. The welcoming celebration lasts for days. This is obviously the best time to visit, because otherwise the barren, mountainous terrain and the large sprawling town might convince one that Kalymnos is just another island.

Patmos
(Greece Map E6; 1270km) Although the main town of Patmos, perched in the hills, has a light Cycladic charm and would be a very pleasant place for a quiet holiday, most foreigners go to Patmos for sentimental reasons; for it was here that St. John the Divine wrote the *Book of Revelations*. The fortress-like **Monastery**, where he received the word of God, is open to the public and affords a panoramic view of the island.

THE EASTERN AEGEAN ISLANDS

Samos
(Greece Map E6; 315km) Separated from Asia Minor by a narrow strait, Samos is fertile and majestic. Unlike many Aegean islands, which spell out a single classic mood, Samos is full of variety. The cool mountain scenery contrasts greatly with the fertile plains; the vineyards and tobacco fields keep the long lines of olive trees from seeming monotonous. And although the towns of Vathi and Tigani are typically white and clean, one can notice a vague and exotic Turkish influence.

Samos was an important island in ancient Greece. Its wine was greatly valued, its architectural triumphs applauded, and its tyrant, Polycrates, feared. It was also the birthplace of Pythagoras, one of the most influential philosophers of ancient Greece, and of Aristarchus, an astronomer who formulated a heliocentric theory of the universe nearly two thousand years before Copernicus.

The most notable relics of this age are the **Tunnel of Eupalinos**, an aqueduct built through a mountain (often used as an escape tunnel) and the **Temple of Hera,** formerly one of the great wonders of the world, but now reduced to a single column.

Vathi is a pleasant town with many handsome neoclassical houses and a wide bay, but it is on the whole rather staid. The pretty village of **Tigani** (which means frying pan) is beautiful and natural. Here chestnut trees and tiny tavernas line the harbour, and the view of the mountainous Turkish coast is splendid. Those who are energetic and crave majestic vistas, however, need not limit themselves to Tigani; they should climb up to the top of Mount Kerkis, from which not only Turkey but all of the neighbouring islands are visible.

There are daily steamers from Piraeus to Samos.

Hotels. Xenia (B), Samos (C), Hera (D), all in Vathi.

Ikaria

(Greece Map E5; 245km) Famous for its radioactive thermal springs, and endowed with a few beautiful Byzantine buildings and churches, Ikaria is also a hunter's paradise. Wild hare and partridge abound in the interior of the island. The fishing is also excellent, but, as the tourist brochure says, 'There is no need to live only on fresh fish when in Ikaria. The island is inhabited by countless wild goats whose meat is exceptionally tasty and tender.' —an interesting suggestion which those who have previously partaken will seriously debate.

Hotels. Thermae: Apollo (C), Irakarion (C), Radion (D), Thermae (D).

Chios

(Greece Map D5; 280km) This island, one of the many birthplaces of Homer, is largely mountainous with a few fertile plains. It is in the latter areas that mastic—the base for chewing gum and for the very strong local drink, *mastika*—is produced. Before the invention of synthetic substitutes, mastic was Chios' most prized export.

The main town, except for the old Turkish section within the Castro and the mosque which adorns the square, is rather characterless. It is more a commercial than a social centre. The medieval mastic-producing towns of **Pyrghi**, **Mesta**, and **Olympi**, which have ramparts, winding streets, and strange intricate designs on the buildings' façades, are very interesting. These villages were some of the few to escape the Turkish massacre during the War of Independence; twenty-five thousand people were killed and forty-seven thousand carried off into slavery at that time.

Bellavista and the distant **Kardamyla** are two excellent and typical beaches; those who wish to combine historical curiosity with fun in the sun can visit the ruins of a Bronze Age settlement and then go to the beach below, remarkable for its black pebbles.

Hotels. Chandris Chios (B), Xenia (B), Aktaeon (C), Kyma (C). In Kardamyla: **Cardamyla (B)**, restaurant, night-club, beach, roof-garden, tennis, sea sports.

Evening cocktails on a balcony in the Aegean islands

Lesbos (Mytilini)

(Greece Map C5; 320km) Lesbos is a thoroughly delightful island, covered with olive groves. It has two enormous bays which are both almost completely land-locked, thermal springs, and a curious petrified forest at **Sygri**. The main town, **Mytilini**, is a slapdash mixture of Turkish, Genoese, and island architecture, and its streets are cheerfully noisy. To the north-west is the island's second largest town, **Methymna**, which is thought by many to be the loveliest place on Lesbos. An artist and intellectual colony has recently been established here—the tower houses which overlook the sandy bay, the constant breezes, and the view of Asia Minor across the sea create what would seem to be the perfect setting for creative geniuses and their imitators. After all,

147

it was at **Erissos**, only a few kilometres down the coast, that the tragic poetess Sappho was born.

There are daily steamers from Piraeus to Lesbos and three or four flights every day.

Hotels. Mytilini: **Blue Sea (B)**, **Lesvion (B)**, **Xenia (B)**, **Rex (C)**, **Sappho (C)**, **Lycabettus (D)**. Methimna: **Delfinia (B)**, restaurant, swimming-pool. Thermi: **Blue Beach (B)**, **Votsala (B)**.

THE NORTHERN AEGEAN ISLANDS

Limnos

(Greece Map B5; 115km from Kavalla) Now a barren, rather uninteresting island, Limnos has quite a few amusing mythological associations. It is supposed to have been the home of Haphaestos, the god of smiths, metalworkers, and jewellers. Since Aphrodite was always cuckolding him, the Limnos wives refused to pay her any dues to show their anger; she expressed *her* anger by making the wives so smelly that their husbands would not touch them. The wives, once again enraged, murdered their husbands. A few years later, the Argonauts sailed through and stayed for two years to repopulate the island.

There is an excellent luxury hotel in the main town of **Myrina**.

Hotels. **Akti Myrinis (L)**, restaurant, tennis, sea sports. **Lemnos (C)**, **Sevdalis (C)**.

Samothrace

(Greece Map B5; 60km from Alexandroupolis) Samothrace, with its sharp cliffs and its heavily-wooded mountains, is remote and mysterious. The name is known to the western world through the statue of the Victory of Samothrace, now displayed in the Louvre. But even without the celebrated statue, the ruined city of **Palaiopolis** on Samothrace is one of the most impressive sites in Greece. Hidden in a lush valley on the west side of the island and totally free from tourists, it contains the sanctuary of the strange Kabeiroi cult, a theatre, an Arsineon, and the ramparts of the old city. The setting of Palaiopolis is nothing less than enchanting.

Hotels. **Xenia (B)** (at Palaiopolis).

Thasos

(Greece Map A, B4; 40km from Kavalla) Thasos is another green island; its central hills are covered with a forest of fir, pine, plane, and chestnut trees, and its coast is dotted with white sandy beaches. The main town of

Limin is built on the same site as the ancient city, so modern buildings co-exist charmingly with the sanctuaries of Herakles, Artemis, Poseidon, and Dionysus, the Gate of Silenus, and the remnants of an Agora. There is also a fine Greco-Roman theatre, where several plays and concerts connected with the Phillipi-Thasos Festival are performed every summer.

Makriammos is the island's most famous beach. In addition to a luxurious bungalow hotel, there is a marvellous taverna in the hills above which is ideal for a long and lazy lunch. One can also drive from Limin over the mountains to two very pretty villages—**Panayia** and **Potamia**—to another even lovelier beach on the far side of the island.

Hotels. **Limin (B)**, **Timoleon (B)**, **Xenia (C)**, **Angellika (C)**, **Glyfada (C)**, **Lido (C)**, **Makriammos Thassou (A)**—Bungalows, restaurant, night-club.

There are several ferries a day from Kavalla and Keramoti.

EUBOEA AND THE NORTHERN SPORADES

Euboea (Evia)

(Greece Map C, D3, 4; 88km from Athens) Euboea, 180km long, is the second largest island in Greece after Crete. Parts of Euboea, especially in the more heavily-wooded north, have beautiful scenery, and despite its proximity to the mainland it remains one of the most remote and unspoiled parts of Greece.

Chalkis, the capital, is primarily a commercial and industrial centre. It is separated from the mainland by the Straits of Euripus, whose current changes direction inexplicably every six hours or so. Aristotle is said to have been so frustrated by his failure to explain the phenomenon that he threw himself into the water. There have been bridges over these narrow straits since the fifth century B.C. Chalkis is also well known for its seafood.

Other points of possible interest are **Limni** (86km from Chalkis), a small town good for fishing and surrounded by excellent beaches; **Aedipsos** (160km), formerly a fashionable Roman spa, and still popular today; **Eretria** (23km), which has temples to Dionysus and Apollo, and a ruined theatre; **Kymi** (92km), a dull town which is near some fascinating ruins and **Karystos** (128km), a holiday resort near a remarkable grotto. There are an increasing number of high-class hotels being built on the island's most attractive beaches.

Hotels
Chalkis: **Lucy (A)**, restaurant, tennis, sea sports, night-club. **John's Hotel (B)**, restaurant, roof-garden. **Palirria (B)**, **Ethnikon (C)**, **Hara (C)**.
Limni: **Avra (C)**, **Plaza (C)**.
Aedipsos: **Aegli (A)**, **Avra (A)**, **Petit Palais (A)**, **Hermes (B)**, **Heracleion (B)**, **Kentrikon (B)**, **Thermae Styla (B)**.

Skyros—the mill and the town

Aghios Minas: **Saint Minas Beach (A)**. Restaurant, night-club, tennis, sea sports.
Aghios Giorgos: **Gregolimano (A)**. Bungalows, restaurant, night-club, tennis, sea sports.
Karystos: **Apollon Resort (B)**.
Eretria: **Holidays in Euboea (B)**. Restaurant, night-club, roof-garden, swimming-pool, tennis, sea sports.
Malakonda Beach (B). Bungalows, night-club, mini-golf, swimming-pool, restaurant, tennis courts, sea sports.

Skyros

(Greece Map C, D4; 22 nautical miles from Kymi) Although Skyros has extremely fertile sections, one's first impression is of a classic, bare island. The main town, **Chora**, is arranged amphitheatrically around a ruined Venetian fort, which sits on the jagged rocks above. The scattered houses seem to be Cycladic from a distance; they are typically whitewashed and flat-topped. But when one walks through the cobble-stoned alleyways, one will notice that all of these rough houses have very fine woodwork in the windows and the doors as well as beautifully-carved furniture inside. Skyros is one of the few places in Greece where folk art is still truly vital. The rush-bottom Skyros chairs are now classics, but the islander's creativity is most evident in their loom-weaving and embroidery. The naturalistic motifs, e.g. roosters, mermaids, ships, flowers, men and girls, which they use are rare in a country so enamoured of geometric designs. This is an island whose souvenir shops are really worth a visit.

Below Chora is a long, gentle beach with several tavernas; the most remarkable of these is a converted mill, owned by the wonderfully disorganized Balabanis family. The mill itself is divided into two rooms which can be rented in the summer, and the taverna is on the large shaded porch surrounding it. The wide bay in front of the mill is filled with crayfish; if one takes a boat out, the sea is so clear that one can actually see them resting on the sea floor.

The interior of the island is filled with fig trees, watermelon fields, and wild miniature ponies. To the south is the small **Achillion Bay**, where Odysseus found Achilles—despite the fact that his mother Lito had disguised him as a girl—and carted him off to Troy and immortality.

Rupert Brooke, the English poet, who died in 1916 on the eve of the Dardanelles campaign, is buried in an olive grove some few hundred yards inland from **Trebuki Bay**, in the remote and almost inaccessible southern part of the island.

There is a regular service from Skyros' dull port-town, **Linaria**, to **Kymi** in Euboea, and frequent buses from there to Athens. Another boat runs between Skyros and the other Sporades twice a week.

Hotels. Xenia (B). Modern, on the beach, restaurant.

Skiathos

(Greece Map C3; 30km from Volos) This beautiful, heavily-wooded island, which has long been popular with middle-class Athenians and British villa-owners, is now beginning to attract a larger, more varied crowd of tourists. Its coast is lined with perfect white beaches, and where the sand ends, the pine tree forest begins. **Koukounaries**, the long, crescent shaped beach of the picture postcards, and **Lalaria**, a unique beach with large pebbles and unearthly rock formations, are the most famous ones. The latter beach is only accessible by boat, but there are numerous day-trips around the island which stop off at the nearby grottoes. Another interesting spot is **Castro**, where the islanders lived for several centuries to protect themselves from the corsairs. Built on a rocky peninsula, this ghost town is practically inaccessible but full of the most fascinating ruins. The present port town of Skiathos, with its red shingle roofs and sparkling round cobblestones, looks terribly carefree in comparison to the deserted Castro.

There is a boat-bus every day from Athens to Skiathos, and several boats from the mainland town of Volos. There is also one flight from Athens every day.

Hotels. Esperides (A). On the lovely Achlades beach; air-conditioned, roof-garden, swimming-pool, restaurant, night-club, sea sports. **Skiathos Beach (A)**. On Koukounaries beach. **Xenia (B)**. On Koukounaries beach. Restaurant, beautiful terrace overlooking bay. **Koukounaries (C), Akti (C), Avra (D), Sporades (D)**.

Restaurants. Talagria is a garden taverna which has live bouzoukia music and good professional singers. The food here is expensive but really excellent. The cook manages to make even *moussaka* into something special.

Skopelos

(Greece Map C4; 45km from Volos) An imposing island whose high hills are littered with 123 white churches. Although the main town, **Chora**, with its blue slate roofs, is attractive, the small village of **Glossa** on the other side of the island is more interesting. Here the matriarchal tradition is so well-established that the women run the coffee houses while the men do the dishes. The island has several adequate beaches which are best reached by caïque.

Hotels. Xenia (B), Aelos (C), Avra (C), Amerika (D).

Alonissos

(Greece Map C4; 100km from Volos) Alonissos is a small and pretty island near Skiathos, famous for its quiet white-sand beaches and ideal underwater fishing opportunities. Like its neighbour, it is thickly wooded. There are boats connecting it with the other Sporades and Aghios Nicholaos on the mainland which run four times a week.

Hotels. (C) Marpounta Residence Club. Extraordinarily inexpensive bungalow complex designed to look like a traditional Cycladic village. Comfortable rooms, good beach, tennis courts, facilities for waterskiing and sailing, volleyball, restaurant, and a pine tree forest in the background. **Alonisos (D), Artemis (D)**.

Crete

Crete (Kriti) is one of the largest and most important islands in the Mediterranean. The island is 160 miles (280km) long and only 30 miles (50km) wide, and is dominated by a rugged mountain range which extends along the full length of the island.

Crete may well be an island, but it is so much more than a collection of typical white towns on pretty harbours. The astounding landscape alone would put Crete into a category of its own. As one drives along the coastal road, wild, rocky mountains block out half the sky, but between these and the sea one sees gentle hills bursting with brightly coloured flowers, and fields of olive and citrus trees. Life on this large island, so harsh and so luxuriant at the same time, is predictably different from that on the mainland. Crete has a separate reality, and its people have a separate soul. Seldom will the typical fishermen strike a joyous dancing pose on his nets to please the amateur photographer; he would glare indignantly at such a suggestion. For Cretans are proud and independent, and no number of attractive hotels, improved roads, and air-conditioned buses will make them comply with the tourist façade.

Although Crete is famous in the western world for its fascinating Minoan ruins, the visitor walking through the major cities will be struck by the buildings from the Venetian and Turkish occupations. Huge Venetian forts hang over the sea, and tilted Turkish lighthouses guard the entrance to the ports. Many streets in the old sections are reminiscent of Naples' slums, decrepit but nonetheless picturesque, but the occasional minaret destroys the illusion.

One should bring or rent a car in order to explore Crete. The four main towns, all along the tamer northern coast, are reasonably well connected by bus, but there are an unlimited number of beautiful spots along the road, which should not be missed. One will also want to visit the isolated mountain villages, the plateau of Lassithi, the more remote Minoan sites, the remarkable Gorge of Samaria, and the cave which, tradition claims, is the birthplace of Zeus. And those with cars will find the southern coast more accessible. Here, huge mountains jut dramatically into the Libyan Sea, cutting off the few small coastal villages from the rest of the world almost completely. These towns are, therefore, very natural, and the sea is warm enough for year-round swimming.

One should be wary, however, of the futuristic map which is sold in all the island stores—the great red line suggesting a super highway is merely a road-planner's dream for the Crete his children will live in. The present road-network is a horror show of scenic hairpin curves. But the fact that one cannot cover ground fast is certainly not the only reason why one must spend more than a few days in Crete. The island's unique mood, so well described by the narrator in *Zorba the Greek*, cannot be understood immediately:

> To my mind, this Cretan countryside resembled good prose, carefully ordered, sober, free from superfluous ornament, powerful and restrained. It expressed all that was necessary with the greatest economy. It had not flippancy, no artifice about it. It said what it had to say with a manly austerity. But between the severe lines one could discern an unexpected tenderness; in the sheltered hollows the lemon and orange trees perfumed the air, and from the vastness of the sea emanated an inexhaustive poetry.

Those who rush through Crete will be unable to read poetry in the landscape, and they will leave with nothing more than an unpleasant memory of a greasy roast chicken dinner in Heracleion.

HERACLEION (IRAKLION)
Greece Map G5

Heracleion, often referred to by its medieval name of Candia, is the biggest city in Crete and the fifth largest in Greece, with a population of 75,000. Although the town itself is not as intrinsically interesting as others in Crete, it is a central point for excursions all over the island, and it has also one of the most important museums in Greece.

Eleftherias Square, the centre of modern Heracleion, is bare and undistinguished during the day. Buses leave for Knossos from under the carefully-planted palm trees and the plastic chairs in the gigantic cafés shine dully in the sun. In the evening, when the great crowds of carefully-dressed townspeople arrive for their daily stroll, the square buzzes with new life. One can notice this same tendency in the city as a whole. Heracleion is architecturally dull, but its inhabitants give its grey streets a certain vitality from time to time.

Founded in the ninth century by the Saracens, Heracleion quickly became Crete's administrative and commercial centre. It continued to grow during the four centuries of Venetian occupation, and the city was fierce enough in the seventeenth century to live through a twenty-one year Turkish siege. Although the city was never made capital of modern Crete, it continues to be the island's most important city. It has good connections with the mainland, both by air and sea, and it is the centre of the tourist trade. There are five flights daily to Heracleion from Athens and at least two daily boats from Piraeus. There are also sea and air connections to Rhodes.

However, beyond the fact that Heracleion has more hotels than any other Cretan city, tourists will, after a brief look at the Venetian fortifications, the Morosini fountain, and perhaps Kazanzakis' tomb, find little to hold them. Most people use the city as a base from which to visit the impressive **Archaeological Museum**, Knossos and Phaistos.

The Museum is located just off Eleftherias Square. This is one of the truly great museums of the world, and its vast collection of Minoan antiquities is unrivalled. The Museum's collection covers the entire span of ancient Minoan sites in Crete: Knossos, Phaestos, Mallia, Aghia Triada, Tylissos, Gortyn, Gournia, and Zakro, to name only the most important. The artefacts from these excavations give one a remarkably vivid picture of the cultural life of this extraordinarily advanced and creative civilization, whose very existence was virtually unknown less than a century ago. Ideally, one should visit the museum at least twice; once before seeing the various archaeological sites on the island, and again afterwards, when one can place the artefacts in their proper context.

(Opening hours. Summer period: daily 8 a.m. to 1 p.m. and 3 p.m. to 6 p.m.; Sundays and holidays 10 a.m. to 1 p.m. Winter period: 8 a.m. to 1 p.m. and 3 p.m. to 5 p.m.; Sundays and holidays 10 a.m. to 1 p.m.)

When in Heracleion one should also visit the **Historical Museum of Crete**, which stands near the Xenia Hotel. The various exhibits here take one through all of the later periods of Cretan history: Christian, Byzantine, Venetian, Turkish, and modern Greek.

(Opening hours. Summer period: daily 8 a.m. to 1 p.m. and 4 p.m. to 6.30 p.m. Winter period: daily 8 a.m. to 12 noon and 3 p.m. to 6 p.m. Closed Sundays and holidays throughout the year.)

Hotels (Recommended)

(A) Astir, 25 Avgoustou. Tel: 282-222. Beautiful terrace over main street. Old elegance. Restaurant.

(A) Astoria, Plat. Eleftherias. Tel: 286-462. On main square. Excellent view from roof-garden, which has salt-water pool. Huge balconies, restaurant, air-conditioned.

(A) Atlantis, Meramvelou and Hygias. Tel: 288-241. Air-conditioned, roof-garden, swimming-pool, tennis courts.

(A) Knossos Beach, Kokkini Hani. Tel: 288-450. Bungalows. Mini-golf, sea sports, restaurant.

(A) Xenia, Archiepiskipou. Tel: 284-000. Large and comfortable.

(B) Mediterranean, Plat. Daskaloyanni. Tel: 289-331. Bright roof-garden; modern décor elsewhere. Air-conditioned, well-run. Restaurant.

(C) Knossos, 37 25 Avgoustou. Tel: 283-247. Marble staircases, beautiful tiled bedroom floors. Well-run and central.

Other hotels. Cosmopolite (B), 44 Evans. Tel: 283-313. **Castro (B)**, 20 Theotokopoulou. Tel: 285-020. **Esperia (B)**, 20 Idomenous and Meramvelou. Tel: 288-211. **Domenico (C)**, Plat. Daskaloyanni. Tel: 289-331. **El Greco (C)**, 14 Aimyrou. Tel: 288-231. **Heracleion**, Kalokerinou and Delimarkou. Tel: 281-881. **Olympic (C)**, Plat. Kornarou. Tel: 288-861. **Palladion**, 16 Chandakos. Tel: 282-563. **Park (C)**, 5 Koroneou. Tel: 283-934. **Posseidon (C)**, Posseidon St. Tel: 285-859. **Selena (C)**, 7 Anrogeon. Tel: 287-660.

Restaurants

Knossos, El. Venizelos Square. Typical but respectable food for reasonable prices. View of Morosini Fountain.

Caprice, El. Venizelos Square. Routine food, view of fountain.

Glass House, Sofoklis Venizelos. On the sea and has a good *bouzoukia* show. A bit more expensive than most.

Nea Ionia, 5 Evans. Noisy, brightly lit, specializes in meat on the spit which can be good.

Klimataria, Daidalou. Rather good taverna with music.

Kallithea, Viglas. Straw-roofed taverna with music.

Rafina, Sofoklis Venizelou. Very cheap, on the waterfront. Mostly grilled foods.

Kostas, Daidalou 6. Very cheap, good selection of food.

EXCURSIONS FROM HERACLEION. Virtually any one of the Minoan sites on Crete can be visited easily in a one-day tour from Heracleion. By far the most important of these is the great **Palace of Knossos**, which lies 5km from the city.

The Palace of Knossos, first excavated by Sir Arthur Evans in 1900, is a vast complex of royal dwelling places, public rooms, servants' quarters, processional corridors, monumental halls and stairways, places of worship, storehouses, dependent buildings, and royal tombs. The enormous extent and complexity of the palace are a testimony to the power and wealth of the Minoan ruler, whose gypsum throne with its attendant griffins can still be seen in the magnificent Throne Room of the Palace. The first palace on this site is thought to have been built in about 1950 B.C., when the majority of the palatial residences on Crete were originally constructed. Knossos and many other palaces in Crete were destroyed in a great earthquake in about 1700 B.C. The Palaces were rebuilt not long after the earthquake, and the structures, which we see today, date mostly from that period. This was the golden age of Cretan civilization, which flourished until its sudden end in *c.* 1400 B.C., when all was totally destroyed, probably due to the explosive eruption of the volcanic island of Santorini. The ruins were buried under ashes and earth for more than three thousand years until they were unearthed by the archaeologist's spade at the beginning of the present century. The rediscovery of the Palace of Knossos represents one of the very greatest achievements in the history of archaeology, and adds immeasurably to our knowledge of the life and culture of ancient Greece.

(The archaeological site at Knossos is open during the following hours. Summer period: every day from 8 a.m. to 1 p.m. and 3 p.m. to 6 p.m. Winter period: every day from 8 a.m. to 1 p.m. and 3 p.m. to 5.30 p.m.)

There are many other possible excursions from Heracleion. In addition to **Phaistos** (62km from Heracleion), the Messara plain has two other major Minoan sites: the **Royal Villa of Aghia Triada** (66km) and the scattered remains of ancient **Gortys** (45km). Along the coast towards eastern Crete is the Minoan Palace of **Mallia** (37km), also very impressive. Not far away from the city is the little village of **Fodele** (28km), the birthplace of El Greco, which has a commemorative pillar and a bust of the artist, and which is surrounded by fragrant orange groves. One of the most spectacular day-trips would be to visit the **Plateau of Lassithi** (69km), hidden between Crete's fiercest mountains. The plateau's 600 working windmills are so beautiful as to be not quite believed, and the nearby **Diktaean Cave of Zeus** is as diverting as a mythologically important cave can be. The village of **Archanes** (15km) has spectacular vineyards, where the apparently famous *rozaki* grapes grow; the village has two good tavernas where one can occasionally see authentic Cretan dancing. The **Idean Cave** (55km), on the plateau of Nida, is reputed to be the birthplace of Zeus. One can also go to the tiny settlement of **Arvi** (90km) on the Libyan Sea, which is remarkable because of its banana-palm forest. And finally, if one does not mind battalions of hippies, one can go to see the famous **Matala Caves** with the spectacular beach on the Libyan Sea below.

A dock worker (Sotiris) loading marble

AGHIOS NICHOLAOS

70km from Heracleion
Greece Map G5

This small whitewashed town, beautifully situated on the Bay of Mirabello, could be anywhere in Greece. It has none of the dramatic quality which distinguishes Crete from the rest of the country. But even those who complain that Aghios Nicholaos is a very pretentious little resort must admit that it is terribly pretty and that the sea is the clearest on the northern coast. Adjacent to the harbour is the small 'bottomless lake', **Voulismeni**, around which there are cafés, restaurants, and exquisite white houses. Along the waterfront are some of Greece's most attractive luxury hotels. They are open all year round, because the bright blue water is warm enough for winter swimming.

Hotels (Recommended)

(L) Minos Beach, Akti Ilia Sotirchou. One of the most beautiful hotels in Greece. Whitewashed bungalows amid gardens look out onto tiny bays. Small beaches with excellent water. Rowboats, sailboats, canoeing, water-skiing, swimming-pool, tennis courts. Restaurant is the best in town but one.

(A) Mirabello. 1km from town; air-conditioned, roof-garden, swimming-pool, beach, sea sports, good restaurant.

(A) Hermes, Akti Koumoundourou. Very new hotel on waterfront; classical décor with a difference. Palatial hallways, large, comfortable rooms with wall-to-wall carpeting, huge balconies, and refrigerator. Swimming-pool, restaurant whose terrace has stone arches and a spectacular view. Highly recommended.

(B) Ariadne Beach, Gargadoros. Bungalows, private beach, sea sports.
(B) Corali, Akti Koumoundourou. Next to the Hermes. Original lobby decorated with plants, skins and swords. Bar, restaurant, roof-garden, private beach of sorts.
(C) Akratos, 19 28 Octovriou. Overlooking lake; roof-garden and restaurant.
(C) Du Lac, 17 28 Octovriou. Very attractive, overlooking lake.
(C) Alcestis, 30 S. Koundourou. On waterfront.
(C) Rhea, 10 Marathonon and Milatou. Night-club, restaurant, roof-garden and swimming-pool.
(D) Lato, Josif Koundourou. Very clean and cheap hotel.

Restaurants

Popi's Restaurant, Josif Koundourou. A luxury-class establishment with surprisingly low prices considering what you get. Popi's is beautifully decorated with brass pots, wall hangings, jugs, straw Skyros chairs and other handicrafts. Exceptional food: lobster and shrimp soup; *hirino krasato*, pork chops in wine; pepper steak; piccata of veal with mushrooms, shrimp and bacon on a skewer. Desserts include almond pudding and crêpe suzette. There is also an expresso-machine.
I Limni. Pleasantly situated on the lake, Limni has typical entrées in addition to a few shrimp dishes served in clay pots. Reasonable.
Kallithea. On the seafront, serving grilled fish and meat for reasonable prices.
Flissos. On the harbour. Extremely simple; cheap.
Vasili's. Tables on the quiet harbour; all varieties of meat for reasonable prices.
Ellas. This is only a simple café on the lake, but it is a marvellous place for a before-dinner *ouzo*. *Ouzo* comes in small jugs with an incredible plate of hors d'oeuvres.

EXCURSIONS FROM AGHIOS NICHOLAOS. From Aghios Nicholaos one can take any number of excursions to various points in Eastern Crete. **Gournia** (19km) and **Zakros** (114km) are the two most interesting Minoan sites. One can also drive along the Bay of Mirabello to the salt lake of **Elouda** (11km), which, besides being spectacular, has the best fish in the area. At the entrance to the salt lake is the rocky island of **Spinalonga**, upon which a Venetian fortress, rather similar to a battleship, stands. (There is an excellent bungalow-hotel, the **Elouda Beach (L),** here.) **Kritsa** (11km) is a typical pic-turesque Cretan village; Jules Dassin filmed *He Who Must Die* here. The view of the bay from this mountain town is panoramic. Those who are not bothered by rough roads can go to the remote fishing port of **Siteia** (73km), which is distinguished by yet another Venetian fortress. The waterfront in Siteia is very pretty, with a line of cafés and tavernas shaded by tamarisk trees. Near Siteia is the rather militaristic **Toplou Monastery**, built 600 years ago. And next to this is the remarkable beach at **Vai**, set in the middle of a palm-tree forest. **Ierapetra**, Crete's fourth largest town, is only 36km away on the Libyan Sea. This town is famous for its scythe-shaped knives, but it has little to offer the peace-loving tourist besides its long beach.

There is one boat a week which connects Aghios Nicholaos with Santorini and Rhodes.

RETHYMNON

81km from Heracleion
Greece Map G4

Built on a small strip of land extending to the sea, Rethymnon is hauntingly

The harbour of Rethymnon, Crete

beautiful. It has the atmosphere of a medieval city waiting for the onset of the plague: dark, sullen mothers stand in Venetian doorways; laundry hangs from the enclosed wooden balconies of the old Turkish houses. The army of motorcyclists in the narrow, winding streets brings one back to the twentieth century in a way which is far from soothing. The dilapidated Turkish and Venetian buildings on the waterfront are unforgettably picturesque, but all four cafés now have television sets on their front walls, and nothing is spookier than to walk past them when the 10 p.m. soap-opera is blasting out to four silent café audiences.

Rethymnon was a cultural and commercial centre during the Venetian occupation; the famous Malvasia wines were shipped from here to all parts of Europe. Turkish pirates burned and pillaged the town very badly in 1571; to safeguard Rethymnon from a similar disaster, the Venetians built the impressive **Fortetsa**, which still stands on the great hill overlooking the sea. Less than a hundred years later, however, the Turks conquered the city, making it one of their principal military bases. The scattering of minarets, and the exquisite white lighthouse are relics of this era.

Modern Rethymnon is the capital of one of Crete's four prefectures; this is the extent of its commercial, political, and cultural significance. The museum, housed in the old Venetian Loggia, contains interesting local finds. At the end of July, the **Cretan Wine Festival** is held in the Public Gardens (formerly the Turkish cemetery).

Hotels (Recommended)
(B) Ideon, Platia Plastira. Bright modern furnishing; balconies with good view; restaurant, café on street.
(B) Xenia, N. Psarou. Predictable comfort.

Other hotels. Acropole (C), Pl. Agnostou Stratiotou. **Valari (C)**, 78 Koundouioti. **Park (C)**, Igounou Gavriel. **Emboron (D)**, Ethnikis Annistaseos. **Minoa (D)**, 62 Arkadiou.

Restaurants. There are a string of tavernas on the tiny old harbour—**Taverna Halona, Zefros, Kosmiki Taverna**, etc.—which serve a small variety of excellent fresh fish. Another good restaurant is **Apostolis**, at Kaliris Paren Siganou St., near the park. Here there is traditional food for reasonable prices.

EXCURSIONS FROM RETHYMNON. The closest point of interest is the **Monastery of Arkadi** at Platanes (7km). When 1,000 people took refuge in this monastery during the struggle for independence, they decided after three days of desperate fighting against the Turks to commit mass suicide rather than surrender. This is where their famous motto: 'Freedom or Death', became internationally recognized. One can also go to the **Preveli Monastery** (32km) on the Libyan Sea. On the way, one goes through the **Gorge of Kotsifas**, where the wind passing through makes strange noises. 14km away from Preveli is the beautiful beach of **Plakias**. **Aya Galini** (63km) is a lovely fishing village with rocky beaches and shocking blue water. Because of the great publicity given to the nearby hippy cave-dwellers, Aya Galini is now packed with young nature lovers.

CHANIA

156km from Heracleion
Greece Map G4

Chania is similar to Rethymnon in appearance, but its faded Venetian buildings and Turkish mosques are less oppressive. The Inner Harbour, which is no longer used for anything but small fishing boats, is even cheerful. And behind the coastal layer of vaulted arsenals, bombed out castellos, narrow alleyways, and pleasant cafés is a very noisy industrial town. Perhaps it is the abundance of motorcarts and smelly machine shops along the main streets which make Chania seem less haunted than its neighbour, but the constant roar of progress is very trying.

The modern town is built on the foundations of the ancient Greek town of Cydonia. It has been an important trade centre since the Arab occupation, and when the Turks took over the island, they made Chania the capital. Chania has retained this honour throughout all of the political upheavals of the last few hundred years.

Six kilometres away is the excellent bay of Souda, which serves as a port for Chania. There is also a large naval base and an airport here.

Those who wish to swim should avoid the town beach at Nea Chora at all costs. Instead they should take a bus from 1866 Square to **Glaros** or **Kalamaki**. These beaches are almost completely deserted after 2 p.m. and their tavernas serve excellent fish. A good spot to visit in the early evening is the promontory of **Akrotiri**, from which the view of Chania and the White Mountains is spectacular. On this hill are the statue of Cretan Liberty, the grave of statesman Eleftheros Venizelos, and a very good luxury restaurant, **Asteria**.

Hotels (Recommended)

(A) Kidon, Plat. Venizelou. The most attractive hotel in the city. Bar with balcony overlooking the square.
(A) Xenia. Comfortable, modern, with swimming-pool and polluted beach.
(B) Lissos, 68 Vas. Constantinou.
(B) Canea, 18 Plat. 1866. Clean airy rooms. View of busy square and mountains.
(C) Cyprus, 17 Tżanakaki. Cheerful, clean, filled with flowers. No rooms with bath.
(C) Lukia, Akti Koundourioti. On the Inner Harbour. Beautiful view of port and lighthouse.

Other hotels. Criti (C), Nikoforou Foka and Ciprou. **Dictina (C)**. **Doma (C)**, 124 El. Venizelou. **Elyros (C)**, Milonoyanni 5. **Plaza (C)**, 1 Tombazi. **Hermes**, 23 Yannari.

Restaurants

Faros. Very large and brightly lit, the Faros has the atmosphere of a hotel restaurant. Rather expensive, but with a good selection of European dishes, e.g. tournedos, escalopes, etc.
Kavouria. Near the Faros on the harbour, this is the only other restaurant in the vicinity with good food. The prices are reasonable, the fish excellent. Also try the *arni stifado*, lamb cooked with onions and wine.
Annitsakis, between Plat. Venizelou and Plat. 1866. A marvellous taverna for people who want a good night of drinking. It is a very deep cavernous hall with twenty enormous barrels lined up on the wall. The owner is an eccentric who calls his taverna '*I Vouli*' (the Parliament) because it is for serious drinking. The parliament has not changed in forty years and the cooking is still done over charcoal stoves. There is no music because it is a church, and water is strictly forbidden. There are two kinds of wine served—red and *retsina*. The upstairs balcony is for im-

portant senators, but the atmosphere downstairs is much better.

To Mini. This is actually a café on the harbour, but its *mezedes* of shrimp, octopus, and the like are large and expensive enough to make a healthy meal.

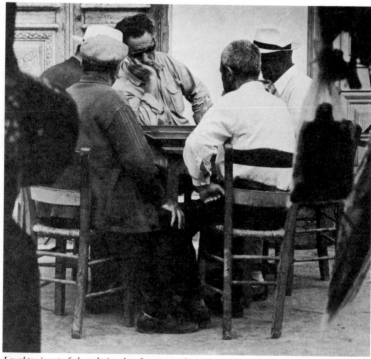

Laughter is out of place during the afternoon tavli game

EXCURSIONS FROM CHANIA. One should not miss seeing other parts of western Crete while in Chania. The **Plain of Chania** has a number of little villages hemmed in by densely-planted orange groves; they are most beautiful when the trees are blossoming. 77km away on the Libyan Sea is the small town of **Palaiochora**, which is on a flat strip of land between two extremely long beaches. On the promontory between the two beaches is the ruined fortress, Castel Selino. Life is very simple in the village, but it is warm enough here in the winter to swim. At least twice a week there is a boat from the village to **Gavdos**, the small island which is the southernmost point in Greece. Another village on the Libyan Sea worth visiting is **Chora Sfakion**. The drive across the White Mountains is hair-raising and unforgettable. One can take a caïque from the village to **Frangocastello**, yet another Venetian fort on another marvellous beach.

The most remarkable excursion is to the **Gorge of Samaria**. It is one of the longest, deepest, and narrowest ravines to be found anywhere—18 kilometres long, 330–600 metres high, and 3–40 metres wide. The narrowest points, called *sitheroportes* or iron doors, only admit light for a few minutes every day. The scenery throughout the seven hour hike is wild. The ravine ends on the coast at **Aya Roumeli**, and the NTOG operates a caïque service from there to **Chora Sfakion** during the summer. It is probably better to go with a tour to the Gorge; otherwise one can take the 6.30 a.m. bus to **Omalos** and hope for the best.

SUGGESTED TOUR ITINERARIES

One week
Athens—3 days.
Delphi—1 day.
The Argolid (Mycenae, Nauplia, Epidaurus)—1 day.
Olympia, the Gulf of Corinth and the western Peloponnese—2 days.

Two weeks
Athens—4 days.
Cape Sounion and the environs of Athens—1 day.
Saronic islands—1 day.
Delphi—2 days.
The Argolid—2 days.
Olympia—2 days.
Mistra and the central Peloponnese— 2 days.

Three weeks
Athens—5 days.
Cape Sounion—1 day.
Saronic islands—1 day.
Delphi—2 days.
The Argolid—2 days.
Olympia—2 days.
Mistra—2 days.
The Greek Islands—6 days.

Six weeks
Athens—5 days.
Cape Sounion—1 day.
Saronic islands—1 day.
Delphi—2 days.
The Argolid—2 days.
Olympia—2 days.
The western and southern coasts of the Peloponnese—2 days.
Mistra—2 days.
Ioannina and Epirus—2 days.
Thessaly and the Meteora—2 days.
The Chalcidice and Mount Athos— 4 days.
Kavalla and Thrace—2 days.
Kastoria and Macedonia—2 days.
Salonica—2 days.
The Greek Islands—6 days.
Crete—5 days.

In addition to the day trips in and from Athens, travel agencies such as Chat Tours offer more extended guided tours of Greece and the Aegean coast of Turkey.

Index of Localities